ACCLAIM FOR
BONES WOULD RAIN FROM THE SKY

"Unique and insightful . . . Challenges us to examine our own actions and beliefs."

—*Dog & Kennel*

"A top-shelf selection . . . challenges us to think more deeply about what we know about dogs . . . The greatest gift in Clothier's work is realizing we can learn to be whisperers."

—*Golden Retriever News*

"Clothier offers what many people want to know: how to deepen and enhance the connection between dog and owner."

—*Pet Life*

"Fully delivers on its promise to deepen the relationship between humans and dogs . . . It is impossible to read this book about dogs and not learn some surprising and provocative things about yourself. I can't recommend this book highly enough . . . A must-read."

—Susan Chernak McElroy, author of
Animals as Teachers and Healers

"At long last, we have an accurate analysis of the mind and motives of our best friend, the dog . . . This absolutely delightful book has my highest recommendation. Read [this book] and learn how to read your dog."

—Ian Dunbar, PhD, MCRVS, host of the British television series
Dogs with Dunbar and founder of the
Association of Pet Dog Trainers (APDT)

"Riveting. Clothier's book has depth, wisdom, good humor, and challenging insights . . . Learn from this wonderful work."

—Marylee Nitschke, PhD, animal behavior therapist and
professor of psychology, Linfield College, OR

more . . .

BONES
WOULD RAIN
FROM THE
SKY

*Deepening
Our Relationships
with Dogs*

BONES
WOULD RAIN
FROM THE
SKY

Suzanne Clothier

GRAND CENTRAL
PUBLISHING
New York · Boston

Grand Central Publishing
Hachette Book Group
1290 Avenue of the Americas
New York, NY 10104

www.HachetteBookGroup.com

Printed in the United States of America
Originally published in hardcover by Hachette Book Group.
First Trade Edition: October 2005
13

Grand Central Publishing is a division of Hachette Book Group, Inc.
The Grand Central Publishing name and logo is a trademark of Hachette Book Group, Inc.

The publisher is not responsible for websites (or their content)
that are not owned by the publisher.

The Library of Congress has cataloged the hardcover edition as follows:

Clothier, Suzanne
    Bones would rain from the sky : deepening our relationships with
dogs/Suzanne Clothier.
        p. cm.
    ISBN 0-446-52593-6
        1. Dogs—Behavior. 2. Dogs—Training. 3. Human-animal relationships.
    4. Human-animal communication. I. Title.

    SF433 .C56 2002
    636.7'0887—dc21   2002024987

ISBN 978-0-446-69634-0 (pbk.)

Cover design by Julia Kushnirsky
Cover photo by John Lamb/Getty Images
Book design by Mada Design, Inc./NYC

FOR GRAS,
CHRISTIAN
AND BEAR

CONTENTS

*If a dog's prayers were answered,
bones would rain from the sky*

TURKISH PROVERB

BONES
WOULD RAIN
FROM THE
SKY

1

IN THE COMPANY OF ANIMALS

*You have to leave the city of your comfort and go into
the wilderness of your intuition. What you'll discover will be wonderful.
What you'll discover is yourself.*

ALAN ALDA

MY ONLY MISTAKE WAS LICKING HER KNEE. Until that moment, they had
been quite tolerant of me panting quietly under the dining room table,
a good place to lie on a warm summer's evening. I was a smart dog. I
knew I might have been cooler lying on the slick tile in the bathroom,
or even outside, shaded by the bushes along the foundation. But I would
have missed being with my family. Seen from beneath the table, framed
by a tablecloth, my family appeared as a collection of limbs and cloth-
ing: plump knees, knobby knees, scabby knees, tired-looking ankles rising pale and thin from sensible white socks, pleasantly grubby feet idly
rubbing the rungs of a chair, a flip-flop dangling from a swinging toe.

I shifted to lean against a woman's knee, eyes closed as I breathed in
the sweetly familiar perfume that rose from a hollow on her ankle.
Absently, she reached down to pat my head, and grateful for the attention, I licked her knee. With my aunt's startled cry, my blissful moments
as the family dog came to an end. It was not fair, I thought resentfully
as I was hauled out from under the table and placed unceremoniously
in a chair with the command, "Sit here and eat like a human being!" All
I wanted was a dog. If I couldn't have a dog, the least my family could
do was allow me to be a dog. And everyone knows that dogs lick the
people they like.

It was a typical middle-class family that owned me—no more dysfunctional than most, and certainly not one that encouraged such odd behavior in its eldest child. While tolerant of and kind to animals, neither of my parents were "animal" people. It was not for want of love or acceptance that I was drawn to animals, though for many children animals do freely offer the unconditional love and acceptance often lacking in young lives. Yet long before I knew disappointment or anger, long before I learned how hurtful and complex human beings could be, there was an instinctive gravitation toward animals. Animals of every description drew me to them simply because they existed; they were, and are, my Mount Everest—ultimately defying any explanation of their magnetism, unbearably inviting—there to be seen and possibly known if I am willing to undertake the expedition.

It was not enough to watch animals, or even to touch them. I wanted to see their innermost workings, to be inside their minds, to see and feel and smell and hear the world as they did. My experiments in "being" an animal were usually carried out in private, since my mother's tolerance for my animal behaviors had pretty much vanished by the time I had licked one too many knees. In playing house with my sisters, however, these skills and experiments were encouraged, as they allowed for exciting new story lines to be developed. Typically, my middle sister would play mother (a role in which she was and is extremely fluent), and our youngest sister would accept whatever role we assigned her. Without exception, I played the family pet. Sometimes I was a dog, sometimes a horse, and sometimes, stretching myself to more exotic roles, I played a cougar or a lion or a tiger until the requisite fierce roars had exhausted my throat.

IF BERLITZ HAD OFFERED DOG

In my lifelong quest for fluency in animal languages, fluency in Dog was the first and the easiest. After all, native speakers lived in my neighborhood and could be readily studied. Whether in the company of a living, breathing dog or only conjuring the countless fictional dogs in my head—Bob, Lad, King, Buck, Lassie—I practiced. I practiced panting, to the annoyance of my sisters and to my own dismay when I discovered that far from cooling me as I had read it did for dogs, panting only made me dizzy and left me wondering if dogs ever hyperventilated as I did. I tried lapping water and eating from a bowl on the floor, wishing each time my muzzle were longer and more suited to the task. I truly loved (and still do) gnawing on bones from a steak or a chop, and understood at least in part why dogs look so blissful when granted such a treat. I practiced not turning my head when I heard a sound behind me but instead cocking an ear in that direction. It frustrated me that lacking highly mobile and visible pinnae I was unable to display publicly just how skilled I had become. Tail wagging presented problems not easily solved—a rolled shirt or towel gave a rather dead effect, no matter how much I wiggled my hindquarters. Ultimately, I settled on a wag much like my ear movements—refined, subtle, and known (most regrettably) only to me.

I perfected several growls, a snarl and a snap that ended with a delightfully audible click of my teeth that rarely failed to alarm those at whom it was directed. My hurt-dog yelp covered the complete range of having my paw accidentally stepped upon to mortally wounded and was realistic enough to stop people in midstep. And of course, my barks were convincing—so much so that I was occasionally employed to bark menacingly if my parents weren't home and someone came to the door. In college, my one-man "dog fights" were guaranteed to liven up a boring night in the dorm bathroom. It's amazing how easily you can convince otherwise intelligent people that there are two poodles at war in a shower stall.

There were other languages to be mastered as well. Horses eclipsed even dogs on my passion scale, and when at age ten I began riding lessons, a new language of movement, gesture and sounds opened to me. By age twelve, I had mastered the basics: the greeting exchange of slow, careful breaths in each other's nostrils; the nicker; the whinny; the alarm snort; the head tosses and snaking neck movements of an annoyed horse; the slitted eyes and pinned ears of anger; even the high-headed, wide-eyed sideways retreat of a spooked horse. To this day, when startled, I sometimes revert to a horselike shying. Annoying childhood pranksters attempting to dunk my head into the water fountain while I was drinking failed to realize that I had my ears turned back to hear them. They were always surprised when, as any horse might, I kicked them with great accuracy. Of course if they'd been able to speak Horse, they would have seen the pinned ears and the slitted eyes and known that they'd been given fair warning.

My only regret in learning the basics of Horse when I did was that it came too late to be truly useful. Between ages six and eight, I worked on my most ambitious role—the simultaneous roles of a Canadian Mountie, his horse, and his dog. If at that tender age I had known more than rudimentary Horse, my gallops through the neighborhood would have had far more authenticity.

ANIMALS EVERYWHERE

To the best of my ability, my love of animals was incorporated into every aspect of my life. My mother encouraged my interests even though she did not always understand them or share my curiosity and delight in all aspects of the natural world. She learned to check with caution any container in my possession. A mere Dixie cup might be home to a frog or a collection of shed locust skins or even a deliberately grown mold. Her laundry basket might contain newly washed socks or neatly folded pajamas; just as easily, it might be home to a naked baby bird with hideously visible internal organs. Her card table, turned upside down and wrapped in chicken wire, became home to Buster and Dandy, a pair of Rhode Island Red chickens who, as much older chickens, repaid her tolerance by merrily eating every blossom on three flats of Mother's Day plants.

Without a single question and little more than a raised eyebrow, my mother supplied me with pie pans, flour, molasses, and a paintbrush. Though she may have idly hazarded a wild guess as to what I had in mind, nothing prepared her for the reality of what I did with these items. I had just finished reading *The Yearling*, as she well knew—she'd been the one to find me sobbing so fiercely on the living room sofa that she actually feared one of my friends had died. But seeing the book in my hand, she ventured sympathetically, "I suppose you've gotten to the part where he shot Flag, huh?" I nodded and sobbed louder. "Well, dinner's ready whenever you are." Once I had recovered from grieving for the yearling deer, I decided to use Jody and his pa's method to track honeybees in my own neighborhood to their hive. The book had discussed at length the seemingly simple matter of using molasses to attract bees who would then receive a dab of flour on their behinds, said flour then serving as an easily followed visual marker of the bees' flight. I can now categorically state that my Great Bee Experiment proved only that this classic book was entirely a work of fiction, and that bees object rather violently to having flour dabbed on their behinds. It was not the last of my Great Experiments, but it was one of the more painful ones.

Only occasionally did my enthusiasm overrun my mother's considerable tolerance. I'll never know what rare gleam in my eye warned her when I asked for a small kitchen knife one fine summer afternoon, but she hesitated as she reached into the kitchen drawer. When further questioning revealed that I meant to carry out an exploratory autopsy on a dead rabbit I had found, she flatly refused me the loan of even a spoon. To this day, I am left wondering if a potentially brilliant career as a veterinary surgeon ended there and then.

But it was probably just as well. The proficiency in math that veterinary schooling requires was not my strong suit. Very often, school bored me. I might have fared better as a scholar if the rather dull Home Economics class had been replaced with a truly interesting course, say Barn Economics or Kennel Management 101. Had my teachers been wise, I could have been encouraged to love algebra at a tender age if only the math problems had been: "Seventeen zebras who left at noon are traveling west at nine miles an hour. Six lions who left at four o'clock are headed east at eight miles an hour. When will the zebras and lions meet, and how many zebras will be alive after that meeting?" The requisite cars, planes and trains usually invoked in these problems left me cold and disinterested.

BLESSED ARE THE BEASTS

Even my spiritual life was woven through with animals. Despite the emphasis our church placed on Jesus (who, I noted, did not even have a dog!), I felt a more natural alliance with Noah, my childhood hero.

(Jonah, having had such an intimate relationship with a whale, was another favorite of mine.) Given a Bible with a concordance, I immediately looked up every verse—and there are many—that contained mention of an animal: eagle, ass, horse, sparrow, lion, dog, sheep, lamb, cattle, goats, swine. I took to heart the notion that all of God's creatures were his creation, just as I was. As such, I assumed they were as welcome in Sunday school as any of the little children. And so it was that at a very tender age I had my first crisis of faith, which began with a coonhound I met on the way to church.

He was a grand dog, black with rusty tan, just the perfect size for draping a companionable arm across his back as we walked. And he was an agreeable dog. It took little effort to convince him to accompany me down the stairs and into my Sunday school class, where he settled politely next to my chair. How the teacher missed our entrance, I'll never know. I was not being secretive; it had yet to dawn on me that this was not a perfectly appropriate guest. In fact, I thought as I settled down to hear the day's Bible story, a dog and Sunday school was a heavenly combination.

Singing out the names for roll call, the teacher would glance up from her list to bestow a beaming smile on each child as they answered. "Suzanne?" she asked brightly, her teeth gleaming as she turned her head my way. Perhaps it is only in my imagination that she gasped and stepped backward; perhaps I've only dreamed of how her lips twitched and snarled with unspoken horror. At any rate, I do recall her question, "What is that dog doing here?" There was an unpleasant emphasis on the word *dog*.

I thought it was fairly obvious and said so. "He's here for Sunday school."

Her response shook my innocent acceptance of the church's teachings: "He does not belong here."

I was dumbstruck. Doesn't belong? Isn't he one of God's creatures? Didn't God make him too? Surely Jesus would be glad to have a coonhound in church, especially one that wasn't bothering a soul. If I could bring this scene to life on film, I would cast an articulate, passionate child who, with tremendous presence, argues the dog's case, quoting Scripture so fast and furious that the teacher eventually bows to the greater command of the Bible as a weapon, yields to a deeper understanding of God's love for dogs, and allows the dog to stay. Unfortunately, I was not articulate in the face of wrath and could only weakly protest as I squirmed under her glare.

"He smells." With that final statement, the teacher revealed the limits of her love for all of God's creatures. (In retrospect, I realize that had I brought in a real leper with stinking bandages or a drunk down on his luck and reeking of the gutter, the teacher's Christian charity might have fled as quickly. But I am older now, and a touch more cynical.) I was outraged, and protested with vigor: The dog did not smell. Well, to be perfectly honest, he did not smell bad, he just smelled the way some dogs do. And that's how God made him!

My arguments fell on deaf ears. The teacher insisted that I take the dog outside and return, sans canine, to my chair. Sadly and slowly, I climbed the few stairs, opened the door and stood for a moment with this dog. I apologized to him, and though I lacked the words to express my deep sorrow at the powerlessness of being only five years old, I think he understood. He must have, for his power and mine were similar; his world was also full of larger, stronger people who set rules that had to be obeyed. I hugged him—the memory of that warm, slightly greasy black coat, of that rich musky dog scent has stayed with me all these years—and he leaned into me, wagging his tail. With tears in my eyes and newfound doubt in my heart, I left him standing in the sunshine and returned to Sunday school, infinitely older and wiser.

Love Me, Love My Beetle

How people interacted with and reacted to animals was endlessly educational. I learned, for instance, that many adults were not nearly as brave as they seemed. The summer that I was ten, I carried a coffee can with me at all times. Sweetly patronizing adults would ask what it was that I had in there, and ever eager to share the amazing world of nature, I would open the top and show them my pet stag beetle, Benjy. I do not know what they expected from a ten-year-old kid and a coffee can, but the three-inch-long, impressively fierce-looking Benjy was decidedly not it. A few shrieked before they could recover their composure and smile weakly at me; some actually blanched. All looked at me with new eyes after that, and quite a few never again asked what I had, no matter how provocatively I might carry a container.

I suppose every child blessed with siblings carries resentments for youthful incidents long past. Ask me what I remember of being four years old and I'll tell you that was the year I had turtles. Ostensibly, one of the two turtles was mine and the other belonged to my sister Sheryl. Two years younger than I am, Sheryl wanted to do everything that I did, though our interests were considerably different. She found babies (human babies!) indescribably fascinating; I found them of far less intrigue than an earthworm drying on the sidewalk after a rainstorm. Happily playing with my turtles, enjoying the prick of their tiny claws on my hand, I was mildly annoyed when Sheryl asked to hold one. But at my mother's urging, I agreed to share the joy. More than three decades later, my lips still automatically lift into a sneer of disgust when I recall how, upon my placing a turtle upon her outstretched hand, my sister squealed, "He's got claws!" or something to that effect and flung the hapless turtle across the room. The turtle survived the incident, which in my memory has far outlived the turtle itself.

Sheryl has grown up since then. She now has the sense to avoid handling reptilian creatures, and I know better than to let her. Endlessly kindhearted, she loves animals best from a distance, though she does not always understand them; and there have been a few animals that she has loved up close and personal, muddy paws, drool and all. She earned high marks from me the day she discovered that an intermittent ear problem was caused by a lone dog hair curled neatly upon her left eardrum, the result of a bed shared with her dog. I love my sister, but despite that redeeming dog hair in her ear, I'll go to my grave remembering the turtle incident.

My father and I frequently tangled over animals. There was a pair of kittens I recklessly accepted and hid in the car overnight. It was his car, and despite my best intentions to wake up long before he did and sneak the kittens into the house, I never stirred until his roared "Suzanne!" broke the morning wide open. Those kittens taught me several lessons. First, set an alarm if you really do have to get up early. Second, don't put kittens in your father's car, at least not without informing him first.

Last, providing food (and lots of it) and water (lots of it) is not entirely sufficient for a kitten's needs. One must provide a litter box as well. The kittens went off to the local shelter, and I lost my allowance and quite a few privileges for a while.

I also forgot one night to mention to my father that a large Collie had followed me home (quite nicely once I took off my shoelaces and my belt and hooked the makeshift leash around his neck) and that I had hidden him in the small shed that housed our garbage cans. How was I to know that my father would finish his supper early and decide to take the trash cans out then? He normally didn't take the trash out until much later. Since I had momentarily forgotten the dog, the combination of deep barking, surprised swearing and the bellowing of my name came as a shock. My allowance took yet another hit.

A good deal did happen to me in my youth and adolescence that easily qualifies me for membership in any number of support groups and twelve-step programs. But somehow, I came through it all relatively intact, bearing only a reasonable load of baggage to sort out along my life's journey. It may be that any child with a consuming passion is buffered against life's blows by that very passion; it may be that the animals themselves served as both buffers and healers. I have a hard time imagining that a stamp collection would have done as well as my animal friends did.

Where the Animals Lead Me

Through childhood and beyond, a veritable Noah's ark of animals have accompanied me on my life's journey. Long before I read Joseph Campbell's wise advice to "follow your bliss," I was already following my heart's desire. There were other opportunities available to me in life—my high school art teachers urged me to attend art school, my English teachers pushed me toward a career as a writer. My grandfather, aware of my great love of books, offered to pay my college tuition if I agreed to become a librarian. I was surrounded by disapproval and dire warnings of inevitable failure if I pursued my dreams. My stubborn insistence on following my bliss created conflict and pain in my relationships with those who could not understand why I spent my teenage years at a nearby stable, why I pursued an animal husbandry degree only to abandon that to leap at a chance to work with a guide dog organization and then move on from there to manage a stable and kennels and to ultimately become a trainer. At every crossroad, I took only the path that would lead me where I wanted to go—toward a deeper understanding of a life shared with animals.

I write this book in a house filled with wonderful animals—seven dogs, seven cats, a pair of tortoises, a parrot and a box turtle. From my window, I can glimpse my horses, the donkey and some of the Scottish Highland cattle that grace our pastures. There is mud on my jeans, left there by Charlotte the pig's affectionate greeting. I know that in the warm glow of the barn lights, my loving husband is tending to the nighttime chores, talking to calves as he hands out treats of stale bread, settling the turkeys, chickens and quail in for the night. In my relationship with each of these much-loved and complex beings, including my husband, there are ghosts and echoes of all the animals that have shared my life, and the seedlings of a wisdom crafted from both joys and sorrows. I am grateful for the immeasurable love bestowed upon me daily by my husband and my animals. Sometimes, I question whether I deserve such blessings. If I have somehow grown into a person who deserves what she has been given so freely, it is in large part the reflection of the grace and forgiveness granted to me by the animals who have accompanied me thus far on my life's journey.

Those who do not know better label me simply as an "animal lover" and find it charming, if odd, that a parrot flies freely through the house, that a turtle tells me quite clearly he'd like a cherry tomato for lunch, that my dogs find it not at all unusual to go for a walk in the woods with a turkey or a pig. I give these people amusing tales of waking to find a cat's gift of a dead mole on my pillow or the inexplicable presentation of a live, unhurt baby bird, and we laugh at the dogs' latest adventures. While sometimes impressed by my knowledge of animals and their ways, many people are bemused by my insatiable lust for an ever-deeper, fuller understanding. For them, it is enough to have a pet, to "love animals." And they leave our farm with an incomplete view of our life and of who I am.

I am not an animal lover or a pet owner. I am, perhaps, an animal husband in the oldest sense of the word, but it is much more than even that. These animals are my friends, my partners, my fellow travelers on life's journey. I do not "have" animals as I have collections of art or books. I have relationships with each animal; some are more intimate than others. I try to listen as carefully to each animal as I would to any human friend.

To be sure, tending to the needs of so many creatures gives shape and rhythm to my life and to my husband's. Our plans and goals are often delayed or altered in response to crises as simple as an unexpected puddle on the floor or as complicated as caring for a critically ill or dying animal. There are times when we chafe, individually and together, against the constraints of a life with so many animals in our care. But the immediate and undeniable reality of the animal world grounds us in ways we cannot fully articulate though we can feel it working its peaceful magic deep within our hearts and minds. Fortunately, my husband understands that he did not marry an "animal lover" but someone who travels daily in the company of animals, forever trying to be open to the places they may take me, to the sights and sounds I might have missed were it not for them.

To travel in the company of animals is to walk with angels, guides, guardians, jesters, shadows and mirrors. I cannot imagine how it is to travel bereft of such excellent companions. In my journey, seeking to know animals more fully, wandering in their foreign lands, struggling for fluency in these other tongues, I found much more than just the animals themselves. As all travelers do, no matter how far they may go, no matter how exotic the terrain or bizarre the culture, I discovered myself.

The thirst for a deeper understanding of animals and the desire for relationships with them is not unique to me. Everywhere I go, I find others who are equally passionate about animals, who want to know more. With great joy, I have made it my life's work to help others better understand the dogs with whom they share their lives, and to help them explore new depths in their relationships with animals. This is not a one-sided process of simply explaining the beautiful nuances of canine communications or the structures and protocol of canine culture. It *is* important to understand how and why our dogs behave the way they do and to open ourselves to a different perspective on the world: the dog's perspective of life, love and relationships. This book offers the reader the knowledge that is necessary to more fully appreciate these gentle predators who share our beds, and with this knowledge comes new insights and greater awareness.

But more than that is needed. Relationships—if they are to achieve the depth and intimacy that makes our souls sing—are built on far more than good information about how and why others act as they do. As with any relationship, a fuller understanding of ourselves and what we bring to the table is necessary. Of all the gifts that animals can offer, perhaps the greatest is this opportunity to delve deep inside ourselves. Without judgment or timetables, with patience and an amazing capacity for forgiveness, animals are the ideal guides through our inner landscapes. In moments of glorious agreement as well as moments of frustrated disconnection, our relationships with our dogs serve us well, gently nudging us to a greater understanding of the dynamics of two beings in willing partnership and to new insights into who we are. Once we begin the journey toward the authentic connections we long for, we cannot help but be profoundly changed, often in ways we did not expect but welcome wholeheartedly. A life lived in relationship with an animal has the power to make us both fully human and more fully humane. And this spills over, as a fullness of soul inevitably does, to other relationships, weaving its magic across our entire lives.

This book is for those who also may have spent their youth considering the world from beneath the dining room table, for those who wished as desperately as I did for a tail to wag. It is also for those who never once licked a knee or barked at the pizza deliveryman. It is a book for those who would become fluent in Dog and other tongues, and for those who would learn for the first time these most eloquent of languages. It is for those whose hearts have been shaped and filled by animals now gone, and for those whose hearts have yet to be broken as only an animal can break them. Most of all, this book is for those who would journey through life with dogs and other animals as their fellow travelers, and in doing so, perhaps discover themselves.

2

A BLACK DOG'S PRAYERS

With an eye made quiet by the power
Of harmony, and the deep power of joy,
We see into the life of things.
WILLIAM WORDSWORTH

I BELIEVE THAT I HAVE SEEN DOGS PRAYING to whatever gods dogs pray to, their prayers as silent but surely as heartfelt as our own. And this dog was praying for the leash to break. He did not strain against the tether that bound him to his owner but sat quietly as far away as the long tracking lead allowed. He sat with his back to us, a gleaming black stillness of dog against the lush green field. As he stared intently across the pasture and beyond, I had no doubts that should the leash break, his escape route was already plotted. The pasture fence that stood between him and freedom served more as a reminder than a meaningful barrier, meant to contain only content dogs who did not pray such prayers and my gentle, elderly horses, who obeyed even a thin string as a boundary. In my mind's eye, this dog would clear the sagging wire fence with one effortless bound and be gone, a black arrow moving quickly away from us to somewhere more interesting. But his prayers went unanswered, and so he sat, the uninterested blankness of his back a clear message to us as we watched him.

If dogs do pray, it may be that they pray as we do, for what we long for, for what we need, and for solutions to situations they can neither solve nor escape. Not all dog prayers are serious ones. My husband's Golden Retriever, Molson, prays frequently and gleefully while we are cooking. As far as we can tell, she prays for us to drop entire cartons of eggs (which we sometimes do), to lose control of whatever is on the cutting board (which happens frequently), and for us to turn our attention away from fresh bread cooling on the counter (we are slow learners). Molson sometimes smiles in her sleep, and we suspect that she is remembering our wedding day, a day when her prayers were answered in a way that may well rank as one of the greatest moments of her life.

The wedding cake had been carefully transported home to the farm, where we were to be married, and placed in the cool of the basement, an area unavailable to the dogs. The cake's arrival and resting place did not escape Molson's notice. Ever watchful, she waited for her opportunity amidst the chaos of preparations for an at-home wedding and reception. Inevitably, someone left a door open, and without drawing any attention to herself, Molson seized the moment and disappeared.

I had finished bathing the horses so that they looked beautiful for their part in the ceremony, and as I stepped into the basement to put away the bucket and sponge, I was surprised to be greeted by Molson. The ecstatic look on her face was quickly explained by the mound of icing on her nose. Groaning with disbelief, I looked at the cake, which now read, "Congratulations Suzanne and—" The entire corner of the cake with John's name had been eaten. For a long superstitious moment, I stood wondering if this was an omen to be heeded or some form of canine commentary on our wedding plans. (Our guests, when served the mutilated cake, also ventured a few interpretations, but they nonetheless ate the cake without hesitation.) Never before or since have Molson's food prayers been answered in such a spectacular way. But she continues to pray, and sometimes, the kitchen gods answer.

Molson's prayers are simple ones, easy to interpret. But this black dog's prayers were complicated ones, filled with sorrow and anger and love and pain. To step into a dog's mind requires that you step into his paws and see the world through his eyes. To understand his prayers, you must look for what lights his entire being with joy, and look also for what dims that light. As I talked with Wendy, the dog's owner, I was searching for an understanding of what might make a dog hold himself apart from us. He was clearly loved and cared for with meticulous attention—every inch of his body glowed with well-being, and there was no evidence of his past, when he wandered a city's street, unloved and fending for himself. The intervening years of good food and love had polished this nameless street urchin into a handsome, funny and intelligent dog named Chance. And yet there he sat, removed from us, his mind distant and uninterested. Something had gone wrong; why else would a dog pray as he did for the leash to break so that he might gallop away?

Any relationship is a complicated thing at best, springing as it does from an intersection of two lives; two sets of desires, interests and fears; two different perspectives and understandings of the shared world. In our relationships with animals, we find additional mysteries of other languages and cultures quite unlike our own. While the differences between us and animals both charm and attract, they also serve to complicate the whole affair. I am quite certain that every dog on earth goes to his grave mystified by certain human behaviors. My own dogs adore water in any form except that which is found in a bathtub accompanied by dog shampoo. As a result, they are very often wet, especially in the summer when their wading pool is constantly available to them. While on most nights I welcome the comfort of their warm bodies as I sleep, there is something less than delightful about snuggling up to hot, wet dogs. As I shoo them from bed for reasons they cannot comprehend, they throw themselves on the floor with dramatic sighs and expressions that reveal the truth of John Steinbeck's comment, "I have seen a look in dogs' eyes, a quickly vanishing look of amazed contempt, and I am convinced that dogs think humans are nuts."

Whatever dogs may think of us, it is also true that it is no easy matter to have an intimate relationship with an animal who communicates in variations on a theme of ears and tail, who mutters under his breath in dark rumbles when displeased, and who enjoys rolling in decomposing creatures. But for all the difficulties and differences that lie between us and our dogs, we love them, and we want to understand them. We look at our dogs and they look back, and the sense that our dogs are trying to speak to us is unshakable. Equally unshakable is the nagging feeling that we often fail to understand what they have to say. We are right on both counts. But what we long for is not necessarily what we get, at least not without having to learn some hard lessons along the way.

What Wendy wanted from Chance was companionship and more of the joyful connection she had shared with her first dog, Mel. What she got were knots in her stomach and a very complex relationship with a dog she loved but did not understand. This was not Wendy's first experience in dog ownership. Her first dog, Mel, had died at the grand age of nearly seventeen years old, every one of those years spent as Wendy's constant companion through troubled teenage years and into young adulthood. Confident, gentle, intelligent, Mel was easily trained, and her excellent manners—no matter what the situation—made her welcome everywhere. Whether on the leash or off, Mel was never far from Wendy, quick to respond to any command. Wendy had only to ask, and Mel gave all that was in her power to give. In everything she did, this dog lived as if she had but one purpose in life: to be with the person she loved most and make her happy.

When Mel died, Wendy's grief was immense; she had truly lost her best friend. She did not want another dog—somehow, this seemed disloyal to Mel. But as her grief became unmanageable, and the emptiness left by Mel's death became more insistent, she began to consider another dog. One morning, on impulse, she drove to the county animal shelter, hoping to find a dog who needed a second chance at life. And there he was, his face so much like Mel's that she knew instantly that this dog was coming home with her. But from the very first moments, Chance made it clear that he was not Mel; he was a decidedly different dog.

Ten months old, Chance had already spent six of those months in the shelter, surrounded by the chaos and sadness of so many unwanted animals, his world limited to what he could see from the confines of the narrow kennel run. Set free in Wendy's living room that first day, he was overwhelmed and could only spin in circles, the same behavior he had used in the kennel to entertain himself, the only game he knew. For hours, Wendy watched in amazement and then growing dismay as he paced and circled, unable to relax until she put him in a crate where he promptly fell asleep, exhausted. He did not understand this new freedom; he only understood the limited world of confinement. Nothing in Wendy's experience prepared her for this challenge. As she lay in bed after the first exhausting day of trying to help Chance learn about the newer, larger world she could offer him, she wearily asked herself, "Who knew dogs were so much work?" Looking back, she says now that if Chance had been her first dog, she probably would have returned him to the shelter. But she did not take him back to that terrible place. Mel had taught her what was possible, and Wendy was determined to find a way to help Chance enjoy the same life and the same freedoms that Mel had enjoyed.

For all his problems, Chance blossomed under Wendy's patient care. In their first obedience class, he proved himself a quick learner, and they graduated at the top of their class. At the next level of training, problems began to appear. Though extraordinarily precise and happy in their practice at home, Chance seemed capable of only three responses in class: He performed well, he lay down as if in complete surrender, or—given the opportunity—he bolted away. This puzzled Wendy. How could a dog who worked so well at home be such a problem in training class?

Trying to understand his paradoxical behavior, she received a bewildering array of assessments. One trainer informed her that his problems were the result of a nervous system that didn't develop correctly due to having spent six months in the shelter. While she agreed that perhaps he had missed important puppyhood experiences, Wendy could not understand how this explained why his behavior was so different outside of class. Surely if this was a lack of proper development, the behavior would appear in many contexts. Another trainer, pointing to Chance as he lay on the floor, labeled him "fearful and submissive." Yet another trainer claimed Chance's frustrating behavior sprang directly from his "will to displease"—that while the dog knew what he was supposed to do, he was deliberately choosing to be obstinate. And each offered different solutions for the problem, none of which made sense to Wendy and none of which ultimately made any difference in her dog's behavior.

It seemed to Wendy that she owned two dogs—the exasperating dog she had in training class and the funny, intelligent dog who lived with her. She desperately wanted to understand Chance and to give him the life and freedoms she wanted him to have. Like countless dog owners trying to understand their dogs, Wendy asked every question she could think of. She asked about the dog's health (he had a few allergies and she adjusted his diet), tried to figure out how his mind worked (were food or toys or some reward the best way to restore his enthusiasm for working with her?), considered his puppyhood and everything he had missed while living at the shelter. She even tried to figure out what breed characteristics might be floating around in his Heinz 57 background—was his behavior in part a genetic legacy? And like so many determined, loving owners, Wendy tried different training methods and training equipment, hoping to find the magic technique or perfect collar that would resolve the conflicts. Telling herself that these were the experts who knew more than she did (or why would she be having these problems?) she ignored the uneasiness in her heart when trainers recommended techniques that seemed harsh to her. But no matter what book she read or what trainer she turned to, no matter how many questions she asked, the answers were not what she was hoping to find. Though she did not know it yet, the answer was always right in front of her, clearly written in her dog's eyes. She simply didn't know what the question was.

In Douglas Adams' *The Hitchhiker's Guide to the Galaxy* series, there is a running gag where the characters are reminded, "The answer is forty-two." What no one knows, of course, is what the question is to which that is the answer. Not surprisingly, whatever questions are proposed turn out to be the wrong ones. The people who come to me or any other trainer are looking for answers. But sometimes, even though the answer is right before them, they are asking the wrong questions.

Magic Knots

At a seminar years ago, I was asked to work with a difficult and very powerful dog. After perhaps half an hour, I had him sitting quietly beside me, able to control himself no matter who ran in or out of the door or who walked by with another dog. This was tremendous progress for a dog who earlier that day had literally blown the door off a crate and bounded across the room to grab another dog. We had started our work with the dog wearing his usual leash, a massive thing that would have been entirely appropriate for restraining an elephant. As the dog had relaxed and learned some self-control, I had switched to lighter and softer leads, first a sturdy but light canvas lead and, finally, dredged up from the bottom of my bag, a thin leather lead with many knots. I remember being surprised when someone handed me this lead—it was my "show" lead, used only when showing my German Shepherds, the knots useful in maintaining a grip on the lead. But it was suitable for my use with this dog, and I thought nothing more about it—all I really wanted was the lightness in my hand.

The dog's progress was remarkable, and I could see wheels turning in many audience members' heads. Mentally, I thanked the dog for having given such a lovely demonstration of how quickly simple concepts could translate into changes in a dog's behavior without the need for force or punishment. "Any questions?" I asked the audience. A woman raised her hand, frowning a bit as she said, "I can see that really made a difference. But I'm not sure how to apply that to my own dog." Before I could shape an answer, she continued, "Where exactly do you tie the knots?"

The knots? I stared stupidly at her, completely stumped, unable to answer her at all. She leaned forward and pointed at the dog. "He got much better after you used the leash with the knots. What I want to know is exactly where I should tie the knots in my leash. Is there a specific formula you use depending on the dog's size?"

My husband later pointed out that I should not have laughed while trying to explain that it was only an accident that my show lead was even in my training equipment bag. Right then and there, he noted with a Barnumesque side I hadn't seen before, I might have sold her (at a hefty price no doubt) a "Magical Knots" lead, or at least have offered to customize a Magical Knots lead for her and her own dogs. Even though she had watched me at every step as the dog progressed, she had latched onto the lead as the key ingredient in my success with the dog and so had been stuck in the wrong question, "Where exactly do you tie the knots?"

All of us, at some time or another, in a variety of ways, ask about the magic knots. What we really want to know is how to deepen and enhance the connection between ourselves and our dogs, how to encourage the moments where we and our dogs move together through life in harmony and mutual understanding. Books and videos can tell us how to teach them tricks or how to stop our dogs from digging in the garden or can help us care for them throughout their lives. And we read all that and impatiently shake our heads, because there's something else we want, something else we're actually trying to ask when we ask about magic knots. Though we may not be able to articulate it, what we want is what Antoine de Saint-Exupéry described in *Wind, Sand and Stars*: "Love does not consist in gazing at each other but in looking outward together in the same direction."

But finding our way to such a relationship is not easy. And even if we've been there before, as Wendy had with Mel, we cannot take the same path when we begin another journey with another dog. Each relationship walks its own way. Complicating matters even further, Wendy's relationship with Mel was a blessing, a gift of grace, not the result of knowledge or deliberate choice on Wendy's part. While such relationships are powerful and take us to a point of connection we may not have dreamed possible, we may be in for a rude awakening when we find ourselves back at the first step, with a new dog at our side, and not sure how to get where we want to go. We've been there, and we think we know the way; and then, when we're the ones who must set the course and choose the path, we realize that we've not done this before. While we have been where we want to go again, we realize with humility and gratitude that it was the old soul of a dog like Mel who had carried us safely there. And now, we need to find our own way.

IN SEARCH OF WHAT IS POSSIBLE

Though she had enjoyed the beginner's class, Wendy had become increasingly uneasy with what she saw in the more advanced training. It was common to see dogs being dragged across the room by their collars or shouted at or jerked off their feet with fierce leash corrections. Unwilling to do this to her dog despite the instructors' adamant "this is how it must be done," Wendy began to attend classes only intermittently, using the situation to work with Chance as she wanted to, trying not to see what was happening to the dogs around her.

The night came when Wendy could no longer ignore what she saw. In disbelief and horror, she and Chance watched as the instructor pinched a young dog's ear to force the dog to open her mouth and accept a dumbbell, a common technique in use for many decades and hotly defended by those who use it as the only reliable method for training a dog to retrieve on command. In her pain and confusion, the dog only tightened her jaws and fought to get free. Declaring the dog to be particularly stubborn, the trainer instructed the dog's owner to help her in a "stereo" ear pinch, meaning that while the trainer pinched one ear, the handler would be doing the same to the other ear. The dog screamed in protest, struggling to get away, but the trainer did not stop until—after many minutes—the dog went limp. Looking at this sweet dog who now lay dazed, eyes filled with fear and pain, Wendy felt sick. She looked down at Chance to promise him that she would never do that to him, no matter what. As her dog raised his eyes to hers, she saw an immense sadness in his face. Within her head, she heard him ask clearly, "Why are we here?" It was a very good question, and Wendy knew the answer. She never again returned to that training class.

Although Chance had already earned his first obedience title, Wendy—unable to find a trainer whose approach felt comfortable and right to her—had lost interest in formal obedience training. But she was still deeply worried about Chance's tendency to bolt. Each time he had run away, she could see that his mind and body were no longer connected. His eyes were flat, empty, his body moving in panicked flight from whatever had upset him. Until he calmed down, he would not return to her unless she or someone managed to catch him. Each time he ran away, Wendy knew his life was in danger; living in suburbia, it was only a matter of time before he was hit by a car and injured or killed. Concerned for his safety, Wendy had tried everything that had been suggested by various trainers but with no success. At times, Chance still ran as though his life depended on it. Although her experience in training class had left her shaken and distrustful of trainers in general, she sought out a well-known trainer and author who promised a "motivational" approach. After briefly working with Chance, the trainer told Wendy that an electric shock collar was the only solution that might save his life. Reluctantly, Wendy agreed.

The private lesson began innocently enough. The trainer carefully fitted the shock collar to Chance's neck, then suggested that they wait for half an hour or so for the dog to forget about this new collar before they worked with him in a large, fenced-in field. As they waited, Wendy noticed that even though nothing much had happened yet, Chance was already showing signs of feeling stressed. His ears, normally pricked with interest in his world, were held flattened sideways in a position she thought of as "airplane ears." This was not a good sign. Out in the field, he became even more apprehensive when Wendy removed the leash as the trainer directed and, leaving Chance on a sit stay, walked roughly twenty feet away.

"Call him," the trainer said, and Wendy did, but even as the words left her mouth, she knew her dog was no longer in his mind. His eyes went blank in that all-too-familiar way. Ears now folded back tightly against his head, Chance bolted past Wendy and began to run in frantic loops along the field's fence.

"Call him again!" the trainer urged, but Wendy's command did not register on the dog, who ran on and on. The trainer hit the button on the remote transmitter that sent a signal to the collar. When the shock registered, Chance leaped off the ground, screaming and snarling in surprise and pain, twisting in the air as he tried desperately to bite at the collar itself. Noting, "He probably can't hear you over himself," the trainer told Wendy to call him again and again, but nothing penetrated Chance's terror. At that moment, Wendy's heart spoke up loud and clear: This is not what you do to a dog you love. No longer caring what the trainer had to say, Wendy moved to catch the frantic dog in her arms. Only then did the trainer take her thumb off the button—she had been sending shocks to Chance all that time.

"Well, that should fry his little brain," the trainer noted with satisfaction, adding that he might need a "tune-up" session as a reminder in a few months. She pointed out how successful this training session had been. Indeed, Chance now stood anxiously watching Wendy, afraid to let her move more than a few feet from him. It was true that the bolting behavior had disappeared; what was not evident in that moment was the new behavior that had taken its place. After that session, Chance was unwilling to stay in any position for any reason, even if Wendy went no farther than the end of a six-foot lead. For months afterward, Wendy had to return to the baby steps of puppy training to rebuild the confidence destroyed in just a few wretched minutes. Worse still, when Chance was able to once again successfully hold his stays, the bolting behavior reappeared with a vengeance. But now he would bolt in almost any situation, and without showing any of the early warning signs that had previously alerted Wendy to a potential problem.

More than two years later, they stood in my training field, the cumulative weight of mistakes and misunderstanding heavy between them. Riddled with guilt for what she had allowed to happen, Wendy had slowly resigned herself to the fact that Chance was going to have a limited life. Only the gentle insistence of a mutual friend had convinced her that I might be able to help without hurting Chance in any way. After attending one of my seminars to watch me work, Wendy had agreed.

Watching Chance and Wendy as we walked out to my training field, I had no doubt that she loved her dog and that he loved her. But I knew from a lifetime of mistakes with animals that love alone was not always enough to carry someone where they longed to be. I understood how bewildering it was to stand lost at the end of a road that had been taken in good faith, each turn made in hope, every step fueled by a deep desire to get someplace that looked nothing at all like this unexpected destination. The road she had taken was a road whose twists and turns I knew all too well. But I also knew the way back. And I knew that all Wendy needed to find her own way back to where she had meant to go all along was contained in one simple phrase: *What is possible between a human and an animal is possible only within a relationship.*

The relationship between Wendy and Chance had been damaged, not destroyed; without repair, the damage would forever limit what was possible between them. The restoration of trust and joy that had once flowed between them began when I asked her to see the world through Chance's eyes. He was simply a dog, and for all his intelligence, his understanding of his world was shaped by what the person he loved and trusted had done and allowed to happen. He did not understand good intentions. He did not realize that her mistakes had been the result of misplaced faith in trainers. He knew only that there was no joy left in working with her, that she had repeatedly ignored or misunderstood what he told her when he lay on the ground in mute resignation or when he fled fearfully away, pushed beyond his limits. In every way he could, Chance had told her how he felt, but she had not heard him. He was simply a dog, and he had no way to solve this. He was left only with his prayers. Once, perhaps, he had prayed to be heard; now he prayed for escape.

Gently, for I had been in the same place where this sad, sweet woman now stood, I asked, "If you were Chance and all that you just described had happened to you, would you feel safe? Would you trust your person? Would you look forward with joy and anticipation to working together? Would you want to be in a relationship like this?"

Her face sagged as she shook her head. For a long moment, she stared at her feet, then raising her head, looked me in the eye: "I love my dog. I never wanted to hurt him. I just wanted to train him, give him freedom. And I trusted that those damn trainers knew more than I did." She paused, struggling not to cry. Taking a deep breath, she asked, "What do I do now?"

To reclaim the trust that had been lost, Wendy and Chance were going to have to learn new ways to work together. In everything she did, she had a choice: She could either support and enhance the relationship with her dog, or undermine it. She would need to learn to see the world from her dog's perspective, so that she could understand how and why her actions either dimmed or encouraged the light in his eyes. With consideration for the differences between herself and a dog, she needed to treat Chance as she would want to be treated, with the loving respect she would treat any beloved friend. Communication would improve when she learned to say what she meant in ways the dog could understand, when she was able to listen to what Chance told her in his body language and responses. Her dog would never lie to her, but she had to learn to trust that what he told her was his truth at that moment. Everything she did with Chance had to be guided by this one elemental point: Does this help or harm the relationship?

"But where do I begin?" she asked. In my head, her question was an echo of so many other students who had also asked, "How do you do this?"—as if building or repairing a relationship with an animal was a specific skill that could be explained and taught like teaching their dogs to heel or come when called. In trying to answer them, I have always felt a bit like the artist who, when asked how to paint, responded, "It's easy. You put the red where the red goes and the green where the green goes and the yellow where the yellow goes. . . ." I also remember Matisse's response to a woman who thoughtlessly asked how long it had taken him to paint a picture: "A few hours . . . and my whole life."

I know what it is to long for a recipe, to hope for magic knots, to want a shortcut to knowledge that can be gained in only one way—practice, persistence and experience. When I was first studying with Linda Tellington-Jones, I asked her which place on an animal's body was the best place for beginning the hands-on work. Linda replied, "Anywhere is fine. Unless the animal tells you otherwise. Then pick another spot." This answer initially maddened me. I wanted what I did to be perfect, and I wanted the precise recipe to achieve the results I so admired in Linda's work with animals. But I slowly came to realize that the reply that so frustrated me was a completely truthful answer, one that contained a great deal of the wisdom that informs Linda's work with animals. To begin the dialogue between human and animal so that a relationship may develop is like starting any conversation. You have to pick a starting point, and if that doesn't work, you pick another one, and if necessary another, until at last you find a point of agreement. And then you begin to explore the common ground, feeling your way as you go, always listening to the animal, the only one who can tell you when you've got it right.

"All right," I told Wendy. "Here's how we're going to start repairing this relationship. Leave Chance where he is—it doesn't matter that he's not looking this way. I want you to say nothing but take a step parallel to him. Don't move toward him; just keep taking slow steps until Chance notices. He will. And when he looks your way, don't say a word. Just toss him a treat."

Puzzled, she did as I said. Still deep in his prayers at the end of the leash, Chance glanced over his shoulder when he caught Wendy's movements in his peripheral vision. He was surprised by the unexpected treat that landed next to him. Briefly, he looked at Wendy before reaching for the food and then turning away to resume his prayers. She took another step, and again he glanced over his shoulder. Another treat and this time a long contemplative stare from the dog before he turned away. A few more steps, more tidbits, and then it happened. Chance swallowed the food and then slowly approached Wendy. He stood looking up at her, clearly questioning this unusual turn of events. She fed him a little more, and while he ate, we could see the wheels turning as he thought over the situation. As if to test what he believed might be happening, the dog turned away from Wendy and stared off into the distance. "Wait," I told her, "don't move and just wait." For what seemed an eternity, Wendy and her dog stood motionless, frozen in a tableau of disconnection. Then, deliberately, without being asked, because he chose to, Chance turned back to her and looked straight into her eyes, his tail wagging.

From that moment on in that training session, there was no getting rid of him. Like Mary's lamb, wherever Wendy went, Chance was sure to go. Amazed and delighted, Wendy moved in every possible direction, even trying to run away from him, but Chance was always there beside her, his eyes shining. Over and over she kept shaking her head in disbelief, saying it couldn't be as easy as that.

"I know it sounds too simple," I agreed, "but look at your dog. What is he telling you?"

With a wistful smile, she looked at the dog who stood watching her with bright eyes and a softly wagging tail. "He's telling me that he's happy."

"Then believe him!" I smiled. "He's never lied to you, and he never will. If you want to know if something works for Chance, ask him. He doesn't care how silly or simple something may seem to you. If it works for him, that's all that matters."

For Wendy, the repair efforts of the next few months required concentration and focus, but it was work she gladly embraced. With each day, their relationship grew stronger. In Chance's resistance, she no longer saw a dog with "a will to displease." She saw a beloved friend saying "I don't understand" or "This bores me" or "I can't do that." And then she helped him understand, or made it more interesting, or switched to something more exciting, or asked for something he could do. She opened her eyes to the subtleties of his every movement and began to understand what a flick of an ear or a glance really meant. Chance no longer needed to bolt away or lay down to be heard. He began to trust that Wendy saw the quieter messages written in the slight drop of his tail or the folding of his whiskers against his muzzle. Confident in her support, he began to try harder, now willing to work with her in partnership as they joyfully mastered new skills together.

NO RECIPES

At work in all our intimate relationships is a desire for harmony, for togetherness, for friendship; we long to both love and be loved, to understand and be understood. What is the recipe for such a relationship? There isn't one. There can't be. Recipes are only a beginning, a guide by which you begin to learn the basics. Without recipes, we must reinvent the wheel, which, though possible, is time-consuming and not always successful. Imagine if each of us had to learn to make a cake from scratch, but we had no guide as to what ingredients went into a cake. Even though we have seen cakes and eaten them, unless we had watched someone else make one from scratch we might stare at the cupboard for a long time (eternity?) before thinking to blend some butter, sugar, flour and eggs to create a tasty treat. A recipe is a shortcut to a limited form of knowledge, though not necessarily to experience or even success.

The basics of dog behavior and the training of dogs *can* be learned through recipes. At this simple level of training and relationship, there are basic ingredients that you will need to know about. This book trusts that at some other time, through the many "cookbooks" available, you have already mastered the basic recipes for a life shared with animals. But there is a limit to what such books can offer. There are only a limited number of ways by which you can teach your dog to sit on command or walk politely at your side, just as there are only a limited number of ways to make an ordinary cream pie. This book trusts that you want to know more. While an ordinary pie is delicious, it is possible to create something even more remarkable and memorable, something that satisfies far beyond a basic level.

In cooking, there is a level where the basics have been thoroughly mastered so that recipes are no longer necessary or even desired. At this point, experience and knowledge become a springboard for cooking as an art, each creation as individual as the cook herself as she selects the ingredients and proportions that delight her. Beautiful improvisations on a theme become the goal. A chocolate cream pie previously concocted of instant pudding, Cool Whip and a store-bought crust may now be made of the finest Belgian chocolate laced with elegant swirls of raspberry liquer and nestled atop a delicate crust of hazelnut and gin-gersnaps. Because such a creation springs from a desire to take the experience to new heights of intensity and subtlety, because it is created from feel from a little of this and a touch of that, the cook herself may be unable to offer a precise recipe. Attempts to get such a recipe creates the maddening scenario where a budding cook tries to get Grandma to surrender the recipe for her famous piecrust only to discover that Grandma long ago lost the need for measuring cups and just puts in what's needed until "it feels right."

It is not possible to develop a deep relationship with an animal simply because you know and can recite the basic ingredients, no more than you can match Grandma's famous pastry armed only with the information that a piecrust is made of flour, shortening, and a splash of ice water. While you need to know these basics, such knowledge is not enough. You're going to have to make as many piecrusts as Grandma did, until it feels right in your hands, until the sense of what makes a piecrust right is in your bones. Grandma may give you useful tips to help you as you practice, but the experience and excellent results will come only with time and effort. You may choose a poorer-quality flour or a different shortening or decide not to invest so much time in perfecting your piecrusts; the results will reflect your choices.

In reaching for this book, you are moving toward the deeper levels in a relationship with an animal, where recipes are no longer useful or even possible. The stories in this book will not help you create predictable, wonderful results with the animals in your life; instead, they offer useful tips that when combined with experience and practice, help you get it "just right." I can tell you what ingredients seem to be common in healthy relationships, but it's up to you to create your own special recipe, one that uniquely reflects how you share your life with animals. The specific techniques that worked for the relationships in this book may not be appropriate or useful for you. From this point on in the journey, you must collect your own ingredients and brew them, stew them or swallow them whole as it suits you and your dog and your relationship.

I do have one recipe I can pass along. It may seem all too reminiscent of Grandma's piecrust, but it's a good one.

Take one lifetime with animals. Grind it hard against mistakes and misunderstanding. Season heavily with the desire to get it right, and layer generously with the forgiveness of every animal who passes through your hands. Stew for years, being sure that gifted teachers (animal or human) stir the mess from time to time as needed so it keeps cooking. Serve when it begins to get clear. Yield: a few precious drops worth having.

Each relationship with an animal and a human is a bridge uniquely shaped to carry only those two, and so must be crafted by them. Though the work of a lifetime, the building and repairs are done slowly, in the heart's time, one beat after another. And it is thirsty work, as work of the heart always is, for the heart thirsts after the things that are invisible to the eye, things you cannot grasp with your hand. Simple notions, these few drops I've thus far distilled from a lifetime of learning from animals. But they are surprisingly satisfying to a thirsty heart.

Chance and Wendy have become my good friends. They live not far from us, and happily, they share our passion for the farm's open spaces and hemlock woods, for shaggy cattle with horns and afternoon walks with a pig or a turkey. Chance now has the life and freedom that Wendy had always wanted for him. Some days when Wendy works, Chance stays here with us, and the black plume of his tail waving in the tall grass is a familiar sight as I look out my office window onto the yard and the pastures beyond. My nickname for Chance is Einstein, meant as a tribute to this dog's intelligence. When I call him by that famous name, he always smiles. I know that his namesake long ago defined the speed at which light travels, but each day, this good black dog reminds me of an even more amazing phenomenon—the speed at which forgiveness travels in a dog's eyes.

Through the grace of a dog's forgiveness, and by keeping the relationship with her dog as the defining factor in all she did with him, Wendy and Chance ultimately achieved more than she had ever dared dream possible. One day, a trophy unexpectedly arrived in the mail, accompanied by a certificate declaring Chance the top-scoring obedience dog among all mixed breeds in the Northeast, an honor Wendy was unaware they had won. But how far they have come in their relationship is not best defined by any trophy. For Wendy, the watermark was an incident at a practice competition. Competing at an advanced obedience level, she and Chance had done very well. As Wendy set him for the final exercise, the broad jump (an exercise that requires the dog to stay while the handler walks away and then—on command—jump a low, wide hurdle), she was extremely pleased with their performance. Turning to face the jump, she noticed that the trainer who had tried to "fry his little brain" was standing outside the ring, only a few feet from where Chance sat. Realizing that Chance had also seen the trainer, Wendy understood the message contained in what her dog did next. Chance looked at the jump, at Wendy, and then, with a brief glance at the trainer who had been the source of so much pain, quietly got up and walked away.

The judge, not understanding that the dog had good reason for what he had done, was surprised when Wendy softly called Chance to her and prepared to leave the ring. "Don't you want to take him back and try that again? It's a practice show, so you can try again if you like."

Wendy knew it was impossible to explain what Chance had said so clearly in his behavior. "No, sir," she said. "I think my dog has done well today, and I am very pleased with him."

The puzzled judge shook his head, questioning her decision. "All right," he said with a shrug. "It's your dog."

With a big smile, Wendy agreed. "You're right. He is my dog." And she and Chance walked out of the ring as they had entered it—together.

I haven't seen Chance pray in a long, long time. He has no need. All his prayers have been answered.

3

DANCES WITH DOGS

Folk will know how large your soul is, by the way you treat a dog.
CHARLES F. DORAN

I DO NOT KNOW WHAT THE TURTLE THOUGHT. I hope that any fear it may have felt quickly disappeared, leaving only a vague, dreamlike recollection. For me, the memory is a sweet, clear picture: It is a summer's evening, and as I ride, the tall grass brushes in whispers against my feet, keeping time with my pony's steps. At the edge of the field where the grass grows thin and short under the shade of the trees, I can see my dog Bear sniffing at something. I turn my pony in that direction, and as we approach, Bear looks up, his eyes bright with excitement. "What have you found?" I ask, and in reply, he turns to gently pick up a box turtle.

"Give it to me," I tell him, leaning down from the saddle, and he strains to offer me this gift. I cannot reach that far, and seeing this, Bear stands on his hind legs, bracing his front paws against the pony's shoulder. I take the turtle from him, thanking him for this lovely surprise. As I examine the intricate tracery of colors and grooves, the size and the wear on the shell tells me this is an old turtle who has seen much, though I suspect his brief journey in Bear's mouth was a new experience. As my pony stands patiently waiting, I hold the turtle level on my hand, hoping he will peek out. Cautiously, the wrinkled head appears, and for a moment, the tables are turned—one deep orange eye unblinkingly considers me, the color shocking against the dull brownish gray of the turtle's head. Finding me of little interest, the eye snaps shut and the turtle closes into himself once more.

"We need to put him back now," I tell Bear, and once again he rears

31

to stand against the pony. With surprising delicacy, his powerful jaws close on the turtle, and with infinite care, he places the turtle on the ground right side up before stepping back to stand watching for what might happen next. Impatient, Bear gives it a little push, his wet nose cutting a trail through the dust of the turtle's back, revealing a splendid dark tapestry of color. But the turtle doesn't move. I turn the pony away, and calling my dog, we continue on our way.

When I think of Bear, it is memories like this that fill me with joy. But our journey together was not always as uncomplicated as that summer's evening ride that had no purpose but to move through the fields on an old gray pony with a dark wolf of a dog beside me. It would be nice to report that all my moments with animals were sweet and good ones, that from the day I was born, people mistook me for the sister of Saint Francis of Assisi, or perhaps Dr. Doolittle's daughter. I would prefer to write a self-congratulatory tale of how I instinctively treated all animals with the utmost respect and tenderness. I wish that I could claim that I cannot fathom how or why people who say they love animals are nonetheless willing to use horrific techniques in the name of training. But none of that would be true, though most of my mistakes and selfish acts went largely unnoticed, private affairs between me and an animal.

Here's a memory that is not a beautiful one: I am fourteen and—desperate for a dog of my own—I spend so much time with the neighbor's Collie that everyone considers me his surrogate owner. I have taught him many tricks, some so subtly signaled that gullible onlookers believe the dog has magical powers. Frustrated that I don't own a dog, I have trained Brandy to jump the weird assortments of chairs, broomsticks and lawn furniture that I drag from the garage and arrange in some semblance of an Olympic show-jumping course. He is an athletic dog, and willing to please me in anything I ask of him. One afternoon, after he has sailed clear over my head on command, I cockily inform kids from the neighborhood that this dog could probably jump anything—even my mother's Buick station wagon. When they scoff at my boast, I point to the car and tell Brandy to jump. He flies joyfully through the air, his sable-and-white fur flowing, and then he lands hard on the car's hood. As he scrambles for some purchase on the slick metal, he spins slightly toward me, and I see his eyes, surprised and afraid, silently questioning me. I am sick with the knowledge that I have betrayed a trust.

Becoming truly humane in my relationships with animals has been a slow and painful evolution that required me to look carefully at the darker corners of my soul. Unlike the external evolutionary pressures on a bird to grow extraordinary feathers in order to attract a mate, the selective pressure on the soul comes only from within. You can hear this force at work if you listen closely. It may be what the psalmist meant when he wrote of "the small still voice inside you." But it can also be quite easily ignored.

I was twenty-one years old with a whopping three years of experience as an animal professional already under my belt when I acquired Bear, my first German Shepherd. Though my enthusiasm for training animals far outran my skill, Bear managed to figure out what I meant. In our daily life, he was a wonderful companion. Whether walking through dense, hectic crowds at a concert in Central Park or exploring nearby woods with me, I had but only to say a word or give a hand signal to get a quick, happy response from Bear. He was as comfortable lying quietly in a department store dressing room as waiting outside the local post office. He was a very good dog.

The problems began when I decided that we should enter obedience competitions. It seemed a simple matter to meet the requirements; after all, he'd handled much more challenging situations in real life. Ever the perfectionist, I became unpleasantly focused on the importance of precision in performance, worried about the points that might be deducted if his response was a hair slow or his sit a wee bit crooked. I began to nag at him, bemoaning his stubborn refusal to practice the same thing over and over again. At times, during practice of heeling off leash, Bear would veer away from me to lie on the porch ignoring my pleas, impervious to my demands. I grew frustrated with his lack of desire for retrieving the official wooden dumbbell. How could this be the same dog who would fetch sticks or balls until my arm grew weary? This was the dog who would voluntarily retrieve turtles, but my commands to fetch a simple wooden dumbbell were met with reluctance or even downright refusal.

Had anyone asked, I would have confidently insisted that Bear and I had a wonderful relationship. But there was a difference between our relationship during training and what we had when he lay at my feet watching the sunset or happily galloped along next to my pony. At a level I could not yet define, training served to push us away from each other. Somehow, it weakened our relationship; we were out of synch, frustrated and even downright unhappy at times. There were times when I decidedly did not like Bear—specifically when he refused to do what I wanted—though I never stopped loving him. I know there were also many times when Bear did not like me very much, and for good reason: Our communication became a one-way street that went my way or no way. This bothered me a great deal—but not enough to let go of my goals and pay attention to what my dog was telling me.

Sure that technical knowledge was the key to what I felt was missing, I devoured books on training and behavior, attended seminars, read more, watched other trainers at work. Along the way, I acquired new training skills and a deeper understanding of dogs. This knowledge was useful; in learning a more structured, analytical approach to unraveling the mysteries of behavior and training, I became a better trainer. As the Royal Air Force motto says, "Every handler gets the dog he deserves." And through diligent effort, an endless desire to know more and a passion for becoming an ever-better trainer, I began to deserve and thus received more of Bear's willing cooperation. Proud of my mastery of both jargon and technique, I did not realize that much of what I had learned had clouded the clarity of my connection with animals. Though increasingly technically proficient, I had lost (or more accurately, misplaced) something I could not quite define, something that had existed before the adult me knew more, knew better. Unable to articulate just what was lost, I was still uneasy enough to need to account for this uncomfortable feeling. In the end, the only explanation I could offer myself was that it was not so much a matter of something missing as changed. My previous experiences had been due to a childish view of dogs and training, and now, I assured myself, I had a more mature, adult perspective of the matter, which included sometimes unpleasant but necessary realities. Earnestly trying to follow the example of the trainers I admired, I turned my focus to an intellectual mastery of my chosen profession—and away from my heart.

In time, people began to seek me out for help with their dogs, and a dog training school was born. In retrospect, I shudder when I look back, well aware that though I had proclaimed myself a trainer (and had made serious efforts to educate myself in a number of ways), I was really little more than living proof that a person with a little knowledge can be of some help to those with even less. Often quite uneasy with many of the popular training techniques I read about and saw used by other trainers, yet not totally satisfied with the results I helped people achieve, I kept searching for more—more kindness, more harmony, more joy between dog and human. Always nagging at the back of my mind was an awareness of the gap between training and how I lived day to day with all my animals. I wanted a way to bridge that gap so that there was no sharp distinction between real life and a training session. I needed to find a way to the point where moving between daily life and formal training was only a shift in my focus, not in the relationship between me and the animal.

A new approach began to form in my heart. Or, more accurately, a philosophy shaped by my heart began to define my thinking. There was no single moment of epiphany, just a growing awareness that I need look no further than a dog's eyes to find the precise moment when my connection to that dog shifted away from clear and free agreement between us. Did my approach to the dog create resistance, fear, distrust or pain, dimming the clear trusting light in his eyes? Then I had to find a better way. At first unconsciously and then with deliberation, I began to evaluate all methods, philosophies and techniques against just this simple standard: the light in a dog's eyes. Over and over I asked myself, "Does this allow the light to shine?" And in every dog's eyes, I found my answer. Held to this standard, many of the popular theories and principles proved poor guides to the greater intimacy and deeper, more joyful connections I knew were possible with animals. Slowly, I abandoned much of the parochial wisdom and began to open my heart and mind to learning what I wanted and needed to know from those who could best teach me—the animals themselves.

In many instances, my desire for another way was unmatched by my ability to find the better way, leaving me frustrated and uncertain where to turn. Unhappily, I found myself using the only techniques I knew, though as softly and effectively as possible. I did not like having to apol-

ogize to dogs, telling them, "In the long run, this is for your own good."
I watched the light in their eyes dim, and I moved as quickly as I knew
how to restore the joyful clarity to those unfailing reflections of what I
had done. In my soul, I was quite miserable at times. When I was not
too arrogant or self-importantly busy to listen to that small still voice
inside, I heard the protest deep inside me. I saw all too clearly the pain
and confusion in far too many animal eyes. Always, I kept searching for
an understanding of how and why what I did dimmed the light. And
always, I kept looking for what my heart told me must exist: a way to
keep the light shining.

A GIFT HORSE

Ironically, the direction I sought came from the horse world. This was
the world where in my teenage years, I had learned to apply force quickly and effectively in order to control and "master" animals. (And I had
learned my lessons well, which at the time earned me great praise from
my mentors. But it was hard work indeed to unlearn these same lessons.) On a snowy March morning in a frigid indoor riding arena somewhere in Maryland, I found what I had been seeking.

I cannot recall just how I found my way to that weekend seminar
taught by Linda Tellington-Jones, an internationally respected horsewoman. I was surprised that there were no dull lectures or demonstra-
tions with fully trained horses. Instead, after a brief introduction, this
trainer began to teach by example, working directly with the horses who
had been brought to the seminar for one problem or another. The first
horse was a Thoroughbred mare, who, despite sterling bloodlines and
considerable monetary value as a broodmare, was so dangerous that both
the veterinarian and the farrier refused to deal with her; just one farm
employee could handle her at all. The horse's participation in the seminar was made possible only by the fact that she lived at the farm host-
ing the weekend. For perhaps half an hour, I watched as this gifted
horsewoman worked with this horse, slowly helping her to shift from a
desperately flailing blur of hooves to a horse who was trying hard to
cooperate despite her fear and anger.

Riding invisibly on the back of this troubled, beautiful mare, the gift of understanding made its way past the defenses of my intellect and directly to my heart. As I watched, first in arrogant internal argument and then with humble gratitude for what I could not deny, much of what I had diligently learned and faithfully applied was shattered. Learning theories and principles became dry, one-dimensional, inadequate explanations for the rich, multisensory experience of connecting with an animal in a humane and truly holistic way. Tellington-Jones' philosophy, which had sounded good to me on paper, was given authentic form in her every gesture and in her responses to the horse. There was no lip service to "humane training"—this was an integration of heart and mind on a profound level. Watching her work with that seemingly impossible mare, I was moved quite literally to tears; had someone asked me to speak in those moments, I would have been unable to respond.

The communication and relationship that I saw between this woman and a horse reorganized portions of my brain in such a way that the pieces never again fit together as they had in the past. This elated me only slightly more than it scared me. It was not easy to accept that my view of the world needed to be redefined, that the map I had created to guide me in my world was now useless for taking me where I wanted to go. In my mind's eye, my old map was crumpled and tossed aside. Armed with fresh crayons, I was going to have to start mapping my world and my understanding of it all over again. Though frightening, I knew that it was also necessary. I had to know more.

In the next several years of my study with her, the woman who would become my greatest human teacher shifted me to a whole new level of connection with animals. I thought that I had great respect for animals; she showed me what respect really meant in her attentiveness and responses to the animal. Already known as a kind trainer, I learned that the greatest act of kindness was to see with compassion what the animals told me about their feelings, their fears, their limitations and their abilities. I thought I understood how to communicate with animals; she showed me that I also needed to listen. Respected as someone who had "soft hands," I learned to be softer yet, to ask and not demand, and to patiently wait for the response.

When I was ready to hear it, Tellington-Jones stunned me with succinct advice that shot like an arrow to my heart, piercing the arrogance and pride that lay at the root of my failings as a trainer: "Learn to train without ego." And I did, with the help of countless dogs who have kept me honest, some with a few well-timed growls. Slowly, I discovered how to carry the dance of relationship into training sessions.

This was not an easy transition for me. On paper, it seems like a joyful and painless process: Trainer finds new way, takes it, animals and people are happy. In reality, finding my way along this new path meant years of work, sorting out excess baggage from the important stuff to be carried along, experimenting with anyone who would stand still long enough for me to test my next theory or idea. The impulsively crumpled previous map of my world had to be retrieved; much of what I had learned was still useful and valid. I struggled along, trying to blend the old and the new, trusting that eventually I would find the balance of technique and philosophy that sat comfortably on my heart. There were extraordinary moments of success when I was able to move in harmony with the animal in a joyful, mutual dance. There were also moments of failure that made me consider closing down my training school or simply giving up and reverting to the old ways. The intense joy of even incomplete successes drove me past my repeated failures, my lifelong reputation for stubborn pursuit of a goal now working in my favor.

Years passed—years of experimenting and thinking and getting that blessed connection just right, years of discarding any technique or philosophy that moved me away from an authentic connection of relationship with the animals. Slowly, without my full appreciation or awareness, brief connections became longer moments and then short but joyful dances. Though it required considerable focus and deliberation, finding the connection became easier. Always, I looked for the light in an animal's eyes, trying to move past the fear or distrust or confusion to find the clear light of understanding and being understood, the light of joy and confidence and trust. And then one day, it happened. Without thought or effort, I could find the cool white space within myself where no ego existed, where I had a goal but also no goals at all, where there was only the dog who accepted my invitation to dance, and the world fell away. From that point on, there was no question but that all I did would be directed toward this place where the dance is possible. There was no question but that the only paths I could follow were ones that led me here.

DANCES WITH DOGS

When I first met Hobbs, he was leaping like a hooked trout at the end of his lead as his owner led him toward my training room. From our phone conversation, I knew that this little black-and-white dog had bitten five people, and that other trainers had recommended he be put to sleep. I also knew that his owner considered me this dog's last hope. The woman was high strung, anxious, fluttering in her agitation, but I could see that she loved this dog. We talked a little while I watched him. Vibrantly alive, Hobbs quivered with energy that had no outlet, living on his toes, in his skin, barely able to control his own mind. Every sound or slight movement drew his instant attention.

When his eyes briefly contacted mine, I saw intelligence and distrust in nearly equal proportions. With my mind, I reached out to him and asked, "Do you want to be this way?" For a moment, there was no response. Then slowly he turned his head and looked into my eyes for a long time. His answer was clear in my head: "No one listens to me." I promised him that I would, and taking the leash from his owner, I began to search for how best to begin.

I asked Hobbs to simply walk with me, but he leaped away, pulling hard toward the training room door. I moved with him and stood quietly as he pawed at the door in irritation. In his quick glances at me, I could see that he wished both that the door would open and that I would go away. But the door remained closed, and I stood waiting, gently persistent, softly toning to him. Gradually, he settled down, his breathing normalized, his eyes beginning to lose the hard, quick look of a trapped animal. Again, I invited him to walk with me, and this time he agreed, though he was cautious and still wanted to leave.

As we reached the center of the room, he suddenly stopped. When I gave a little tug on the lead, I saw him begin to tense, his whole body stiff with an unspoken challenge, his eyes shifting in a split second to the hard eyes of a dog who is growing angry. He leaned back to set himself against the lead, and I quickly offered a little slack to release the tension. Surprised by this, he relaxed a little but stood watchfully waiting for my next move. I knew he was anticipating that I would insist on going forward, and I could feel him mentally preparing to resist. From the history the owner had provided, I knew that Hobbs would bite me if I pushed him. Though she had claimed that he bit without "any warning," I could see now that this was not true. Hobbs was quite fair. He did give warnings. The problem was that people ignored these warnings, which undoubtedly both frustrated and confused him. Biting, he had learned, was a clear communication that even very unobservant people take note of and respect. He did not know that he was writing his own death sentence.

Quietly, I turned back the way we had come, inviting him to join me, which he did without hesitation. We continued to work on simply walking together, asking him to be with me but going only where he was willing to go. Silent until now, his owner spoke up: "Why did you give in to him? How can it be a good thing to let him get away with that? Why don't you just make him do what you want?"

I reminded her that precisely that approach had led to this dog biting people. "There is no point in winning a battle but losing the war. This dog no longer trusts that anyone hears him when he says no, and so he's ready for a fight. I don't want to fight with him. If I'm going to help him, I need him to cooperate with me. He's got to do it willingly, freely and with trust that I will respect what he tells me. And he is cooperating—he's just not ready to cooperate in that particular spot just yet."

As I said this, we approached the same spot where Hobbs had balked a few minutes earlier. For whatever reason, he stopped again and looked at me. I asked him to go forward, but he did not move. For a long moment, he stood there looking at me. I waited, watching for the signs that he had reached a sticking point. But they never came. The dog took a deep breath, and when I asked one more time, he stepped forward past that mysteriously difficult place and we went on, together.

For the next hour, each time we found a point where Hobbs told me he could not go on, I listened. We changed direction, we did less, we tried again. There was a dance between us now, the dog and I, and he had given me the lead. I did not step on his toes in any way. He was soft in my hands, so that a mere flutter of a finger on the lead became a meaningful signal. He was soft in his mind, and it showed in his eyes; the distrust slowly gave way to a cautious belief that I was listening. Soft in his heart, Hobbs gave me all that I asked for. I cannot say where we went or precisely what we did. The world had slid away, and this little black-and-white dog was all I could see or hear.

The client spoke up, startling me since I had nearly forgotten she was there. "I can't believe he hasn't bitten you yet." I did not know whether to laugh or cry. I tried to explain to her that I had given this dog no reason to bite me, that by listening to his quiet signals of protest and refusal, he never felt the need to make his point with his teeth.

There was no instant cure for this dog. Teaching him trust and learning to read his subtle warning signals would take time, I told his owner. "This is not an easy dog," I reminded her, "but he will teach you a great deal." In her eyes, I saw a quickening of hope and a fierce determination, and I knew that she would find a way to this dog's heart and mind.

A year later, I received a Christmas card with a photo of Hobbs that I treasure as a reminder of our wonderful dance. To anyone who does not know the whole story, it seems an insignificant though cute picture of a black-and-white dog perched in a pet store Santa's lap. But I remember the first steps that started Hobbs and his owner on the journey to that happy moment, just as I remember my own journey that led me to this place, with this dog, and this dance.

LISTENING FOR THE MUSIC

Learning to find the dance that is possible within a relationship is not simply a matter of hope or desire. It is a journey of a lifetime. In order to develop profound and intimate relationships with animals, we begin with a shift in our awareness. When we open ourselves to believe that the dance exists, that there is new music that our souls might dance to, we have taken that first, important step. From that moment on, moving forward in our journey means that we need to learn new ways of thinking and behaving while at the same time we sort through, question and perhaps discard the old beliefs that once shaped our thinking and informed our actions. Philosophically speaking, in opening ourselves to new possibilities, we put on our dancing shoes.

More than a little stands between us and the joy of mutual connection. The scientific approach so favored by the Western mind insists that we view the dog as an intelligent creature whose behavior is merely the result of either instinct or conditioned responses (like Pavlov's dogs drooling in response to a bell). There is a powerful taboo that insists we not anthropomorphize, or assign human features or characteristics to something nonhuman like a dog. While appreciative of the dangers of anthropomorphizing, I have never understood why the Western mind works so hard to maintain this distance between us and the natural world. I have often wondered, How am I made any less human or my dog any less canine if I am willing to grant that animals feel pain, joy, grief, love, anger, loyalty and more? Respected anthropologist Franz de Waal, writing in *Natural History Magazine*, points out that this taboo is a terribly lopsided one. While it is acceptable to use words like *enemy*, *hate* and *rage* when describing animal behavior, it is not acceptable to say *friend*, *love* or *grief*. While we are all too willing to share the uglier side of emotional life with the animals, we'd like to reserve the really good stuff for ourselves. Even the rules of correct grammar dictate that it is never an animal *who* behaves but rather an animal *that* behaves—a rule that is deliberately broken throughout this book to continually underline the idea that a dog is someone *who*, not something *that*. We hold ourselves above them as if something dreadful might happen if we allow ourselves to embrace the notion that perhaps the dog lying at our feet chewing on a tennis ball is also a sentient being with feelings and emotions and thoughts and humor and language and loves and fears and creativity, and we may choke hard on the idea of the dog as a spiritual being. Of course, that something dreadful is just this: If our dogs do feel and think and reason (though not as incomplete versions of us but as fully splendid versions of themselves), then we'd best think long and hard about how we've been treating man's best friend.

To be sure, there is a very real danger when we see our dogs as merely little people in fur coats. When we do this, we cannot see past our projections to the real animal that stands before us. Not only does this inevitably limit the full expression of that animal's life, it also undermines our relationship with that animal. When we cannot see an animal or anyone as they really are, we are bound to be disappointed. We are also bound to act in cruel ways. Think of the grief created by the mother who sees her son as she chooses to see him—a future doctor—when the reality is that her son wants to be a baker. Our dogs cannot be little people in fur coats, nor should they be asked to be. The glory of any relationship is not in finding ways to shape the other to suit our needs, but rather in celebrating the fullness of who they are.

In accepting the view of the dog as an attractively packaged, user-friendly blend of instinct and conditioned responses, we put on blinders that work to exclude anything that does not fit neatly within that explanatory framework or that cannot be "proven" via scientific method. Even the great scientist Albert Einstein pointed out, "Everything that can be counted doesn't necessarily count; everything that counts can't necessarily be counted."

If we cling to a stubbornly Western notion of animals, we may deny the mystery and beauty of what we experience in our daily lives with animals and build barriers that keep us from what is possible in deeper levels of relationship. It is sobering to remember that until relatively recently, the mute or deaf among us were considered inferior in countless ways simply because they could not share the largely verbal language that we use. What makes Helen Keller's story so timelessly compelling is that one person, Anne Sullivan, was able to reach past the known and embrace the possibility that within the damaged physical shell of a blind, deaf and mute child, there was nonetheless a mind and a heart as fully human as her own. In that simple but profound perceptual shift, Anne Sullivan was indeed a miracle worker who opened the floodgates of possibility. To explore the possibilities, we must be willing to shift our view to include dogs as thinking, feeling beings who—while vastly different from us—are very much like us in many ways. In the shift to a view of the dog as a thinking, feeling being, we open floodgates of our own.

The technicalities and mechanics of behavior and training are useful and valuable to our understanding of dogs, and I urge all readers to educate themselves continually. As Goethe noted, "There is nothing more frightful than ignorance in action." Limited knowledge means limited choices and limited expression. Every artist, every craftsman, every practitioner of an art (such as animal training) strives to master the tools of their trade for one reason: to allow the full, clear expression of their heart to shine through. To long to express one thing but actually create another, lesser or incomplete thing is a terrible thing to the soul.

Still, it is good to balance knowledge with the reminder that the Western mind's rigidly scientific approach to animals is a recent development in the long history of man and dog. Long before learning theories and jargon such as *positive reinforcement* or *stimulus control* crept into the world of dog training, long before Skinner ran a single rat through a maze, men and dogs had found ways to dance together. Science cannot explain the beauty and mysteries that deeply move us. It cannot explain the power of a dog's head laid on our knee, or why a man might lay down his life for a friend, or even why we love as we do. Nonetheless, even scientists fall in love, and it is said that some even talk to their dogs.

An intellectual understanding of canine psychology, behavior, learning theories and more is helpful and sometimes necessary. By degrees, our knowledge combines with what our hearts tell us, and we move forward in our search for a way to dance with our dogs. To learn to dance with a dog or any other being, the desire must come from within, from your heart. In our search for deeper, more meaningful relationships, we must be careful to recognize that while knowledge is helpful, it can also be limiting, serving to block our view of what is possible, weighing us down so that we cannot move lightly without stumbling. A dancer who concentrates on technicalities may forget to hear the music.

On the Way to the Dance

As already noted, finding your way to the dance is not simply a matter of making the right turn somewhere in childhood or when you first acquire a dog. In one way or another, and most often without meaning to, we will stumble against the realization that there are levels of relationship. This is something we already know from our human experience. From the intense bond of parent-child to the very casual one of, say, that with your local dry cleaner, we understand that there is a wide range of possibilities encompassed by the word *relationship*. As we mature and learn more about ourselves and develop greater awareness, we come to understand that even within a single relationship, there are levels, beautifully explained by Stephen Sloane in his brilliant essay "Spirit of Harmony," which appeared in *Equus* magazine in July 1995.

The first level is what Sloane calls the "mechanical" or technical level of relationship. At this level, the relationship between man and dog is a matter of mechanics: You apply the stimulus, the dog responds. The relative simplicity of this level is best exemplified by Gary Larson's cartoon showing two amoebas, one complaining to the other, "It's always the same old thing—stimulus, response, stimulus, response." Though simplistic when placed in the context of a relationship, this mechanical approach can be used to train an animal to perform quite complex tasks. Problems are solved mechanically, often through the use of force. If the dog won't do x, y or z, you make him. The dog won't sit? Push down on his rear and pull up on his collar until he does sit. The puppy bucks and pulls when the collar and leash are put on? Tie him to a doorknob and let him fight it out there.

Recipes are not only possible but quite popular at this level. To be sure, if the recipe is a good one, a large percentage of dogs will respond nicely, especially when such a recipe is applied by an expert hand. With a high degree of skill and a thorough understanding of learning principles, a trainer may never move past this purely technical level yet still be very successful (assuming that success is measured solely by the animal responding in the desired way). It is also possible to be technically proficient and yet fail at a deep, soulful level. Notable in its absence at this level is a sense of partnership—the animal is little more than a living, breathing machine, though he may be taken care of diligently. Technical proficiency is a dispassionate thing, though it may be admired for what it is—competent workmanship. My view of relationships is that they are living works of art. And so when I consider the purely mechanical as the basis for a relationship, what rings true are the same four words considered the most damning commentary on any work of art: "It has no heart."

The leap from the mechanical level to the next level, what Sloane calls the "motivational" or psychological level, is a fairly easy one, requiring only that you become curious about why an animal will or will not do something. Motivation is defined as "the psychological feature that arouses an organism to action." In trying to understand what motivates the dog, you begin to learn more about him. At the mechanical level, the question is how to make the dog do what you want him to do. At the motivational level of relationship, you are trying to figure out how you can make the dog *want to do* what you want him to do. The trick is to discover in what way (or ways) your dog is motivated to act as you'd like him to. There are many ways to motivate a dog: food rewards, toys, play, freedom, praise, attention.

That sounds good and pleasant, doesn't it? When we think of *motivational*, we often make this word synonymous in our minds with a pleasant, happy approach. But there are other, darker ways to motivate. Waving cash in someone's face may be a good way to motivate them (if cash is a meaningful reward for them); waving a gun in their face is also motivational. A dog may be motivated pleasurably or through pain, fear and deprivation. Pain is delivered in any number of ways: collar "corrections," remote-control shock collars and, of course, the human hand. Fear is another great motivator, and it is possible to make a dog more afraid of one thing than another. For example, a dog may break his sit stay because he's afraid of being left by his owner. If the owner dashes back, shouting imprecations, and shakes the dog to "correct" him, the dog can quickly learn to be more afraid of the consequences of getting up than of being left behind. Deprivation of food, social interaction and even water are also used in dog training. Though depriving a dog of water is rare, social deprivation is not. A hungry, thirsty or lonely dog is "highly motivated" to please the person who controls these critical resources. Take great care to find out what the motivation actually is when someone claims to be a motivational trainer, and be sure to carefully consider just how your dog is being motivated in any situation.

It is possible to progress no further than the motivational phase and have a good relationship with a dog, especially if there are no real conflicts and the level of achievement is agreeable to the trainer. If through motivation you can get where you want to go, why go any further? Understanding how to motivate a dog (through pleasant or unpleasant means) can result in successful training, though not always in a great relationship. If the motivation used is largely positive (i.e., reward-based training), it is also possible to be quite humane.

Many training problems can be resolved when the training shifts to a purely motivational level. But not all problems will yield to a romping game of ball or a fistful of tasty treats. While Wendy was able to improve much of Chance's performance in training when she incorporated food rewards, his bolting behavior could not be altered by this approach. And as Chance proved, new problems may arise from the training technique itself if pain, fear, and/or deprivation are used as motivation. While the motivational level offered Wendy some answers, there were other questions that could not be satisfied because the answers did not lie in technique but in the dynamics of two hearts in relationship. Like Wendy, many dog lovers go just this far and, failing to find the answers they long for, assume that there is nowhere else to go. As Wendy nearly did, many resign themselves to making the best of what they have been able to achieve.

The motivational or psychological level is where I got stuck as a trainer for so many years. It was easy enough to do, especially when the majority of dogs I worked with were successful and happy in their training. Two things kept me searching for something more. The first was that I knew something more was possible. There was no denying the beauty and joy of what I experienced with my animals. Though I did not yet know of Sloane's essay on levels of relationship, what I was experiencing in those lovely moments was the third level, and I wanted more of that experience. The other driving force of my search for more (that indefinable thing!) were the dogs that I could not reach and the dogs who only partially succeeded. While it would have been easy to blame the dogs or their owners for the failures or incomplete successes, it would not have been honest or fair. Nor would I have been motivated to continue my search. The sense that I could help these dogs if only I knew another way nagged at my heart, and it still does. If I could go back in time and bring with me what I have learned, I would go to these dogs and apologize for what I did not know, and ask for a chance to try again.

What I found that cold morning in Maryland as I watched a woman and a horse was what I wanted: the dance. The true dance of relationship is possible only at the third level, what Sloane terms the "spiritual" level. Here, the focus shifts from how to make the dog do something or how to make the dog want to do something, and the question becomes, "How do *we* accomplish this together?" Such a simple question, but to even ask it, we have to make a profound shift within ourselves.

Remember the trainer's advice to me? "Learn to train without ego." Moving to this third level, the spiritual level, requires that we are willing to set aside our egos and let the relationship between us and the animal take center stage. The focus is no longer solely on the dog, but on the partnership between us, and on us as partners in this dance. At times, I think of this level as the Snow White phase, because once you reach it, you spend a lot of time saying, "Mirror, mirror, on the wall. . . ." This level requires a willingness to look honestly at ourselves and at our motivations—and to look again and again. It is not always a pretty picture we see before us. Staring at the uglier wrinkles in your soul, you'll realize that some hard work with fresh crayons is called for, because the map of the world that you've lived by is going to need to be redrawn. (I'll concede that perhaps your map needs only minor revisions; mine has needed entire new editions on a regular basis.) It is not easy work, but this is where the dance truly begins. I do not know if it's possible to live completely at this level, but I hope so. I keep trying, mirror and crayons at the ready.

While the three levels seem clearly defined on paper, in practice there are rarely such crisp distinctions; many of us drift between all three, though we will spend a majority of our time operating at one level or another. For many readers, there will be a shock of joyful, excited recognition when reading about the third level—"I've been there!" It is the magic of connection that we experience with animals, the moments that we cannot explain or perhaps even understand, moments that only another animal person can comprehend with a knowing nod, moments that keep us coming back for more. But we may not understand that these elusive moments of connection can be more than just fleeting experience, ephemeral and unpredictable as a rainbow. The third level is not a moment but a philosophy, a way of life, an awareness of what we can create every day, in ways large and small. We can, if we direct ourselves to follow the less-traveled trail, find our way more often to this most blessed place of deep connection where the dance of two is possible.

The dance is not a result of specific techniques. It springs from a life lived according to the philosophy crafted by your heart, a philosophy that informs all you do. This cannot be achieved by bringing your awareness and effort only to those moments you call "training." The dog is a dog, twenty-four hours a day. His world is shaped by what you say and do, not just in training sessions but in every waking moment he is with you. Incapable of dishonesty in his own communications, a master of observation, the dog not only notices what you do, but he believes what you do to be an accurate reflection of the relationship between you. The relationship—the pivotal point on which all else turns—is built (or undermined) in every interaction. There are those who recoil from this, saying "That's too much work!" In so saying, they admit they have no desire to put so much effort and time into a relationship with a "mere" dog. But for those who have the desire, those who would dance with a dog as their partner, this reality is a welcome opportunity to use every moment with awareness and purpose.

"Education is an admirable thing, but it is well to remember from time to time that nothing that is worth knowing can be taught," Oscar Wilde wrote. No one can teach you how to dance with a dog. There are no recipes or shortcuts, no magic knotted leashes that ease the way. What this book offers are the cautionary tales of common failings and misunderstandings between man and dog. They are offered so that you need not make the same mistakes, or having already made them, you may reassure yourself that many other travelers on this road have also stumbled. The philosophy offered here is mine, but it points the way to a very real place where a dog will meet you gladly. Perhaps you can use this book to help you find your way to dance, joyfully and with heart.

4

The Quality of Connection

To know someone here or there with whom you can feel there is
understanding in spite of distances or thoughts unexpressed —
that can make of this earth a garden.

GOETHE

WHEN WE ENTER INTO A RELATIONSHIP WITH A DOG or any other being, we are seeking a connection or, perhaps more accurately, what we feel as a result of this connection: comfort, love, acceptance, peace, joy. What we are seeking and striving for is a quality of connection that is—hopefully—a mutually pleasurable state, a dance of two spirits moving in agreement. Though we may be unable to articulate precisely what we seek, we recognize it when it happens. Simply stated, it feels good when it is right, and it does not feel good when things are wrong. And when it is right, it's delightfully, incredibly, inexpressibly right. And when it's wrong, it can be terribly, unbearably wrong. What drives us crazy at times is that even when the connection is powerful and good, we may not know just how that moment was achieved or what magical ingredients helped to create it or, sadly, why it just as mysteriously dissolves into the mundane or routine.

Because this kind of profound connection is elusive (whether we seek it with other people or with animals), we may not understand that it is not a goal or "thing" but rather a process, and a dynamic one at that. Despite the messages from advertisers that assure us that with their product (their car, soap, beer, dog food, jeans) we will be able to have the fulfilling relationships we seek, the truth is there is no particular formula by which a powerful connection may be summoned or created. In our restless searching through books and videos and seminars, we are asking for the recipe that can help us create what we know exists. Such a relationship between us and our animals is possible, though not necessarily easy, certainly not automatic. We've tasted it, or we've seen it or perhaps we've even just read about it—and we want more. We want a road map to There, because we've been there or we know others who have, and we know it's where we want to go.

None of us deliberately sets out to create a relationship filled with conflict, frustration or disappointment. But the deep connection we seek may be missing, especially if we mistake the technicalities of dog behavior, training theories and techniques for a relationship. To find what we are seeking, we need to begin at the beginning, examining the foundation on which the entire relationship will turn: the *quality* of the connection itself.

Rather mechanical in nature, dog training has long been devoid of words like *quality*. Open most dog books and you'll not find this word in the index. This may be due in part because in using a word like *quality* in the context of the dog/human relationship, we step out into murky waters. If we ask "What is quality?" we are now in deep waters indeed. Philosophers have struggled to answer this for literally thousands of years, and the jury is still out on any definitive answer because like most things that deeply matter and powerfully inform our lives, quality will not yield to a simple definition. In *Zen and the Art of Motorcycle Maintenance*, Robert Pirsig addresses the question of quality itself, a tricky concept that proves difficult to unravel and define though he tackles it from endless angles and theoretical stances. One of my favorite ideas from Pirsig's book is this: "Quality is not a thing. It is an event."

In other words, quality is something that *happens*, the result of a coming together. Pirsig poses the thought that while a sunset may be beautiful, that beauty is an event of quality within the beholder. Though splendid, the colors of the sunset are not what move us. If that were true, then each time the sun set, all of us would be moved as we are but infrequently. It is what we bring to the observation of that sunset that moves us as it does. I cannot remember with precision too many sunsets, though I have seen countless ones in my lifetime. I can remember only vaguely the pleasure of flooding my mind with such unexpected colors combined in a way unique to that time and place. I can more clearly remember one particular sun setting over the distant trees, the night breeze chilling me as it dried the sweat raised in digging my dog's grave. That sunset moved me as the one before it or after it could not. On that evening, the setting of the day was more than just a routine moment that signaled mundane shifts such as the need to feed the horses or begin the evening meal. And it was more than my casual attention that was brought to the brilliant but brief display that all too soon disappeared, leaving only the darkness.

A CREATION OF CHOICE

Each time we interact with a dog or any other being, we have an opportunity to create an event of quality, or not. Our relationships with our dogs are dynamic, responsive to and informed by every choice we make. Each of our actions, whether intentional or inadvertent, will move us in only a few possible directions—away from or toward greater intensity of connection, or we do not move at all and remain still.

If quality is indeed an event, then in every moment, we have a choice. Relationships are not mechanical processes, though training itself is very often considered to be. Bob Bailey, a professional animal trainer who has used scientifically established principles of training to train over 140 different species, states it plainly, "Training is a mechanical skill." The problem arises when we mistake the *skill* of training for the relationship itself. It is possible to have extremely good technical training skills and very little sense of relationship; conversely, as millions of dog owners demonstrate daily, it is also possible to have little or no technical training skill and still have a profoundly moving relationship with an animal. Though training can be mechanical, I think it is unfortunate at best that many trainers try to reduce it to that level. We are not mixing chemicals that will react predictably; we are dealing with the intersection of two live, unique beings. We are dealing with something that is dynamic. To view training as purely mechanical is to say that the results are predictable, like gravity pulling a thrown stone to earth. But as any experienced animal person will tell you, animals are not entirely predictable, no more than we are.

If we view our dogs as organisms that will respond in certain ways provided we apply the appropriate and timely stimuli, we are stuck in a very mechanical perspective that does not allow for (because it cannot explain) the mysterious and wonderful possibilities of a deep connection. Though we enjoy the things that Newtonian physics makes possible—our automobiles, planes, bridges, homes—we must turn elsewhere to understand nonthings or processes, such as our own bodies and relationships. Whether we are trying to understand the rich interwoven biological and ecological systems that make up the planet, or to unravel the mysteries of the body/mind connection or move into deeper levels of understanding in our relationships with others, the rigid, mechanistic views based on Newtonian physics fail us. Our world is not one of simple cause and effect, but one of dynamic interactions, right down to the cells within our bodies. As Candace Pert points out in her book *Molecules of Emotion*, our thoughts create definable physiological shifts in our bodies; the biochemistry of the cells help to inform the shape of our thoughts. It is a seamless integration of information, so that it is impossible to say where the beginning or end of it all may lie. A relationship is also—at its core—a seamless integration of information. By the very act of choosing to be in a relationship—even casually—with another being, we open ourselves to the dynamic process of both putting forth and receiving information.

To fully embrace the idea that quality is a dynamic event that we can choose to create is both a heavy burden of responsibility and one of the greatest of all freedoms. We can push away this responsibility with a mental shrug, saying, "Well, that's the way it is" as if life and our interactions with others are some kind of emotional weather over which we have no control or influence. Even worse, we may throw up our hands and, relative to another's behavior, say, "That's just the way they are!" as if we have no influence on the behavior of those around us. Both responses are as common in the dog/human relationship as in our human interactions. Either way, we are not accepting the responsibility for creating our world and are fooling ourselves that we can somehow stand apart from our life and our relationships with others. Though dog training often focuses on the dog's behavior, it is almost impossible to separate the dog from the dog/human relationship, which in turn means that we, as part of the relationship, have responsibilities and choices to make about our own behavior. The event of quality is one that we can actively choose, every day, each time we are with our dogs.

SUNSETS IN DISNEYLAND

Pirsig's second book, *Lila: An Inquiry into Morals*, takes the concept of quality a little further, defining two basic types of quality: static and dynamic. Static quality is predictable, replicable and most often involves people and things, not people and other living beings. Disneyland is an example of static quality. Deliberately set in climates that offer a high percentage of good weather, Disney's attractions are carefully controlled to make sure that to the highest degree possible, all visitors have the same experience, at least in terms of what is presented; no one can control the internal response of any visitor. I disliked Disneyland very much but could not articulate why I found it so flat, almost sterile. Years later, when I read Pirsig's *Lila*, I understood that what I objected to was precisely the static quality of the experience.

There is a tremendous attraction for many people in such static or fixed-quality experiences, as evidenced by the success of Disney and other venues, because there is value in static quality. You would have a hard time convincing the average person to pay an admittance fee to a park where they might or might not see Mickey Mouse, where there might or might not be a parade on Main Street, where rides might or might not be open. It is the static quality of the offered experience that is the attraction. People feel safe when they know what to expect, when they can reasonably predict the experience.

Static quality can be enjoyable, it can please us and make us feel good, but it has its limits. Rarely does it quicken our souls. We often accept the merely static because it requires less energy from us, requires less of us. Within the context of a relationship, an expectation or desire for static, predictable experiences can deaden us to the complex beauty of another being; at worst, such expectations are truly destructive since they do not honor or enhance the connection. For some, a dog is not a living, breathing being with needs and expectations, but something they can "have" when they want to interact with a dog. Like any living thing, dogs do not loan themselves to moments of static quality. They are not appliances or furnishings or instruments that await your need of them. A fine stereo system can provide us with superb-quality music anytime we push a button; you cannot turn a dog on or off like a radio depending on your desire at the moment, ignoring it the rest of the time. But God knows, people try.

Every dog trainer in the world can relate stories of clients who want a dog and are seeking advice as to what kind of dog they should consider. Questioned, the client reports in all sincerity that they want a dog who would happily stay home alone for eight to ten or more hours a day, never destroy anything, perfectly control his bladder and bowels, be delighted to see them and need little more than a walk around the block before settling down to keep them company. They ask, "What kind of dog should I get?" The correct answer is "A stuffed one." For a while, the AKC had a TV commercial that posed a similar situation and answer. There might be a market, I suppose, for a canine version of escort services. You could, for instance, pick up the phone and ask for a beautiful blonde (Golden Retriever) to accompany you to a picnic in the park. Need a four-footed playmate for the kids one afternoon? Request Nanny the Newfoundland, who doubles as a lifeguard. Feeling vulnerable while your spouse is away on a trip? Rent Gunther the Guard Dog—he's delivered, of course, only for the few hours that you actually need his services. Like any professional escort, these dogs would be impeccably groomed, well mannered and pleasant, guaranteed to provide "a quality dog/human interaction." Once done with your need for a dog, you could return him to the Dogs on Demand office and go about your day. All the delight of a dog's companionship but none of the responsibility. But also none of the soulful moments of dynamic authenticity. This sterile, static approach to dogs is not as far-fetched as it seems. In her book *The Animal Attraction*, Dr. Jonica Newby reports that in Tokyo, dogs can be rented by the hour; outside of Beijing, dog lovers unable to keep dogs can visit a special "dog farm." In both cases, it is more the pressures of urban life and society that make dog keeping an extraordinary luxury unavailable to many, not a shallow desire to avoid the complexities of a life shared with dogs.

Dynamic quality is unpredictable, and impossible to replicate. Quite possibly, it is the uniqueness of dynamic quality that makes it so intense or meaningful for us. Moments of dynamic quality occur seemingly at random: a spectacular sunset, a red fox walking out from the woods to stand gazing into your eyes, the fairyland of a tree freshly dusted in snow, the sudden arc of a meteor across the sky. These may be dramatic moments, but there are others less dramatic but equally powerful: the sound of a child softly singing to herself, the silky feel of a dog's ear sliding between your fingers, the warm pressure of a body curled lovingly around your own, the sweet smell of rain in the spring.

Moments of dynamic quality, moments with the potential to move our very souls, are all around us. Though unpredictable, they require only one thing from us in order for us to experience them: We must be available. Because it resides in your response, dynamic quality is everywhere you are, if you are open to the experience, willing to seek it out, interested and alert to what is happening within and beyond yourself. Sweepstakes promoters have it all wrong: In life, you *must* be present to win. If we are glued to the nightly news, we will not see the sunset. We also will not be available to see our dogs or anyone else we love. We must actively seek moments of dynamic quality by being open to and aware of them, by being present in the moment, by bringing ourselves to the world and through the world. Every moment of dynamic quality is possible because of this: You are there, and you are aware. Is the gaze of a red fox any less piercing if you are not there to connect with it? Perhaps. But what is possible when your eyes connect with fox eyes is possible only with you present and aware. Potential connections are all around us, yet we sometimes march through our days without bringing our awareness to each passing moment, moving in a preset lockstep that answers not to natural rhythms or even those of our own hearts, but to some artificial, externally generated beat that we agree to and abide by. This is not without price: We miss the moments of authentic connection, the dynamic moments. Dogs remind us that the only place that dynamic quality can occur is in the moment of now.

For those intrigued by the infinite possibilities of what can happen when we nurture the dynamic quality of our relationships with dogs and others, the only requirement is a constant awareness that at every moment we are choosing to create events of quality. To do so, we must invest ourselves fully in the moment, bringing our awareness and curiosity to even the simplest acts of connection. Nothing in life is free, but our investment of ourselves is richly rewarded in profound and moving connections with our dogs, and in turn, a powerful connection with the natural world around us and with our deepest selves.

5

WALKS WITH DOGS

You ask of my companions. Hills, sir, and the sundown,
and a dog as large as myself.
EMILY DICKINSON

IN JUNE, THE ROAR OF HAYING EQUIPMENT fills our farm's fields. It seems chaotic, this noisy movement of man and machine, but flowing like a cool green wake behind the tractor there appears an orderly row of cut hay, heaped gently to dry awhile before being baled. All day, diesel fumes hang in sunlit haze over the fields but are gone with the cooling breezes of evening. A mosquito buzzes my ear as I walk in the emptiness between the sweet, wilting piles, thinking of the coming winter when these simple grasses will fill our cattle's bellies.

For my dogs, there are no thoughts of cattle or of winter. They have only a passing interest in the cleared areas where I walk, but with an intensity that seems unusual in these familiar fields, they move along the long piles of hay. Methodically, they work row after row, tails wagging furiously then stilled for just a moment as they swallow something before moving on. I know what they are after, though I often do not tell visiting guests who think this scene a most pastoral sight: The dogs are searching for and eating the hapless victims of haying season. Mice, birds, snakes, rabbits, moles, shrews, frogs and voles have all appeared at times in the drying hay. My dogs have learned that hay season means a potluck dinner.

But for all their intensity as they search, for all the delicious (only to dogs) snacks that they find, the dogs never forget that we are together. Between mouthfuls of mouse, they glance up to check my progress through the field. Sometimes, I am content to sit and watch them scavenge, thinking about stories I have read of fox and coyote following farmers who are working to bring in a hay crop; the easy pickings of hay row cuisine are not a secret known only to my dogs. But sometimes, I am headed elsewhere and pass through the hay field only as I must. As I move, the dogs keep track of me as completely as I keep track of them. We share this responsibility of togetherness. Noting that I'm about to enter the hemlock woods and head to the creek, they grab one last mystery morsel and race after me. Though they may range away in search of a tantalizing scent or to furiously mark where the coyotes have left their messages in the night, the dogs circle back to me as I choose another trail or stop to investigate a small patch of hepatica growing under the hemlocks' shade. We are, at every step, together, without the need for words, bound by the heart's invisible leash, unmistakably connected.

A CHOICE OF TWO

Baseball great Yogi Berra summed it up rather neatly: "You can observe a lot by just watching." And he was right—few things tell me as much about the quality of the connection between a person and a dog as what can be observed as they just walk along together. This sounds so simple—to be with a dog as we walk. What I mean by "with" is a connection that is not easily defined but that is evident in its absence. It is a choice of two to be together, not a matter of tying someone to you with leash and collar.

At my seminars, I make a routine practice of standing where I can watch people and their dogs entering the building; at home, I watch clients take their dogs from the car and walk them toward me. If there were a single snapshot moment that encapsulates a relationship, it might be simply this: how a person and a dog walk together.

My friend Rosemary has driven from Illinois to spend a few days at our farm with her four dogs. She is tired from the long drive, and after hugging us, asks if she might walk her dogs. As she opens the side door of her van, I can hear her talking quietly to the excited dogs. Although they are good travelers, even the best of dogs grows weary of confinement after fifteen hours on the road. As she leans into the van and gathers their leashes, I see Teddy's nose appear over her shoulder, nostrils flaring as he drinks in the farm scents. Poking out past Rosemary's hip is Zena's black button of a nose, and though I can see only a little of the graying muzzle, I can tell that she is wriggling in the delight of arrival.

With all leashes securely attached, Rosemary steps back. The dogs stand eager but contained, waiting for her quiet "okay." When it comes, they flow from the van, a river of feet and tails, ears and eyes and noses busy trying to take in the whole farm at once. Despite their excitement, they do not lose track of Rosemary, nor do they pull on their leashes. As she shuts the van door, they glance up at her as if to ask, "Are you ready yet?" While they wait, impatient but polite, she carefully organizes the leashes in her hand and says, "Let's go, guys." And off they go, together in every sense of the word.

Not surprisingly, Rosemary has an excellent relationship with her dogs—in every moment of her interactions with them, she makes it clear to them and to all watching that she is truly with them. In turn, they are decidedly with her, whether in the quiet empty moments or when working on a task. Any difficulties, when they arise, are a matter of miscommunication between Rosemary and the dog or an inability on her part or theirs to work together in just that way, not a failure of clear leadership or the result of conflicts in the relationship itself.

Walking the dog is the stuff of cartoons for good reason. The eternal question: "Who is walking whom?" is amusing only on the surface, just as jokes about henpecked husbands are only superficially funny. Examined at a deeper level, there isn't anything funny at all about relationships or leashes taut with tension. Perhaps the humor arises from a wry recognition that relationships are not always what we'd like them to be, from our unstated relief that others have the same difficulties with their dogs or spouses or bosses or children that we do. But we are uncomfortably aware—if we take a moment to think about it—that an unbalanced or frustrating relationship is no laughing matter.

How important is the quality of connection? How critical is it that we learn on the most basic level to truly walk with a dog? It may be, quite literally, a matter of life and death. The leading cause of death in dogs in Western countries is behavior—unacceptable, uncontrollable, inappropriate behavior. Not disease. Not being hit by a car. Not neglect or abuse (though an argument could be made that a failure to train a dog so that he can act appropriately is precisely a form of neglect and abuse). If we fail to develop a high quality of connection with our dogs, we may fail them in the most terrible of ways, and they may pay for our failure with their lives. Whether we care to admit it or not, we reveal a good deal about our relationships with our dogs in the simple act of walking together. Do we excuse our dogs' behavior? Ignore them? Helplessly allow ourselves to be towed along like so much baggage? Are we really with them as we walk along, attentive to their comments and interests, ready to help or defend or reassure them as needed? Trainer Sherry Holm has a lovely way of looking at the simple act of walking with a dog: Is there a balance between dog and person, or is the energy flowing too heavily in one direction? Pulling on lead, at a very fundamental level, is an exchange of energy. When two are moving together in harmony, there is a balance that gently sways back and forth across the two. Moving together toward a common goal or with a mutual purpose, there is no pull of energy one way or the other.

Imagine that everywhere you went with a human friend, you had to hold his hand and he yours. Now imagine that at every step, he was pulling hard. Would you want to go for walks with such a friend? What we would say to such a friend is this: Why can't you just be with me? Just walk nicely here, by my side, and we'll go together.

Consider how the connection with your dog feels. Do you feel as if you are being towed? As if you must struggle to guide or direct the dog? Does the thought of walking with your dog bring up feelings of joy or is there some frustration? It is considerably annoying to walk with a constant struggle, and few of us like having our arm pulled (sometimes quite hard) by our canine friends. Yet with our dogs, we may think that saying "Just walk nicely by my side" is not possible, or even if we wish it were, we don't know how to say it. If we view the leash as merely a restraint that keeps the dog safe, we may view pulling on the lead as the end product of the conflict between what the dog wants to do and what the leash allows him to do. We resign ourselves to the struggle, never realizing that it is not necessary, unaware that we are perhaps undermining the very quality of our relationship.

Pulling on lead is, for me, a fundamental issue that both reflects on and affects the dog/human relationship on many levels. Looked at within the context of the overall relationship, pulling on lead reveals disturbances in the quality of attention given and received at both ends of the lead and says something about the degree of togetherness at work between dog and handler. I do not know anyone who enjoys being pulled around by a dog. While dogs do pull, I doubt that they find the experience enjoyable—it's hard to believe that being gagged and choked is enjoyable. But lacking our perspective and our ability to change the situation, they may believe it is an inescapable part of being on leash, especially since we most obligingly play our part.

It takes two to tango, and it takes two to pull. A frustrated student once told me that her dog always pulled, no matter what. Unable to resist such an opening, I sweetly asked, "Always? No matter what?"

She nodded vigorously. "No matter what! It drives me crazy." When I asked if the dog pulled even when he was off leash and running around in her yard, she looked at me with disgust. "Of course he doesn't pull then." So then I persisted, he only pulls when he's on lead. What if you drop the lead? Does he still pull? Now a bit annoyed by this line of questioning, she answered sharply, "Of course not. I have to be holding the leash." She stopped as the realization hit her that in order for her dog to pull, he had to have something or someone to pull against. It had never dawned on her that she might be contributing to the problem; she had viewed this solely as the dog's problem.

Any of us would take a dim view of someone who was dragging their dog or a child down the street—it is an act that speaks to the person's insensitivity to or lack of respect for the dog or child they are towing. But we don't think twice about the dog whose person allows him to pull them down the street. We don't think about the lack of respect implicit in the act of pulling, or the lack of leadership that allows it. Simply put, we may move through life spending far too much time simply tied to our dogs by the length of our leash, not bound to them through an investment of our attention.

IN THE UNPLANNED MOMENTS

At this most simple level of moving together, we reveal the courtesy and respect at work in the quiet unplanned moments of life. I am never as interested in how two work together on a specific task as I am in how they are together in the in-between moments, when no focus or goal drives or shapes their behavior. Focus on a task—especially one that is enjoyable or so demanding that attention is literally consumed by the effort required—can conceal a great deal and give the false impression that all is well. Don't show me what your dog can do when you give him a command; just show me how you and he walk down the street together, and I'll know much more.

When a high degree of quality exists, it is unmistakable. There is attentiveness that flows between the two partners, a mutuality and respect that is evident in everything they do. Simple gestures reveal a world and say more than we may realize about a relationship. And whether we do so consciously or not, we look at the quality of connection itself to evaluate the relationships we see around us. What I see in a dog and person walking together is a rough blueprint for the relationship, a brief overview of the quality of the connection between person and dog. I do not pretend or assume that these glimpses into how people and dogs walk together is indicative of the whole relationship. But long experience has taught me that this is a surprisingly reliable predictor for what else will be revealed as I learn more about the relationship.

"How can you judge the connection between dog and person based on just that?" the reader protests. "All you are seeing is the dog when he's excited, going somewhere new, stimulated by the new setting or other dogs or the activity around him."

And I would answer, "Yes, that is precisely what I am seeing, along with how the human in the equation deals with the dog in that situation, how the dog and person work together."

A client, Margaret, arrives at the farm for a consultation with her fifteen-month-old German Shepherd, Luger. On the phone she has told me about their difficulties in working in a class situation, how her dog barks and lunges at other dogs, and how inconsistent he is in his obedience work despite his considerable intelligence and athletic ability. When she can get his attention, he's cooperative, but keeping his attention on her is difficult. She has high hopes for Luger, but she needs help dealing with these training problems.

I stand on the porch, watching as she opens the car door. Luger lunges for the opening, but Margaret is prepared for this. She deftly catches the dog by the collar and wrestles him back into the car, using her body to block his escape route while she puts on his leash. It appears that she's quite practiced in these maneuvers. The word "stay" drifts to me; though it is muffled the first few times, by the tenth time the volume has been turned up, and I'm pretty sure I've heard it correctly. At last she steps back, and a black-and-tan bullet shoots from the car, nose to the ground and moving fast. Dragged along behind him like unwanted baggage is Margaret, fighting to stay on her feet and control Luger at the same time.

"He's awfully excited about being here!" she calls to me as Luger tows her along on his exploration of the front yard. Eventually, Luger is bored with the yard and, lacking anything better to do, turns his attention to Margaret, who leads him to the front steps where I have been sitting for the last few minutes. I mention to Margaret that he is an extremely handsome dog, and she beams at this compliment. I add that I can see that she does indeed have a problem getting his attention. At this moment, the big dog chooses this moment to return to the car, pulling his owner sideways so sharply that I have the impression of an owl turning its head to me as Margaret looks over her shoulder and asks, in all seriousness, "What makes you say that? You haven't even seen him work yet."

Connection is not created through proximity (otherwise everyone on a crowded elevator would become fast friends), though we do use proximity as a substitute for connection, just as we substitute holding a child's hand or holding a dog's leash for actually paying attention to them. Truth be told, we often substitute a leash for attentiveness to our canine companions. Consequently, dogs also substitute a leash for attentiveness to us. In essence, we eliminate the need for any deep attentiveness on our part while also inadvertently teaching the dog that he need not really pay much attention to us—we're right there at the end of the lead. This does not seem to be a terribly bad situation. The dog is safely restrained, and both we and our dogs may move along in some semblance of togetherness. But in the seemingly harmless act of tethering a dog to us and setting off for a walk "together" in this strained fashion, we have already begun to undermine the relationship itself. We have already chosen less quality for the connection between ourselves and our dogs. Ultimately, this choice may come to haunt us at a later time, in moments of far greater intensity and importance than simply walking together. Think of it like this: In allowing our dogs to pull us along, we are practicing, over and over and over, the quality of disconnection. We really have no right to be surprised when in other situations, when we really want or desperately need the dog to be fully connected and attentive to us, he's a bit out of practice.

A healthy relationship maintains a fairly even degree of quality no matter what the circumstances. We'd all look strangely at someone who said that their husband was a very well-behaved man at home but just too excited out in public to act politely. We'd be skeptical of parents who assured us that while at the park they might appear careless and disconnected from their children, they were very attentive to their kids' needs at home. If there are noticeable variances in the quality of connection between you and your dog depending on the situation or circumstances, your relationship may not be as strong as it could be.

Mutual attention—dog to handler, handler to dog—should serve as the first and most powerful connection in all situations. This takes time to create through training and a diligent practicing of attentiveness; a leash can serve as a safety net along the way to handle the bobbles that will inevitably occur, maybe even as a way to begin a conversation that requires no words. Perhaps our language needs to shift so that we no longer "walk the dog" but rather choose very deliberately, with loving attentiveness, to "walk with the dog."

And don't forget—the dog has his own point of view. Interviewed, he might report that at home, you give him loving, careful attention but that out in the world, you are highly distracted, even excitable, and he finds taking you out in public a very tiring experience. Leaning close, his voice low so you don't overhear him, he might whisper to us, "And, gosh, you ought to see how she pulls on that leash!"

6

TAKE IT FROM THE TOP

There are no shortcuts to any place worth going.
ANONYMOUS

HAVING TO GO BACK TO THE BASICS IS NOT FUN FOR ANYONE. What I have always hated in any game and in life was the move that required me to go all the way back to the start and begin again. If I could stand on my head and sing "Ave Maria" backward in Cherokee as atonement, I'd rather do it than return to the beginning. Having to begin again, trying to fill in the gaps left on your first trip—well, it's not something anyone I know enjoys. Why, we ask, can't I just fix it from here? We point to how much we've already accomplished, how far we've already come, and wonder why we have to back up so very far. But the truth is, sometimes you have to back way up, right to the beginning, where the root of a problem lies, and as musicians say, "take it from the top."

Understanding the dismay that accompanies receipt of the "Start Again" card, I had understood why Kate, who had driven a long, long way for a consultation, had looked at me with disbelief and a touch of irritation. She found it hard to believe that she was sitting in my kitchen and being told that one of the keys to her dog's behavior problems is that he pulls on leash.

Kate had worked carefully to train her young dog, Angel, since early puppyhood, and he knew how to do many things. But his behavior was worrying her. She had brought him to me because of the intensity with which he focused on things he found interesting. Sometimes, the intensity escalated into near hysteria, with Angel leaping wildly at the end of the lead and screaming. On a few occasions, he had broken away from her to chase another dog; though he did not do any harm, the intensity of his pursuit alarmed Kate. Angel is a dog she raised and handpicked as her next performance dog. His behavior embarrasses and scares her; she is afraid that he is aggressive, out of control, unfit to perform as she hopes he might.

Ready to learn new techniques, willing to implement even a long, involved training regimen, she was speechless when I told her that she first needed to step back and work on the very foundation of their connection. She had to master the simple act of truly being with him whenever they were together, and insisting—gently, quietly—that he also be with her. If she did not have his mind, I told her, she could only hope to control or at least restrain his body. But if she could stay connected to him and help him learn to stay connected to her, anything was possible within the limits of their joint skills and abilities.

"Oh, come on. I can't even count how many dogs I know that pull whenever they're excited. Lots of them are much worse about it than Angel, but they don't act like he does. I don't see how you can say that contributes to his behavior problems." Kate was frowning slightly, her jaw set in disagreement.

Brilliant, highly responsive, Angel is like many dogs I have worked with—dogs reactive to even minute changes in the world around them, desirable qualities in a working dog. But his keen intelligence is a double-edged sword: almost instantly responsive to a handler's gesture or command, but equally responsive to other stimuli in his environment, including the ones Kate might wish he would ignore. Such dogs are like Mazeratis, beautiful and fast, but they need to be driven with care and precision. With maturity, experience and training, such dogs learn to be selectively responsive, turning their attention to appropriate matters, but Angel was young. He was also impulsive, emotional, volatile. For him, the intense excitement of a training class, Kate's fearful apprehension that he might attack another dog and his own considerable intelligence were proving to be a difficult combination.

Allowing him to pull excitedly on the lead had some unwanted effects: First, Angel's arousal level escalated. Kate simply hung on for the ride, excusing the pulling behavior as something that just happened when her dog was excited. With each step, Angel's excitement built, so that by the time they actually reached the class or practice grounds or even a nearby park where dogs might be playing, he was already aroused to a high degree. By acting as little more than his anchor, Kate had also abandoned any position of leadership, an abdication that did not go unnoticed by the dog. They would arrive at their destination with Angel's heart rate racing and his adrenaline level already high. From a purely physiological perspective, he was well primed to respond to the stimuli of other dogs running. He would stand watching, his excitement growing with each minute, and would soon forget that Kate was even with him. When at last he reached critical mass, he exploded in a frenzy of barking, yelping and leaping, a display that many students in the class interpreted as aggressive behavior. Unable to connect with his mind, Kate had no option left but to drag his body away, frustrated by his behavior, embarrassed and disappointed. Pulling on lead is the spark that starts the embers glowing; everything else that happens is fuel poured on that tiny fire until it is blazing out of control.

I could see the disbelief in Kate's face as I told her that it is here, in the quality of connection, that problems begin or are dealt with, though we will employ a variety of techniques to accomplish this. But first, helping Angel would require a shift in her understanding at a deep, almost philosophical level, and it would require a commitment to being with him and insisting, gently but relentlessly, that he be with her. In even the tiniest steps, she needed to create the quality of connection she wants. There is no way to leapfrog the "unimportant" moments and reserve your full attention for only the "important" times, no more than a builder can create a beautiful house without a solid foundation. In countless ways, some that will seem insignificant at the time, she needed to build the relationship. Kate was not convinced, but she was polite and agreed (though without conviction) to think about this and give it a try. I could see that talk was getting me nowhere, and I silently asked Angel to help me show Kate what I meant. Putting on his leash, we went outside for a walk.

Accustomed to pulling as he pleased, Angel was surprised when I began to insist that he not pull. Since it takes two to pull (ever see a dog pulling off leash?), I didn't give him anything to pull against. Each time the leash grew taut, I gave a gentle tug and then released all tension. At first, he paid no attention to me. This was not unreasonable—we had, after all, just met. Though politely friendly, the dog had no reason to believe that I was of any great interest or concern. To expect him to respond to any direction from me would have been as arrogant as my shaking hands with someone I just met and then giving her orders on how to behave or act. We had no relationship. How then could I find a way to connect with this dog? I needed a way to become someone worth working with, someone interesting and fun. Taking advantage of his love of movement, I called his name and raced away, never letting the leash go tight. I allowed him to just catch up to me before I spun away from him and ran the other way. As his intensity grew, I allowed him to "catch" me and offered praise and some delicious treats before we began again. He found this a delightful game and soon responded happily and quickly to my calling his name. Soon, I was hard-pressed to outmaneuver him—he kept a close eye on where I was and what I was doing, hopeful that I might start the game again. Now we had a connection, although a fragile one, and we resumed our walk. I was still insistent that he not pull, and when I felt as if I had lost him, I danced away, calling him, asking him to reconnect with me. It worked, but not in a smooth, unbroken way. In a series of advances and retreats, it took us nearly ten minutes to go a few hundred feet.

THANKSGIVING COMES EARLY

I decided that I'd take him toward the barn. Our cattle, chickens, pig, cats and horses provide excellent distractions for most dogs. In the absence of competition for the dog's attention, I can only teach so much. To teach a dog to stay connected with me even in the face of distractions requires distractions. Most of the animals who have been with me for a while seem to understand their role as teachers, and they modify their behavior in fascinating ways that I interpret as the assistance of colleagues. (Although the majority of my animals have proven themselves excellent fellow teachers, I must confess that goats may be the animals voted as most likely to tease a student as teach them. One of my goats could be extraordinarily helpful in certain training situations, but at times, she also seemed unable to resist the opportunity to tweak a dog's mind. I once had a college professor a lot like that. . . .)

As we walked, I was planning just where and how I'd introduce Angel to the various animals. The chickens offer a lot of movement but no interaction—they simply pay no attention to dogs unless directly chased, something Angel would have no opportunity to do. Since they can be counted on to move in their brisk scratch-and-peck way, I can choose the appropriate distance and let the dog begin to learn how to think even in the presence of something as intriguing as a hen or rooster. After the chickens, I would have to decide whether it was a good time to meet the cows or go face-to-face with a pig. Have to play it by ear, I told myself. (Charlotte, the pig, is an intense interaction, her sheer bulk and fear-lessness a nice counterpoint for dogs who've begun to believe that they are the biggest, baddest thing on the block. One look at a pig towering more than five feet above them has put more than one dog into a new frame of mind. It's not possible to tell a dog that no pig on earth is actu-ally that tall, no way to explain that Charlotte's standing on her hind legs and balancing on her stall door. But sometimes, I think even if I *could* pass that information along, I might choose not to and let the educa-tional value of seeing the world's largest pig work its magic.)

As we rounded the corner of the drive toward the barn, I realized that in my consideration of how best to use the various farm animals on Angel's behalf, I'd forgotten the turkeys. This, I realized with a silent groan, could be a problem. These turkeys are confident beasts. Endlessly interested in whatever is happening on the farm, it is some-times difficult to accomplish anything without the "help" of the turkeys. Their active involvement is not always entirely welcome, and occasionally worrisome, like the day John was walking into the barn and a turkey carrying a screwdriver walked past him on the way out of the barn. (We're still wondering how the bird got the tool, if he knew how to use it and what he was planning to do.) Exposed since their arrival as day-old chicks to our dogs, they have no fear of dogs. If anything, our turkeys find dogs fascinating, and approach a new dog with interest and an evil glint in their eyes. A rudely inquiring dog nose receives a sharp peck from their strong beaks, and on more than one occasion, a gang of six or more turkeys have surrounded a dog like street toughs surrounding an old woman—with bad intent and a possible mugging in mind.

And now, here they came to help me as I worked with Angel. I knew the turkeys would carefully size up the dog before approaching, keeping their distance unless they felt they could intimidate or safely ignore him. It was endlessly fascinating to me how quickly and accurately these birds assessed every dog they met. I knew the turkeys would keep themselves safe, but I was not sure what Angel would do. Keeping an eye on the turkeys and the dog, I reminded myself to stay soft and breathe and wait to see what the dog would do. Although relaxed, I was ready to deal with what might happen if I had misjudged the situation—I'd have no choice but to simply restrain the dog and steer him to a turkey-free zone where we could start again.

It was quite a scene. Angel stood frozen in his tracks, a wide-eyed statue of a dog, as six turkeys strutted toward him, looking like poster children for some vaguely evil Thanksgiving festival. At that moment, the ten minutes spent insisting that Angel be with me as we walked paid off. I called his name; he turned toward me; and though still fascinated by the turkeys, he came with me as we moved away. While I was busy telling him what a great dog he was, the turkeys moved a little closer, so that when we turned back to them, I discovered to my dismay that the gap had been closed a bit.

Though understandably interested in the birds, Angel was not bouncing around or barking. A casual observer who did not understand canine body language might even have assessed him as standing calmly and just watching. But in the stillness of his body (*rigidity* might be a better word) and the intense pricking of his ears and his fixed stare, I could read just how excited the dog really was. He was internally primed to a high degree, a missile that has been switched on and armed but not yet fired. Now was when I needed to ask him to remain connected with me; waiting until he had exploded was far too late. I called his name, watching for the sign that every dog gives that he has heard you. There almost always is one—whether it's a slight turn of the head, an ear flicking back in your direction, a lightning-fast eye movement or a slight tail wag—and it is sometimes easily missed. But it's almost always there. When Angel showed no sign of being able to hear me, I knew that we were in the danger zone where our connection was broken, so that nothing I said or did would be of help or direction to him.

In such situations, I feel it is critically important to be fair to the dog. I could easily have pulled Angel off his feet with one well-timed jerk of the leash—he was so deeply focused on the turkeys that nothing in his body would have prepared him for that. Just such techniques are employed every day by trainers intent on teaching the dog to pay attention to them *no matter what*. Some even add insult to injury by sweetly inquiring in a cheerful tone, "Oh, what happened? Were you not paying attention?" after jerking the dog off his feet. But what would that really teach Angel except that I might without warning inflict pain on him? It might teach him that paying attention to me no matter what was a good idea since evidently I was psychotic and not to be trusted, a lesson that decidedly would not deepen our relationship. It certainly would not increase the dog's understanding that we were in this together, and that together, we would find a way to deal with whatever situations arose. Everything in the dog's behavior told me that he was truly unaware that I had asked for his attention; his focus was completely on the turkeys. To use force to shift his attention to me would have been grossly unfair. And it would have reflected a choice on my part to take the easy route and not follow the path that led to the quality of connection I wanted between myself and dog.

I'm Sorry—All Circuits Are Busy, Please Try Again

In a laboratory experiment, a cat was wired with electrodes that helped researchers see when an audible signal was received by the brain. When a tone was played, the cat's brain responded with a blip. Tone, blip; tone, blip. Then researchers put a mouse just outside the cat's cage where the cat could see it but not reach it. They were curious to see how the brain processed the competing stimuli of mouse and tone. Their theory was that the brain would register the tone but that the cat would consciously disregard this stimulus in favor of the mouse. To their surprise, when the cat was completely focused on the mouse, the brain did not register the tone at all—it was as if the tone had ceased to exist within the cat's perception of his world. Why they found this surprising is a mystery to me—I have had innumerable experiences where I was so focused on a task or so deep in a book that I failed to hear a phone ring, a teakettle whistling or even the approach of another human being. But no one asked me.

It is difficult—if not downright impossible—to communicate with someone who is not "with" you. Communication is one of the keystones of a relationship, but the prerequisite for communication is a state of connection. When we address another human being, and we can see that they appear engaged in something—be that the football game on TV or balancing the checkbook or getting the decorations on a cake just right—we have both the courtesy and common sense to repeat our question or comment, or allow them to finish before asking for their attention. We understand that they are not "with" us. If we don't realize that they are busy—or worse yet, assume that they are deliberately ignoring us—we can feel both hurt and angry when we receive no response. They in turn can get angry with us, and rightfully so, for our rude insistence that they abandon whatever they were working on and turn their attention to us.

Yet we routinely ignore our dogs when they tell us that they are busy. I am *not* saying that you should stand there helplessly waiting until your dog decides he is finished watching squirrels or whatever. I am saying that you need to respect the reality that your direction or command or request *may not even have been perceived*. Our response to being ignored should not be the same as our response to not being heard. In order to communicate to the dog what you would have him understand, you have to find a way past his focus on something else and turn it back to you. And at a very fundamental level, the dog's disengagement from you speaks to a quality of connection that may need some work. But using force to ask for a dog's attention (unless it is a matter of life and death) is just as insane as slapping someone upside the head because he did not respond to you while his focus was elsewhere. Dogs must wonder at our sudden and unpredictable violence toward them—I do not know how else they could possibly perceive our actions.

That the dog is too engrossed to hear you is meaningful information. A fair response is to take note of that situation and try modifying it a bit.

In Angel's case, having the turkeys less than ten feet away was simply too much—he could not pay attention to me and to them at the same time. Like Edison's comment after yet another failed attempt to create a filament—"Now we know ninety-nine ways not to make a lightbulb"—I had some useful information that I could apply at the next opportunity. This was not a matter of defiance by the dog, just fascination with the largest birds he'd ever come nose-to-nose with in his life. Think about a four- or five-year-old child meeting Mickey Mouse for the first time—would you have their full attention, or might you find yourself peripheral to their wide-eyed, openmouthed wonder at coming face to face with an eight-foot-tall mouse? We sometimes forget just how amazing the world can be to creatures who live fully in the moment instead of "maturely" dismissing an experience with a superficial assessment as we often do. (It is sad that maturity sometimes leads us not into a greater depth of experience and more intense enjoyment of our world but rather to an apathetic belief that we've already been there and done that.) Angel's owner Kate was not immersed in the full experience of what turkeys looked like or sounded like or smelled like or how they moved or how their feathers gleamed in the sunlight or how their wattles changed colors with shifts in their emotional states. But Angel himself was drinking it all in, every sense at work. While such intense focus may interfere with our plans or goals, we might do well to join our dogs from time to time in watching the world with some genuine wonder in our eyes and hearts.

Knowing that Angel was deeply aware of turkeys and little more, I became a bit more insistent with little tugs on the leash, gentle taps on the head with a fingertip or a ruffling of his fur on his rump—anything to get his attention so that we could retreat, together, to a distance where Angel was both able to watch the turkeys and respond to me. The quality and intent of my touches and voice were exactly the same as if I'd been trying to get a human friend to shift attention back to me and away from something fascinating; persistence was part of it, but not pain or even irritation. All I wanted was to get through to him, just as a person might tap your arm repeatedly until the signal actually registered on you. I was looking for the same thing I'd be looking for with a human friend—a shift of the eyes toward me, even momentarily, or a head or body turn toward me even though the eyes might remain focused on the attraction. Both would indicate the beginnings of a shift away from the attraction and back to me. I knew that the split second Angel gave me his attention, I had to make it crystal clear in word and deed that I was thrilled with that response. I also had to try to be more interesting than six turkeys, no mean feat since I'm lacking tail feathers and wings and my wattles aren't nearly as red or obvious.

It took a few tries, but I did get Angel's attention back on me, and we quickly retreated to a turkey-free zone to give Angel a break and to discuss with Kate what was happening. As I suspected, she was a bit confused about why I even allowed Angel to look at the turkeys, why I hadn't "corrected" him for ignoring me and how on earth I thought this was helpful in any way.

Before coming to see me, Kate had (unsuccessfully) tried an approach recommended by another trainer, one that insisted that Angel look only at her and ignore everything around him. In theory, this is the establishment of incompatible behaviors, an approach that at least on paper seems reasonable: A dog engaged in behavior X cannot also be engaged in behavior Y. In practice, establishing incompatible behaviors can be a very effective resolution to some behavior problems. For example, a dog who is trained to run to a special place in the kitchen when the doorbell rings and wait for a delicious treat cannot also be bouncing off the front door and threatening to eat a delivery person. A person who is exercising at the gym can't also be home eating a pint of ice cream. But the use of incompatible or competing behaviors works best when the behavior that is substituted for the undesirable behavior makes it literally (through proximity or posture) impossible for the dog to engage in the unwanted behavior.

For dogs like Angel, trainers sometimes try to apply this same theory like so: A dog cannot remain totally focused on his handler and do anything else at the same time. In reality, this is not exactly true, and such an approach does not work for all dogs. A dog is quite capable of learning to keep his face and eyes oriented on the handler while still listening to or even smelling what's going on around him. Couldn't you? Try this for a moment—look up from this book and make eye contact with someone else or a little imaginary friend. Give the complete impression that you are doing nothing but focusing on that person. But while you're doing that, really bring your attention to whether or not you can wiggle each individual toe. Keeping your eyes on someone's face is not synonymous with being focused on them, is it? The average human being is quite capable of appearing to be engaged in listening to someone else while miles away in their minds, thinking about the existence of the Holy Grail or the speed of an African swallow or where to find the perfect shrubbery. Dogs can figure this one out too, and they do. I've watched many dogs dutifully keeping their eyes fixed on the handler's face as expected, but their ears were swiveling around, picking up all kinds of information, and their noses were busy sorting out even more—all of this stimuli making its way into the dog's mind even though his eyes never left the handler's face. It's a rather insulting assumption on a trainer's part that a dog is incapable of directing his attention as he pleases.

From a purely philosophical point of view, I have trouble with this concept of asking a dog to act as if the world has evaporated around him. It seems insulting to me to insist to an animal—or anyone for that matter—that he should ignore what his senses tell him and just pretend everything is fine. This is particularly true when a dog's attention is fearful, though Angel's was not. As trainer Turid Rugaas says, "If you've seen a green slimy monster in the corner, you're going to have a hard time pretending there's no green slimy monster in the corner." In our loving human relationships, we do not discount others' experiences of the world but instead seek to understand them and perhaps even join them in their point of view. We may not always share their point of view or their fears or their concerns, but if we love them, we deeply respect their reality. When Mom agreed to leave the light on in the hall, it probably wasn't because she was afraid of the dark.

There is nothing inherently wrong with a dog watching the world and what's going on. The world can be a very interesting place, and we'd be more than a little foolish (or rigidly controlling) to ask any intelligent animal to pretend otherwise. There is nothing wrong with a dog watching turkeys or anything else with interest. The world is an intriguing adventure for any intelligent, aware being. There's an old joke about a man who cannot help noticing beautiful women; the punch line is "I'm married, not blind." A dog ought to remain a dog. If truly connected to his people and in control of the impulses that turkeys and other amazements might inspire, a dog need not be blind to the world around him.

And if not deeply connected, if not in control of his impulses, the blame can be laid at the feet of the people involved, not at the dog's paws. If the dog's behavior steps past alert curiosity and interest in his world and becomes annoying, frightening, threatening, fearful or even dangerous, there is a problem that needs to be dealt with at a very fundamental level of the relationship. But the answer is not to deny the dog his dogness or to make him completely dependent upon his handler. A handler who insists that the dog ignore the world is one who is afraid of losing control of the dog, just as the woman who elbows her husband in the ribs for noticing a beautiful woman is afraid and uncertain about the relationship and herself. And always in the face of such fearful need to control, I am reminded of Erik Erikson's provocative question, "Why do we think the face has turned away that only looked elsewhere?"

Unable to detect the difference between interest and serious intent, some handlers set up a rigid system of prevention that does not stretch their understanding but simply limits the dog. A dog who is systematically trained to ignore his world is a fur-clad robot, not a living being. Additionally, this approach gives the animal no coping skills, no new or improved way of dealing with the situation. It does make the dog totally reliant on his handler in what I think is an unhealthy way that smacks of the handler's desire to control the animal's behavior instead of educating them so that they can deal with the world. A more loving, relationship-based approach would be to educate the animal, help him find healthy, productive responses to the world around him, to eliminate or at least minimize his fears—not to offer him temporary fixes or an ostrich-sticking-his-head-in-the-sand approach.

YES, BUT . . .

Taking advantage of physiological facts, it seemed to me a much fairer and, in the long run, more productive approach to help Angel find another way to deal with things he found of considerable interest. Knowing that the longer he stared at the birds, the more likely he was to escalate on the arousal scale until he perhaps lost control of himself, we began to encourage and reinforce any shift in Angel's attention away from the birds. Initially, we prompted this behavior simply by having Kate walk away. In order to rival the fascination of turkeys, she had to dance, stomp and holler as she departed, but Angel did glance over his shoulder to see where she was going—a good sign. It took a fair amount to get him to voluntarily shift his attention away from the birds, but we made sure it was worth his while with lots of praise and treats. Each time he glanced back, the fixation cycle was broken for the moment. At every step, Angel was learning that he could watch the turkeys and keep an ear out for Kate as well.

We didn't want a robot who somehow felt it was bad to watch turkeys. What we were working toward was a dog who would be able to watch the world with curiosity and interest, but also remain connected to his owner, able and ready to respond to her should she ask for his full attention. We worked on this for quite a while, and though I was pleased with Angel's progress, Kate remained unconvinced and unimpressed. Though willing to concede that he was behaving remarkably well, she felt this was due in no small part to the fact that turkeys were not normally a part of Angel's world. What excited Angel beyond control in his everyday world were other dogs racing around and acting wild. In that situation, she noted, he would not be behaving as well, and I'd really get to see what she meant and just how crazy Angel could become. I could not get through to her the idea that whatever the trigger, a high level of arousal was a high level of arousal, and the approach and philosophy would be the same. And so, in an attempt to create a scenario that Kate felt would bring out the worst in Angel, I had John let all of our dogs out into their fenced yard.

As expected and desired, there was a chorus of warning barks from my dogs when they spotted me with Angel on the lawn, and Angel responded with a surge of excitement. But our work with the turkeys had paid off; he was able and willing to remain connected to me, sitting quietly when I asked and watching the dogs with interest but nothing more. I was delighted with his progress, so when I turned to look at Kate, her frown surprised me. I asked if she didn't think this represented progress, and in her response, I could hear her still struggling to accept the concept of the quality of connection as the all-important foundation. Interestingly, she was more intent on finding excuses for why he was *not* behaving badly rather than embracing the positive changes before her: "Yes, but they're not all revved up. Even though they're barking, they're not racing around really excited and playing. That's what really sets him off."

Looking at Angel, who looked right back at me, I realized for the millionth time that what I love most about working with dogs is their willingness to accept new ways and discard old ones. If you show a dog a more comfortable and productive way to experience life, he is usually quite glad to trade in his confusion, anxiety, anger or fear for more pleasant feelings. Humans, on the other hand, can be a bit resistant to change. With an internal sigh, I told Kate that I'd have John race around and play ball with my dogs, working them up to as near hysteria as could be managed. My dogs were happy to oblige, and their usual excited, noisy play just a few feet on the other side of the fence was certainly of interest to Angel. But he did not explode or lose his mind or do anything except occasionally forget himself and get up from the sit I had requested. At a quiet reminder, he promptly sat back down, watching the dogs play, still unmistakably connected to me. I had but to whisper his name for him to instantly turn his attention away from the dogs and to me. At last, Kate had to admit that perhaps what I had been telling her had some merit. She apologized for being so resistant and allowed that on the long drive home, she would have plenty to think about.

There is a beautiful red ribbon that hangs near my desk. Sometimes, a light breeze makes the long streamers dance, and the gold lettering on the rosette gleams softly and tells me that this ribbon was presented for second place in a competition. This is a very special gift from Angel, this first ribbon he ever earned. In the note of thanks that accompanied the ribbon, Kate told me that in his first official competition just a few months after meeting the turkeys, Angel had performed with style and precision, joining her in a mutual dance. Kate had not fully believed that this might ever be possible, and certainly not so soon. Angel had lost first place by only a point when instead of jumping up onto and immediately lying down on the table obstacle as required, Angel just had to peek under the table to see what was there. Kate felt that Angel knew I would understand why he did this, and I did: The world's an interesting place.

Beyond the ribbon that I treasure, Angel gave me a far greater gift, one that exists only in my memory, a snapshot of a moment when we were working with the turkeys. I stand behind him, softly calling his name and giving a little flutter on the leash to say, "Come with me, this way." His beautiful neck is arched as he cranes his head to keep the turkeys in sight for as long as possible. Even though I laugh at his wide-eyed curiosity, I am insistent with my gentle nudges and reminders that this dog be with me. I know he is torn, reluctant to leave these darkly feathered hoodlums who peer sternly past their dangling snoods at him.

"Angel," I call again, and one ear swivels back to let me know that he hears my request. Without taking his eyes off the turkeys, the dog begins to back up in my direction. "Good dog," I say with deeply felt sincerity; this is such tremendous cooperation in a difficult situation. He backs a few more steps, then surprises me by lifting himself up and walking backward on his hind legs so that he can keep the turkeys in clear view. This is his counteroffer to my request—he agrees to come with me but in return he asks for only this, to be allowed to keep his eyes on the birds. I don't need him to turn away from the turkeys; I only need his cooperation, and I have it, though it is styled uniquely in this brilliant compromise that both pleases and amuses me. In this unusual fashion we retreat, Angel walking backward on his hind legs with amazing coordination. At last, we reach a point where the turkeys can no longer be seen, and Angel drops to all fours and turns toward me, the expression on his face one of wonder and pleasure. He prances at my side, smiling up at me, and it is clear that he finds this new adventure a good deal of fun. As we walk together down the driveway, away from the birds, Angel glances longingly over his shoulder and then up at me, his tail wagging. I feel as if I am walking a reluctant but ultimately agreeable child out of Disneyland.

To fix the weak spots in a relationship, you need to begin at the beginning. The quality of connection is created and repaired at the most fundamental level of attentive awareness. In each moment that you are with the dog, you must be aware, gently and persistently shifting the balance toward one of mutual agreement and cooperation. This is not easy, and it requires some thought. Most of all, it requires a desire to create—over and over again—the event of quality, which in turn creates a heartfelt commitment to truly being with the dog.

Learning to really be with their dogs, to truly listen (with far more than their ears) to what their dogs were telling them about that moment's experience, some people I've worked with have found themselves also examining the quality of their connection with others around them. Newly and profoundly aware of the difference that results from a conscious choice to create an event of quality, they begin to apply an equally attentive and loving approach in their dealings with friends and family.

This commitment to truly being with their dog sometimes proves more difficult than some expect, requiring as it does ongoing and greater awareness in every moment. Many have reported to me how exhausting they initially found the work of being truly, deeply attentive to and aware of their dogs. At a very basic level, we are out of practice. Our modern world does not encourage deep, thoughtful listening skills but rather offers us quick "sound bites"—perhaps acceptable when zipping through a quick review of news stories, but hardly supportive of a meaningful relationship. The gift of attentiveness and total focus on what we are saying is so rare, in fact, that when we are truly heard, we often exclaim with pleasure and amazement, "He really listens!"

It is strangely true that while each of us wishes to be heard at length, we often listen to others in only short bursts of attention. Sad that something as fundamental to a loving relationship should so often be incomplete or even missing. If we would understand our dogs, then we begin by shifting our awareness toward understanding that in every interaction, we are in conversation with our dogs. Every conversation begins with a simple connection, a shift of attention away from the world and to another being. It is only when we choose to create an event of quality by bringing our full attention to bear that we open ourselves to truly hear another.

7

CALLING DR. DOOLITTLE

"Lots of people talk to animals," said Pooh.
"Maybe, but . . ."
"Not very many listen, though," he said.
"That's the problem," he added.

BENJAMIN HOFF, *THE TAO OF POOH*

YOU'VE SIMPLY GOT TO LOVE A MAN WITH A DUCK FOR A HOUSEKEEPER. I keep telling folks that the real reason Dr. Doolittle has been my life-long hero is that he trusted his household to the reliable Jemima Puddleduck. As someone who has dealt with her share of ducks (there was that mallard who lived in the living room for a few months and happily swam in the bathtub, bobbing for Cheerios), I can attest to the fact that our web-footed friends are not exactly the kings of clean. Never a fan of vacuuming or other forms of keeping house, I've defended myself over the years by pointing out that I simply haven't yet found the right duck to help me keep an orderly house.

To be truthful, far beyond his choice in housekeepers (she *did* carry her own feather duster with her at all times), what I admired most was the good doctor's ability to talk to the animals. To be able to speak fluent Horse or Dog was, to my mind, the finest of all possibilities. The notion that it was possible to talk to the animals was not a new concept to me when I first encountered Dr. Doolittle at a tender age. Like most children, my earliest books contained countless animal characters, most gifted with memorable personalities and intelligence and the ability to speak. The animal heroes of books I read as an older child somehow—without my noticing—lost the power of speech. The Black Stallion,

Black Beauty, the troubled Flicka, Lad of Sunnybank, White Fang, Old Yeller and others all continued to communicate, but wordlessly. In their gestures, in their resistance and their agreeable compliance, in their misdeeds and heroic actions, these animals spoke volumes. If there was a common thread running through these books and many others, it was that powerful communications were possible without a single word being said. In Jack London's *Call of the Wild*, silent testimony to a dog's utmost willingness is given in Buck's struggle to move the sled that his master has piled high with a staggering load and the foolish freight of human pride. And what more could mere words convey about love and loyalty than a Collie who has traveled the breadth of Scotland to return to the boy she loved? Even if author Eric Knight had given her a voice, Lassie could have said nothing more eloquent than what was told in her eyes as she lay exhausted, nearly dead, outside her young master's school-yard gate.

Though behaviorists and cognitive scientists might insist otherwise, what we see in our dog's eyes is more than just animal instinct or the trained behaviors of dumb beasts. Looking back at us, we see intelligence, humor, joy, disappointment, fear, anger, lust, anticipation, relief, curiosity, delight, boredom, resignation, amazement, sorrow, sympathy, and—undeniably—love. If we honor the dog as a dog, we do not see another human being trapped in a fur coat, doomed to wander through life on all fours at the end of a leash. We see another sentient being who, though science may anxiously remind us there's no "proof," has feelings and experiences that often parallel our own but are uniquely canine. Our dogs look at us, and we cannot shake the feeling that they are telling us something, in fact that they are telling us a lot more than we can understand. And we want to know.

WHAT IS IT, GIRL?

From the time the First Dog crept up to the fireside, man and dog have been trying to understand each other. We have not always been successful, but on both sides we keep plugging along at it. Roughly fourteen thousand years later, communication between man and dog reached its ultimate expression, of course, in Lassie. Not even Rin Tin Tin was as eloquent or as capable of saying so much with just a few barks. Lassie needed only to appear on the scene with an inquiring or urgent look on her face to prompt the classic question, "What is it, girl?" In response, Lassie might say, "Woof. Arf, arf, ARF-rowf!" and Grandpa or Timmy would instantly know that a busload of hungry Boy Scouts was trapped in an abandoned mine just two miles southeast of the farm and that subtle (but detectable by canine senses) seismic activity foretold a collapse of the main mine shaft in the next twenty-four minutes. Whatever the situation and no matter how complicated it might be, Lassie could always find a way to make things crystal clear and rouse the humans to appropriate action.

Few scenarios were as guaranteed to arouse tension and interest in the audience as those dreadful moments when, despite Lassie's attempts to communicate, the humans would not listen or got the message all wrong. "Are these people idiots?" we mutter under our breath, waiting for the lightbulbs to turn on. The director of the show made very sure that the viewers were led by the nose to an understanding of the situation, so that Lassie's barks would be magically translated into meaningful communication. But as someone who was given a collection of Lassie reruns on video as a wedding present, I can assure you that if you miss the first half of the show and tune in just as Lassie makes her dramatic vocalizations, you cannot make heads or tails of what she's saying. Is this, you wonder in vain, the episode where the tiger gets loose from his trainer? Or the one where the greedy rich man from town is tearing up the forest with illegal logging activities? Without the information received in the first half of the show, nothing makes sense.

We would all like to look at the dogs at our feet and ask, "What is it, girl?" and be sure of getting an answer. But our dogs are not Lassie, and it might fairly be said that in our communications with our dogs, we sometimes feel like we've arrived in the middle of the episode. Faced with a series of meaningless barks, you long for clarity like that of the cartoon that shows a Collie at the front steps greeting the lady of the house with a human arm dangling from the dog's mouth. The woman inquires, "What is it, girl? Is something wrong with Timmy?"

Communication is a critical ingredient in any relationship, yet as our human interactions show, even between two members of the same species speaking the same language this is not necessarily an easy matter. On a visit to Washington, D.C., my husband and I were walking near the reflecting pool between the Washington Monument and the Lincoln Memorial. As we walked, I was paying attention to the various trees and plants along the path. John said, "Mint?" in a casual tone, and immediately I began scanning the rather closely manicured area for anything that resembled mint. It is a plant I'm familiar with, but no matter how closely I looked, I couldn't find anything that looked even vaguely like any form of mint: spearmint, peppermint, apple mint or even catmint. Still scanning, I heard him say again, "Mint?" Frustrated, I turned to him, annoyed at his superior observation skills; a former park ranger and an avid gardener, he's famous for spotting wild asparagus from a vehicle moving at sixty miles an hour. "*What* mint?" I asked in irritation. Puzzled by my sudden mood shift, he smiled cautiously and held out the peppermint candy he'd been offering me.

When we add the complications created by not only another language but also another culture, it gets more difficult. And when the other speaks a different language and is from another culture and is also another species, we have reached what is perhaps the most difficult challenge of communication with the possible exception of communicating with the average teenager. How, we wonder, can we communicate with a creature that drinks out of the toilet bowl and speaks in a mysterious blend of growls and woofs and wags of his tail? Though it's tempting (and easy) to focus on the differences between us and our dogs as the cause of problems that arise, the truth is that a great deal of the difficulty lies not in understanding canine communications, but within ourselves.

Many of the problems that complicate our human communications also exist in our relationships with dogs. Dog or daughter, puppy or parent, Fido or friend, we still have to find ways to understand and be understood; such is the nature of communication in any form. We still have to find ways to shape our conversations with respect, curiosity about the other's point of view, a willingness to listen (even when we don't like what we hear), and a compassionate sense of how our communications are received and how the listener may be affected. We still need to find ways to hear with more than our ears; to listen is to tune every sense to another's communication, to the nuance of eyes and gesture and breath and body. To hear our dogs, we must also listen with our hearts.

Within a loving relationship, we must be willing to do the work of choosing the event of quality, aware that in each interaction, we are moving in only one of two directions: toward greater trust, understanding and intensity of connection, or toward greater distance between ourselves and another. How we choose to communicate with our dogs will either enhance or limit our relationships. Norwegian trainer Turid Rugaas is a pioneer in understanding canine communications, particularly what she calls "calming signals"—gestures used by dogs to acknowledge, reassure, calm and defuse tense situations. These gestures are offered by dogs to other dogs, to humans, and even to other species. Observing that in our conversations with dogs we can choose to be friendly, neutral or threatening, Rugaas asks the very good question, "Why would we want to threaten our dogs?" In every communication, we have the power to choose how we communicate with our dogs. If we love them, if we respect them, if we are trying to create an event of quality, then we also have an obligation to listen to what they have to say.

What is inescapable in every communication is this: The common ingredient in all our relationships, whether with man or beast, is us. As they say, "wherever you go, there you are." To an astonishing degree, our beliefs, expectations and assumptions color all of our communications. A well-known experiment years ago involved teachers and how their expectations might impact their teaching. One group of teachers was told that they had been assigned the brightest, most gifted students. Another group was told that their classes would consist of slow learners and poor students. In reality, all teachers were assigned their students on a purely random basis. The results were unsettling. The teachers with the "gifted" students had the test scores and progress to reflect just how smart those kids were; the teachers with the "slow learners" had test results that showed that indeed, these were slow learners. The researchers found an important difference in how the teachers taught as a result of their expectations. Teachers of "gifted" children had viewed any lack of understanding by the student as a teaching problem; since the child was known to be gifted, the only possible explanation for a failure to learn lay in the teaching style. These teachers worked in every way possible to ensure that they were able to successfully communicate with what they knew to be gifted children. The teachers of the "slow learners," on the other hand, viewed a child's lack of comprehension as the unfortunate but inevitable outcome of the child's limited ability: If the students did not understand something as it was taught, the teachers did not change their communication style.

A similar phenomenon is at work among dog lovers around the world. People frequently assume that certain breeds or types of dog are stupid, smart, stubborn, lazy, aggressive, friendly. And their beliefs shape their actions, sometimes most unfortunately for the dogs involved. Very often, what we label as stupid or stubborn has little to do with the dog's level of intelligence. What we really mean when we say that a dog is stupid or stubborn or lazy is that he's not in agreement with us, that he's not doing what we want him to do. When we try to force a dog to accept our particular methodology and ignore what he tells us about its unsuitability for him, we are really saying that our toolbox does not contain a teaching approach that will work for him and that we don't really care. The failure, we feel, rests on the stubborn, stupid, dominant, fearful (pick an adjective) dog, not in our approach to him. A good deal of dog training is rather Procrustean. Procrustes was a mythological fellow who had a special bed that he guaranteed would fit all who tried it. And amazingly, it did—because he would stretch anyone too short for the bed and cut off any parts that were too long and hung over the bed. Perfect fit, every time! And we do this to dogs, stretching them unnaturally to suit our training demands and lopping off the parts we don't like or the parts that don't neatly fit within our paradigm.

EVERYTHING'S JUST PEACHY

In some of my seminars, I have the participants play a little game I call Fruits and Veggies. An adaptation of trainer Karen Pryor's training game, Fruits and Veggies offers a reminder of how much we take for granted in our communications, an empathetic experience of how the dog may feel and a sometimes surprising look at how our expectations can create problems. The rules are quite simple. Participants are split up into pairs, and each person is handed a slip of paper meant for their eyes only. On those slips of paper are three simple behaviors well within the ability of the average person, such as "hop," "blink," "take off one shoe." (The slips are color-coded so that each person in a pair has something different from what's on their partner's slip.) The goal is for each person ("the trainer") to teach their partner ("the dog") to perform those three behaviors. There is one catch: They may only address their partners using the names of fruits and veggies. All normal English is abandoned. The commands, praise and even negatives must all be the names of fruits and veggies. The trainers may use any technique they care to (except painful ones), but they must not take advantage of the human tendency to mimic or mirror what is shown. A trainer may not stand on one foot and then look meaningfully at their "dog"—a human will inevitably guess that an imitation of the trainer's behavior is expected. (While dogs are an allomimetic species, meaning that they will imitate the behavior of others, dogs tend to reserve this for actions that are natural and enjoyable to them—digging, for example, as many gardening enthusiasts have learned to their dismay when Fido decides to "help" with the planting.) Trainers must somehow shape and encourage that behavior without offering an example. The "dogs" are free to act precisely like an off-leash dog—if bored, they may wander away; if threatened, they are free to yelp or growl (no biting allowed).

Quickly, participants discover one basic truth about communication: It is most successful when the words you use are ones that both understand. Faced with "Grape!" or "Carrot" or "Rutabaga" (one that inexplicably shows up frequently), the "dogs" are often very, very confused. Diligently, they search the trainer's face and gestures for clues as to whether "Apple" is a command or is meant to dissuade or is offered as praise. The word itself has no meaning; it is the full context of body language that gives the word meaning, just as our real four-legged dogs come to understand "Good dog" as praise and "Stay" to mean don't move.

At the same time, trainers frustrated by the "dog's" lack of appropriate response resort to the technique used by tourists the world over—in the face of a listener's confusion, they often just repeat the word at increasing volume. Volume, while impressive, never equals clarity.

Trainers find themselves having trouble remembering just what they are trying to communicate, mixing up their words so that they're praising when they meant to give a command or vice versa. As many have complained, "This is much easier when I know what I mean!" From the trainers' point of view, the behavior is one they can easily envision, but they discover that communicating that via a nonsensical language is not easy. Of course, when we know what we mean in using a word, we often slip into the assumption that the listener—our dog—also does. "Heel" and "Down" are just as nonsensical to a dog as "Peach!"

Successful communication requires that we understand the listener's state of mind, their level of understanding and, past that, the information in their minds. The information left out of our communications is what Tor Nørretranders in his book *The User Illusion* calls exformation, and it is as critical a part of communication as what we actually do say. As Nørretranders notes, "Information is not very interesting. The interesting thing about a message is what happens before it is formulated and after it has been received."

When I ask my dog Grizzly, "Where is your bumper?" there is a tremendous amount of unspoken information that I know he already possesses. "Bumper" is simply the key that evokes the response I want, but it works only because he has learned a great deal about a bright orange plastic tube with little knobs and a ratty rope. In his mind's eye (and undoubtedly his mind's nose) there springs up not only his internal representation of the thing itself but quite possibly the memory and anticipation of all the pleasurable experiences that go with it. To a dog who does not have all that information, asking "Where is your bumper?" is as meaningless a message as "Where is Timbuktu?" There is no difference in Grizzly's response to the word *bumper* than in my friend Wendy's response if I say, "Let's go get some ice cream!" I do not need to spell out for her that this will require that we put on our shoes, locate some money, walk out to the truck, drive five miles or so to our favorite ice cream stand, stand in line, decide on our flavor or style of cone, pay the cashier and then begin eating. I also do not need to tell her that ice cream is the sweet, very cold, creamy shapeless stuff that comes in many colors and flavors. The mere words *ice cream* evoke all that in her mind, and her mouth begins to water, and she's out the door before I am. If she were an alien who just arrived on a spaceship, we'd have to have quite a lengthy conversation in order to convey the exformation, all left out of but still contained in the phrase "Let's go get some ice cream!"

This is one of the big problems we have when working with dogs or other animals. When we utter a word as command or direction, we bring to that word a great deal of exformation. Because we are usually quite clear in our minds about what we intend to communicate, we forget that *what is in the listener's mind* will affect to a great deal what the ultimate response to our communication may be. On a frequent basis, we experience a bit of the dog's puzzlement when another person says to us, "Hand me that thingamajig." The purely nonsensical word offers us no meaningful information, because no clear image or sensation is evoked. For our dogs, English or any other human language is a nonsensical one, and only experience helps them understand what we mean when we utter any word.

Training is a way of developing our ability to communicate with our dogs (though like many of our conversations with other humans, sometimes it's much more *to* the dog than *with* him). When we train, we are inventing our own mutual language so that when we say "ball" or "stay" or "come," we can excite within the dog's mind the images, sensations or even scents that we intend to. For his part, the dog learns ways to excite within us what he intends—thus, a meaningful bump of his nose against a doorknob creates in our minds an indication that he needs to go out, and if he is a puppy, we may have vivid images of what our carpeting will look like if we ignore this message.

It's safe to say that one of the most common failures of communication is that we take much for granted and forget how much exformation there is in even a simple request. In our mind, there may be a very complete home movie about what we mean when we say "Sit" or "Stay" or "No." But if we haven't made sure that the dog has also seen and understands that home movie, we're going to have problems. We'll be frustrated, and the dog will be too. We are, quite often, asking our dogs for that thingamajig, and they make the best guesses they can based on what we have taught them.

A common response to Fruits and Veggies is a deeply empathetic understanding of how dogs feel on the receiving end of what we are trying to communicate. Many participants report being seriously confused, and they appreciate that "Potato" is as meaningless as "Sit" may be to a dog. As one woman noted, "No wonder my dogs look confused." Others figure out what each word means, but when asked just a few minutes later to perform Mango, Peach and Kiwi, often confuse which word goes with what action—even though they clearly understand the three behaviors they were taught. You can see them sorting through the behaviors, trying to remember which word goes with what action; they are often wrong. Real dogs of course have the same problem, though if they mix up commands, for example offering a down when they are asked to sit, they may be viewed as disobedient instead of simply confused or unsure. We often expect our dogs to learn and perform with far greater alacrity and precision than we are capable of ourselves.

One man who had been working with a woman who used a lot of physical guidance and actually moved his body in specific ways discovered that he was increasingly angry about being handled while being told "Raspberry." He did not understand what she wanted, and he disliked her attempts to force him into the position, however gently. Suddenly, he understood why some of the dogs he had worked with had twisted out of his hands or even growled—he had thought they were just being stubborn or had bad temperaments. Even years after the seminar, he still remembers his confusion and resentment. Before ever laying hands on a dog or trying to teach them something new, he thinks, "Raspberry" and is careful and considerate in his communications.

But one of the most important messages people carry away from this exercise is an understanding that they began the game with assumptions about the willingness and intelligence of their "dogs." Every participant starts the exercise with the belief (conscious or not) that their dog is willing, cooperative and intelligent. No one looks at their partner and thinks, "Oh, a sneaker-wearing pants-and-shirt type. I know they can be stubborn." No one assumes that a lack of response is due to stupidity, dominance, submission or a desire to deliberately defy. Real dogs, however, are not universally extended the assumption that they are willing, intelligent and cooperative. More than one student has walked into training class on the first night and told me, "This dog is stupid." They know this, of course, not because they've tried diligently to educate the dog but because the dog has failed to automatically become Lassie. The most important goal any instructor has is to open her eyes to just how willing and cooperative and intelligent dogs are when we are able to communicate effectively with them.

Our assumptions and expectations about dogs can lead us down the path to pure frustration for both dog and trainer. But unlike the "dogs" in the Fruits and Veggies game, our real dogs can't offer us feedback in English about how they felt or where we went wrong. But they do tell us—over and over again—using the eloquent language of Dog. Learning how to understand them requires time, practice, study and a desire to know more. Most of all, we must first believe that the animals have something to say. It's strange how difficult that first step can be, though we already know from our human relationships that half of successful communication lies in our willingness to hear what someone else has to say. At work in every episode of Lassie was the understanding that this dog had something to say, and folks who knew her well regarded her communications as meaningful. This simple assumption—that something important can be transmitted from the dog to us—is an essential key to the understanding we are seeking.

In *Kinship with All Life*, J. Allen Boone ponders the many stumbling blocks within himself that prevented him from connecting with the dog Strongheart. He realizes that the problems of communication were founded in his assumptions and ideas about animals, not in the animal itself: "And one of the most arrogant of these ideas was the conceit that while I . . . was fully qualified to communicate certain important thoughts down to animals, the animals . . . were able to communicate little of real value up to me."

While we might wish for a real-life Dr. Doolittle to help us talk to the animals, we don't need one. We simply need to learn what Dr. Doolittle knew all along—the animals have something to say. Dog training places a heavy emphasis on communicating *to* the dog, and not necessarily *with* the dog. Though we spend a lot of time working to make our dogs responsive to what we have to say, a better approach might be to follow the advice of Saint Francis of Assisi: "Seek first to understand; then to be understood."

8

PIGS IN POKES

*Listening means an awareness, an openness to learning
something new about another person . . . listening with the intent to
learn is an approach to a different type of conversation.*

ELIZABETH DEBOLD

A WHILE AGO, I READ AN ON-LINE DISCUSSION between a concerned dog
owner and a professional dog trainer. After describing the dog's behavior in detail, the owner asked for specific advice on how to use a particular training technique. The trainer answered at some length, which
prompted the dog owner to ask if it was important to try to figure out
why the dog might be feeling the need to act in such a way. The trainer's response was essentially that what the dog was feeling was not really important; only what he was doing mattered. This in and of itself is
reasonable advice. But then the trainer went on to modify this by noting that it was not possible to ever really know what another being was
thinking or feeling, and so we shouldn't even guess. She admitted that
perhaps "some" trainers with a real gift for reading body language might
be able to make a pretty educated guess and be right most of the time,
but most dog owners couldn't (and, it seemed implied, shouldn't bother to) develop that degree of skill. After all, the trainer concluded, if we
do guess, "What if we're wrong?"

What if we're wrong? So what if we are? Will the seventh veil of the
temple rend because we've misunderstood another being? Will the stars
fall from the heavens because we thought a dog (or a person or any other
living being) meant one thing when actually they meant something else?
This trainer's response made me intensely sad. Within the context of a

trusting, loving relationship, we needn't be afraid to guess if our guess-es spring from loving curiosity and an honest desire to know. If we are wrong, then we have a chance to learn. To my way of thinking, the ongo-ing process of learning to understand another being is a key point of any relationship, delightful, astounding and valuable beyond description, eclipsed only by the value in learning to understand ourselves. To me, a relationship is a journey into uncharted territories quite unlike the famil-iar convoluted trails of my own mind. Such a journey requires that I be willing to try—even stumble down—new trails. Within a loving rela-tionship, there is no need for fearful caution, only respectful considera-tion. With each new person or animal I embrace into my life, I begin a journey with no clear map of where to go and what to say but nonethe-less excited by the possibilities that lay ahead. Although it is said that every journey begins with a single step, reaching outward to another being is not so much a step as a leap of faith. Agnes de Mille noted that "living is a form of not being sure, not knowing what next or how. . . . We guess. We may be wrong, but we take leap after leap in the dark."

To a certain degree, communication is a lifelong series of guesses. After all, one never really can know another's precise thoughts or experience their exact feelings. But we want to try, and we hope desperately that others will care enough to try to understand us. On the purest level, communication is our attempt to leap across the chasm that divides us from other minds, other ways of thinking and feeling, other ways of knowing and seeing and understanding the world we share. From the very moment we can conceive of Other, we begin a lifelong process of reaching out, past the boundary of our own skin, searching for the con-nections that in many ways help define who we are. We communicate because the world within us is not enough; without others, we are incomplete. Only through what we learn in our most profound rela-tionships can we find the completeness in ourselves.

To the extent that we're trapped in our bodies and cannot even begin to communicate more than a tiny fraction of the internal, lightning-fast torrent of our thoughts and feelings, it could be said that all of us consti-tute "a pig in a poke." Those looking on from outside the "poke" (sack) can only guess based on the gyrations and squeals precisely what might be happening to the "pig" inside. Quiet, for example, could be ominous. The pig might be dead, or merely sleeping, or waiting in silent frustration. Squealing could be pain, anger, or even a particularly loud dream. How then could we possibly know what was going on in that poke? We guess.

How well we guess will depend on a number of factors. One is simply this—are we truly curious about the pig in the poke? If we don't really care one way or another about what might or might not be happening with that pig in the poke, we will not devote the energy required to satisfy our curiosity. Another factor is experience—have we ever dealt with a pig in a poke before? Obviously, a first time Poker is going to have a different set of guesses than someone who deals with pigs in pokes all the time. Most important, though, is this: How much empathy do we bring to the situation?

We can see the pig in a poke in a number of ways. One view is the purely mechanical: the pig is contained, thus we can do what we like with him, though we *do* wish he'd stop squealing. Another option is the pragmatic approach: We feel badly that the pig is contained, but we can't waste time dreaming up better ways to transport a pig from point A to point B. We treat him fairly, expect he'll get over it, and we do wish he'd stop squealing. There is also the empathetic approach: We try to imagine how it might be inside that poke, how we might make this easier on the pig, wonder about possibly better ways to transport pigs— and we do wish he'd stop squealing.

The empathetic approach is, without question, sometimes very time-consuming. It requires that we work in slow, careful ways, going past merely treating an animal fairly as we achieve our goals and moving into working with that animal as a partner. It also requires a willingness to see the world from the animal's point of view, followed by a thoughtful contemplation of that perspective. Empathy shapes our view so that the other's perspective is included as part of our consideration; deeply felt, this may shift our own perspective and our goals considerably. The empathetic approach is the only one that allows dynamic quality of connection; without empathy, we are merely driving toward our own goals no matter how that may affect the other. Intimacy is not possible on such a one-way street. Although it requires more from us, in the end I think the results and the relationships possible when we work from an empathetic point of view far outweigh any drawbacks.

Trying to step into another's point of view, however, is sometimes more easily said than done. As a Cuban proverb sagely observes, "Listening looks easy, but it's not simple. Every head is a world." No matter how empathetic we may be, a lot of bobbles and mistakes can be made as we fumble around, trying to understand, trying to guess, trying to walk a few miles in the other's paws.

THIS LITTLE PIGGY

When we acquired our first Gloucestershire Old Spots pig, a rare breed considered endangered in the United States, we decided that this pig needed to learn some basic life skills so that he could enjoy to the fullest possible degree the freedoms and delights life on our farm might be able to offer. After spending two weeks getting to know the little boar whom we named Connor (a grand Irish name for an intensely English breed; we are nothing if not perverse), we were satisfied that the lack of handling in his first few months of life had been largely overcome. The Old Spots legendary gentle temperament was shining through, and it was time to begin working with Connor in earnest.

Time is always of the essence when dealing with species whose lives are, as Irving Townsend put it, "even more temporary than our own." What it takes a human being fourteen years to accomplish between birth and the deranging onset of hormones, a dog accomplishes in less than one light-speed year. Miss a few stops along the way on that track and you've missed a lot; it's quite safe to say that the first six months of a dog's life can make or break the dog that puppy will eventually become. Canine developmental timetables make humans appear to be moving on a very slow, leisurely schedule. Pigs are also on the fast track developmentally, but they bring another dimension altogether to the challenges created by rapid development—the dimension of weight. It is not impossible for a young growing pig to add as much as two pounds a day, and that translates on an explosive and exponential scale to sheer power. With each passing day, Connor was more mature—you may read that as more fixed in his ways; it can be difficult to keep a pig's mind flexible and accommodating. He also weighed more. A lot more. Now was the time if I was going to train my new pal so that he could enjoy walks in the fields and woods, and so that he'd be safe to handle, a desirable goal in an animal that may weigh close to a thousand pounds at maturity!

In the end, Connor's leash training began with several short sessions a day of having a soft cotton horse lead draped in a figure eight around his neck and behind his front legs. Once accustomed to that, I tried to steer him out of his pen and into the barn aisle, where we could stroll and practice this new life skill. Curious about the world outside his pen, Connor took a few steps forward, snout upward sniffing then furiously skimming along the concrete of the barn floor. He was having fun exploring and didn't seem to mind the leash and harness at all. This is easier than I thought, I told myself smugly as I followed the porcine explorer. You would think by now I'd be a wise enough trainer to know that when anything—anything at all—is done with even a hint of smugness in the presence of an animal, the Dog God begins to chuckle just before all hell breaks loose.

I tugged every so gently on Connor's rope harness, thinking to encourage him to take another few steps, and then the squealing began. It was as if suddenly he realized that he was restrained in any way. Apparently, being steered or restrained is something pigs as a rule see as unreasonable; these guys are the Patrick Henrys of the farm animal set: "Give me liberty or give me . . . No, wait—give me liberty or else!"

It is said that a squealing pig can generate sounds that exceed the decibel level of the Concorde Jet at takeoff. Whoever was man enough to discover this fact has my sympathy for what he faced every day on the job. I'm sure he also has a hearing aid by now. (Seriously, in a report of injuries sustained on the job, swine veterinarians reported hearing loss as one of the long-term effects of spending their days in the company of pigs.) Ever alert to the fine nuances of animal behavior, I could not help but notice the escalation of squeals from rather cute porcine mumbles of annoyance to full-blooded stop-every-cow-on-the-farm-in-their-tracks screams. I think that if I were a predator, such squeals would either scare the hunt right out of me or spur me on to new heights of savagery. Of course, if I were a piglet about Connor's size and some evil wolf crept up and put a rope harness on me and tried to get me to stroll up and down the barn aisle, my screams would have another purpose: the piglet's version of 911. Response is not by police or ambulance, but by Momma Hog, a fast-moving mountain of protection on little trotters. My estimates are that in fair weather under reasonable conditions, Connor's screams could easily have been heard at least a quarter mile away. Thankfully, Connor's sizeable mother was nearly a hundred miles away. It's an old barn, and sound likes to stick around and ricochet from the concrete floor to the stone wall on one side to the soft, rotting wood of the haymow floor; I don't think too many decibels escaped. (One of the roosters may now be deaf, though we can't really tell. He didn't respond to his name in the first place.)

A believer in the value of an empathetic approach to animals, I tried to understand how this seemed from Connor's point of view. (Trust me—empathetic thinking is not easily done under these conditions; my eardrums were vibrating in time with Mother Nature's spokes-pig, a vibration that does not loan itself to thoughtful meditation.) I could understand that being restrained from moving freely might be frustrating. So, abandoning even gentle tugs, treating him like a puppy being leash trained, I simply followed him, letting him set the direction. Up and down the barn aisle we walked, Connor squealing no matter what I did. Even when he was free to set the course, he was quite verbal about the whole experience, mollified only slightly by the occasional jellybean I offered when he stood mumbling to himself.

I tried everything I had learned over years of leash training puppies and even full-grown dogs, halter training cattle and horses. And still the pig squealed, though it varied from full-blown "You'll never take me alive!" squeals to more moderate "Damn you all" mutters. Why, I wondered, was this so difficult for him? It dawned on me that what was missing was the exact ingredient I'd reminded countless students of in training their dogs: relevance. From Connor's point of view, this was not relevant to his life. There was simply no point in this senseless walking up and down the barn aisle. He'd already been there more than twice, and jellybeans weren't very convincing reasons to continue. (Our other pig, Charlotte, has a more typically porcine view of food as possibly worth selling her soul for, and will work on silly tasks like sitting or waving just to get a gumdrop.) It's very easy to forget that while we think something is fascinating or important, our animals may not. If we can appreciate that some of their complaints may be about how boring or pointless something is, we'll go further in being able to understand what they have to tell us. Of course, accepting someone's comment that your plan is boring or pointless requires that you've left your ego at home that day and does oblige you to figure out how to liven up the lesson.

"The point, my dear pig, is that in learning to walk on leash and harness you will gain the freedom to go outside for walks with us in areas not safely fenced for you." My speech, naturally, fell on deaf ears (his squeals may have affected his hearing as well, and if not, I encourage some scientist somewhere to find out why not). Verbal communications are rather limited when addressing animals—they're more of a Missouri mind-set: "Show me." So, I showed Connor why this was important. I took him outside the barn, a short trip made possible with a lot of jelly-beans and careful use of blockades to encourage progress toward the barn door. Once outside, his squeals diminished as he began eagerly snuffling his way across the farmyard. By the time we reached the lush green grass of the lawn, he understood what the point was and settled down to eat his way toward the house. By his second leash-and-harness lesson, he complained only briefly when he first left his pen and until he reached the outdoors. By the third lesson, he stood politely while his harness was put on, and like an absolute gentleman, walked out into the sunshine with nary a squeal.

Since then, just like dogs who leap for joy at the sight of their leashes, Connor has welcomed both the harness and the freedom it allows him (or did until he grew so large that harnessing him was akin to harnessing a Volkswagen with no brakes and a determined mind). We had only one other incident with squealing complaints, and it took me a while to understand what he was telling me. We had set off for a long walk in the woods and fields, accompanied by two guests and a few dogs. Connor was a delightful walking companion who set a leisurely pace and whose motto might be summed up as "be sure to stop and eat the flowers." Halfway through the planned route, one of the guests indicated he was tired and in danger of being carried away by hungry mosquitoes, so I headed for home, retracing our steps. The instant I changed my plans, Connor began to squeal. This puzzled me since he hadn't uttered a peep the entire trip. The farther we walked, the more he squealed, and these were the squeals of complaint, not fear or pain or worry. Eventually, the answer came clear in the shift in his body posture and explorations. He was just trudging along without exploring, and I realized that he looked and sounded for all the world like a portly child who was disgruntled by a fun expedition cut short. To test my theory, I veered off the path into an area he had not yet explored. Immediately his head went down and he was quiet again, happy that we were headed somewhere new. Sadly, the already traveled (and explored) trail was the only comfortable route home. When I resumed walking along behind the guests, Connor once again began telling us just how little he thought of it all. He was the piggy I heard tell of as a child—the one who cried wee-wee-wee all the way home.

IS THIS SO?

It is okay to guess what an animal is feeling, just as it's okay to guess what any human is thinking. This is how we learn to know one another, by guesses based on our own experiences, our (always imperfect) understanding of how someone else communicates what they are feeling or thinking, and our willingness to accept feedback and fine-tune our behavior. It's okay to guess what your dog is trying to communicate as long as you're willing to accept that you might be wrong, correct your misunderstanding and try again. It is not okay to guess what an animal is thinking or feeling if you are unwilling to accept nothing less than absolute compliance with your wishes. Far too common are assertions that someone "knows" why a dog did or did not do something; rarely is that guess tested against the reality of the dog's responses. I make a lot of guesses based on my observations of a dog's behavior, the situation and many years of experience. But I'm also interested in testing my guesses against reality. In one way or another, I create a situation that asks the dog, "Is this so? Is that how it is for you? Did I guess right?" I'm as grateful when I'm wrong as when I'm right. Results I did not expect are evidence that I've guessed wrong and need to try again; they are also opportunities for me to learn more than I knew when I guessed incorrectly. This is how all of us learn anything, and it is how all of us learn to understand others.

A relationship is a learning process, and one that never ends; we never "master" a relationship as we might a skill, like learning to ride a bicycle. But there are similarities that are useful to remember. When you were learning to ride a bicycle, you engaged in what is known as a feedback loop. As you tried to master the seemingly simple act of balancing on two wheels in motion, you had to constantly adjust according to the information your body was getting. At first, the feedback loop was sloppy. This, of course, was due only to your inexperience and misunderstanding—the bicycle, responsive only to the laws of gravity, had no ulterior motives or desire to unseat you. Aware of losing your balance, you compensated too soon or too much or too late. But as you persisted, the feedback loop became tighter, quicker, and you learned to adjust only to actual information received through your feeling of balance and what you saw visually. Eventually, the feedback loop was fast but unimpeded by your fear or anxious, premature adjustments, and you rode the bicycle down the street.

Relationships are the ultimate in feedback loops. The speed, accuracy and detail of a feedback loop offers a good clue to the intensity of relationship. For example, if you are having a bad day, you may seem to casual acquaintances or strangers to be perfectly fine—the feedback loop between you and them is a relatively crude one, so that subtleties of expression or movement are often lost. But to someone who loves you, it may be unmistakably clear in the shape of your mouth or the cast of your eyes that you are having a bad day. They have "learned" you, and they did so because they were curious, because they were willing to guess and pay attention to the feedback loop of your responses and your behavior, adjust their own actions accordingly and try again. When we join the dog in a healthy, trusting relationship, bringing intense curiosity, empathy and a humble willingness to learn, a feedback loop of very high order can be created. Fine distinctions and subtleties become possible, and even minute gestures can take on great meaning. We are well on the road to understanding each other.

All of us—man and beast—move through life trying to be heard, trying to listen. Should I ever lose the power to speak and to write, my two major forms of communication, I sincerely hope that someone loves me enough to guess what I'm trying to say. I sincerely hope someone is intensely curious about what's going on inside me and takes the time to listen to the whole message. I hope someone treats me like a dog they love very much.

9

AND NOTHING BUT THE TRUTH

Honesty is the first chapter in the book of wisdom.

Thomas Jefferson

THE OLD SAW NOTES THAT NOTHING IN LIFE IS CERTAIN except death and taxes. I suspect the author of that little cynicism didn't have a dog, or he'd have known that there is another certainty: A dog will always tell you the truth. (Actually, this is true of a majority of animals, with the exceptions of human beings and our closest kin, the great apes. Nice to know that so much shared DNA also allows for outright deception if not matching opposable thumbs.) Mind you, this is not *the* Truth mankind has sought since the beginning of time, though I'll grant dogs have their fair-share number of that puzzle's pieces. A dog will tell you *his* truth, which springs directly from his understanding and experience of his world. Dogs are ruthlessly, unfailingly, reliably honest. What you see is what you get. There are no ulterior motives, or at least hidden ones— our dogs think nothing of giving us wonderful affectionate hugs while also leaning over our shoulders to lick a plate! This does not mean the dog will tell you what you want to hear.

By honesty, I mean that the dog will report faithfully to you in his body language and behavior what he is feeling at the moment. If a dog is angry, he'll be quite clear about that. If he's happy, he shows it. Assuming we can accurately learn to understand what he's saying, we can rely on the dog to tell us what's going on for him at that moment. Concealed feelings are not part of a dog's world. If you could ask a dog "How are you?" and receive an answer of "Feeling great, thanks!" that is an answer you could bet the farm on without placing anything in jeopardy. Ask a human the same question, and while you may get the same jolly answer, that person may be concealing their anxiety over being fired five minutes earlier or hiding their anger at something you did fifteen years ago. What makes human communications especially tricky is that people have the ability to externally display behavior congruent with one emotional or mental state while internally experiencing something else altogether. This is commonly known as lying. (And when people are very good at concealing such incongruence, sometimes we call them politicians.)

To the best of my knowledge, there are no mechanisms in the canine behavioral repertoire that allow for deceit. The closest thing to deceit I have ever witnessed was a dog who somehow learned that if she barked convincingly at the front door, other dogs would rush to join her, giving up the spot on the couch that she coveted. She did not use this behavior frequently—maybe four times in my experience. (Which begs the question—if this was a deliberate and successful deception, why didn't she use it more often or anytime that she wanted access to her spot on the couch?) Our conclusion was that she was barking at nothing, and had done so only to get the others off the couch. But this conclusion may speak more to our state of mind than to an accurate reflection of dog behavior. Knowing just how keen a dog's senses are and how many times I've incorrectly discounted a dog's communication only because *I* saw nothing outside, I'm not sure that there was "nothing" there. Since I've encountered no other form of deceit in dogs (or many other species), I'm hard-pressed to count that single example of possible deceit as meaningful, though I've heard of other dogs learning the same or similar behavior. If that's the extent of doggy dishonesty, I'll take it.

NOT A MATTER OF CHOICE

Given our tendency to romanticize the noble beast and place animals as superior to (instead of different from) humans in certain aspects, I think it is important to recognize that the dog's honesty springs from an *inability* to lie. The dog's honesty does not arise out of any moral superiority but rather from the fact that he is incapable of dishonesty. Lying is simply not a part of canine communications. I have seen dogs offer behaviors that they thought were expected or wanted, but they did not offer them with an intent to deceive. Those who would place the dog or any other animal on a pedestal for being honest are missing the point—human honesty is noble precisely because it reflects a deliberate choice between lying and telling the truth. Dogs lack the option, thus do not consciously choose to be honest. Just as mercy is the possession of power not brought to bear, honesty is the possession of a capacity for deceit that is not used. While we should be more than a little grateful for animal honesty, no merit should be assigned for not doing what you are incapable of doing anyhow; it's kind of like congratulating a blind man for not ogling a naked woman.

On the other hand, the value of this honesty should not be discounted. Whether the result of conscious choice or simple inability, honesty is an extraordinary gift in any relationship. And yet, we frequently discount the dog's utter truthfulness about what he thinks in any given situation. It may be that we do this for two reasons. First, unfailing honesty is almost inconceivable based on our human experiences. Second, complete honesty is not always entirely pleasant; truth encompasses both welcome and unwelcome messages.

In even our most trusting relationships with people, we remain aware that at some level, the potential for deception is ever present. The human mind is unfortunately quite capable of deceit on scales both grand and petty. And no matter who we are or how wonderful we try to become, each of us is uneasily aware that we possess the capacity for lying; our awareness arises from experience with our own minds and our own behavior. The struggle to become honest is one all humans face, because our needs and fears inevitably bring us into conflict with the needs and fears of others. Lies, small or big, are one way of navigating through unfamiliar waters, though if we are wise, we learn that we have traded on trust for only momentary relief and have quite possibly entangled ourselves further in very dangerous tides.

Though we may give lip service to understanding that animals are honest beings, it is not easy to incorporate that knowledge into our relationships with them. For a moment, really try to imagine living your life where *all* that you hoped for, feared, worried about, lusted after, disliked, hated, loved, adored, longed for or coveted was clearly written on your face and in your body language. Imagine being a dog, if you can, and living a life where you were incapable of telling a lie. What if as a dog, you find yourself among well-meaning but ignorant folks? Since their own behavior includes lies and deliberate deceptions, they would assume that you are also capable of lies. All you said and did would be interpreted through a filter of assumption that though you *appeared* honest, there was quite possibly deception and ulterior motive behind your actions. These might be maddening people to deal with—unable to be completely honest themselves, they also could not believe that you were capable of such. Unless we learn to be aware of our own responses, and to see the dog not as a person but purely as a dog offering his animal honesty, the fullness of the gift of honesty will elude us.

Dogs do not have even the most rudimentary form of deceit—the "white lie," a form of dishonesty that many people consider harmless since theoretically the intent of the white lie is to protect another's feelings. Human culture teaches us that to be polite is to suppress our immediate responses, to not blurt out what's really on our mind. Though the real intent of tactfulness is to shape our communications with respect to the listener's feelings, more often our politeness only means that we have been trained to a fine degree of social dishonesty. If a woman asks, "Do I look fat in this dress?" it is only a fool or a brave friend who confesses that perhaps another style might better show off her considerable assets. (A dog, of course, would wonder why a dress was even necessary; buck-ass naked is just as acceptable to a dog as any designer gown. For dogs, life is a come-as-you-are party.) At best, social dishonesty keeps the waters relatively untroubled and characterizes many relationships in their early stages, at least till we've had a chance to see how our boat floats and how best to navigate on those waters. But within a meaningful relationship, intimacy is closely linked to the degree of honesty within ourselves and the other. In our relationships with dogs and other animals, the barrier to complete honesty lies only in us.

Absolute honesty is not easy to take, especially when it arrives in the form dogs offer it to us: blunt and not tactfully shaped to slide unwelcome information past our emotional defenses. At times, we might appreciate just a touch of social dishonesty from our dogs. One of my clients discovered this when dealing with her dog's eating problems. Bella was not a good eater, though her owner, Beth, had tried over the years to provide her dog with the very finest foods available. As she learned more, Beth began to embrace the good sense behind learning to prepare her own homemade dog food; with full control over the individual ingredients and their quality, she could be sure of providing her beloved companion with the best possible diet. Using one of the many balanced recipes available, Beth had painstakingly assembled the ingredients and prepared the food. But Bella didn't like this new food either. As she had with all other foods, the dog ate only enough to keep herself alive, though she gladly accepted certain special treats. Watching Bella wolf down a chicken sandwich that fell on the floor, Beth was frustrated. Was this dog just playing games with her? Thinking of the hours she had spent preparing the best possible food, she felt angry and rejected.

Ever try to feed an eighteen-month-old toddler a food he didn't like? There's no particular consideration on the child's part for the cost of the food, how good it may be for him according to the nutritional experts, how much effort was required to obtain and/or prepare this magical elixir. If he doesn't like it, he will screw up his face in the universal sign of disgust and refuse to allow you to con him (airplanes, trains and all) to swallow any more of that yucky stuff. Your dog will be equally and brutally honest. Spend all day preparing choice tidbits, and your dog may sniff and turn away. No apology, though some very kind dogs will humor you a tad by taking the treat, wagging their tail and then immediately spitting the food out or placing it gently on the floor.

At first glance, I had noticed the dog's appearance—Bella was hardly the picture of good health. Her coat was dull and dry, and her ribs were easily visible even from a distance. Clearly, this was a dog with serious problems that Beth hoped I might help unravel. I asked what she was feeding Bella, and was quite surprised to discover she was using a long-established and very reputable recipe, one that I'd used with my own dogs with excellent results. Seeing my surprise, Beth nodded in rueful agreement. "I know! I thought I was doing something good for her, but look at her. People have stopped me on the street and scolded me for not feeding my dog! They should know how hard I try to do what's best for Bella."

I asked about the ingredients—raw beef, brown rice, and a variety of vegetables—and Bella's response to her food. "She just picks out a little beef and the carrots and green beans, but that's about it." Beth sighed. But before I could ask another question, she went on, her voice filled with frustration and a touch of bitterness. "Of course, Little Miss Picky here is always right underfoot when I roast a chicken. And in the mornings, she'll walk away from her food bowl to sit begging for some of my oatmeal."

Now it all made sense. "She likes oatmeal?"

Beth nodded, adding, "I have some every morning, and Bella knows it. She sits there begging and going through all the tricks she knows just to get some. I know it's spoiling her, but I give her some every now and then—at least it's something in her tummy."

"Did you ever think of using other ingredients? Like chicken instead of beef, oatmeal instead of brown rice?" Beth shook her head, reminding me that the recipe called for beef, not chicken. I assured her that substitutions were fine, and sometimes very necessary. Not all foods suit all dogs, just as people vary in the diet that best suits them. I went on to explain that in my experience, healthy dogs whose food agrees with them are good eaters, enthusiastic and quick in their approach to doing what canines do—gulping down their meals without much chewing involved. (I've had some clients very concerned about this normal dog behavior and have had to reassure them that the design of a dog's teeth offer good clues about how a dog should eat. The impressive array of canine dental ware is designed for grabbing and tearing, not carefully chewing. The dog's powerful digestive system does the brunt of the work, unlike our weaker stomachs that prefer our food at least partially chewed.)

When a dog does not eat or eats very little, my first thought is to take this as a very important communication. With basic physiology similar to our own, I've long suspected that dogs are as prone as we are to food intolerances as well as true allergies (different from an intolerance in that allergies involve an immune-mediated response). There is no physiological reason why dogs should not experience these same physical sensations we experience after eating food that doesn't agree with us: gassiness, cramping, nausea, headaches, sour stomach. But they cannot tell us this in words—though, as Bella did, they can and do report faithfully in their actions.

Far more attuned to their bodies than we to ours, dogs can quickly become aware which foods do not suit them. Nature arms even the simplest creatures with a good memory for avoiding foods that have made them sick. (We have this mechanism as well, but often disregard what our bodies tell us.) As a baby, I repeatedly refused to drink from a bottle, and sometimes went so far as to hurl the bottle away from me. The pediatrician suggested I was spoiled and that perhaps my mother was doing something wrong. After wading through the Sea of First-Time Parent Guilt, my mother knew that something must be causing this behavior since I would drink water or diluted juice from a bottle. She began to piece things together, and the truth was eventually discovered—I had a nasty response to cow's milk, the basis of the formula I was being given. Given goat's milk, I happily drank my bottle and became a picture-perfect baby. (I outgrew that, but still hate milk.)

Unlike an animal that hunts for its food, dogs have no control over what is put on their plates. Our dogs are unable to gracefully decline and say, "Thanks—you do make a delicious gizzard soup, but gizzards repeat on me something fierce." Worse still, their food often arrives as a blend of many ingredients, and they can't pick out the good from the bad. The whole food therefore has to be suitable or not. All they can do is eat what they must to stay alive, and hope that the next meal might be something more agreeable. Beth confirmed that Bella's behavior fit the profile of a dog trying to communicate a problem with her food. The dog was always hopeful and bright-eyed when her meal was being prepared, but her enthusiasm quickly dimmed when the bowl was placed before her. "She just sniffs, and then looks up at me. Sometimes she eats a little, and sometimes she just walks away. She eats just enough to stay alive."

What Bella was saying in the clearest way she knew how was, "I don't like this." Bella's bluntly honest communication held no acknowledgment of Beth's efforts, just the dog's truth. Interpreted through a human's need for acceptance and appreciation, Beth could not clearly hear what Bella kept saying. Trapped in her own emotional response to the dog's rejection of the food she had worked so hard to prepare, Beth couldn't see that Bella had also clearly told her, "I do like oatmeal, and I do like chicken." This is understandable—after all, even a well-trained doctor who ought to have taken my babyhood behavior as important information found it easier to blame my upbringing for my bottle-related antics than closely examine my behavior for important clues. But sadder was Beth's question as she considered my advice to replace the beef and rice with chicken and oatmeal: "If I do, isn't that just letting her get her way?"

Countless training books and countless trainers urge the dog owner to not let dogs "get away with" misbehavior but forget to mention that behavior is a pure form of communication. If a behavior exists that an owner finds upsetting, there's a problem that needs to be investigated and resolved. The dog has a reason for acting as he does, and it's not always because, given an inch, he wants to take a mile. I found it quite sad that Beth had so thoroughly swallowed the battle cry of dog training—"Don't let him get away with that!"—that she felt it would be somehow surrendering to Bella's demands to feed her chicken and oatmeal. By switching the ingredients to eliminate the things Bella consistently avoided eating and to include the equally nutritious and more agreeable foods, the only thing the dog would be "getting away with" was not being hungry most of the time.

Once Beth realized that Bella was not rejecting her or her well-meant offer of delicious food, she was able to see how clearly Bella had been trying to communicate. When I assured her that she had been on the right track, and that her intentions were laudable, Beth cheered up. She brightened further when I explained that she and Bella already knew what the solution might be; all she had to do was give it a try. I also reminded her that in a world filled with rigid recipes, she wasn't going to find too much advice on listening to the dog's body as an important piece of creating the ideal diet for that dog. (This is not the same as the old Bill Cosby routine where a father listens to his children and agrees to serve them chocolate cake for breakfast.) She agreed to try substituting chicken and oatmeal.

A couple of months later, I got a call from Beth to report on Bella's progress. The dog was eating eagerly, had put on quite a bit of much needed weight, and her coat was thick and shiny. After telling me about

Bella's new enthusiasm for her food, Beth went on: "You know, it's funny. When I realized Bella was always telling me the truth, I finally figured out it was my job to figure out what she was telling me. And it's not just about oatmeal and chicken. In training class one day, I asked her to pick up her dumbbell. She trotted out, started to pick it up, and then just dropped it. I was surprised: She knows how to do this—she's done it for years. She just stood there and stared at me. At first I got angry. My trainer was telling me to go make her pick it up but then I remembered how Bella used to stare at me at mealtimes. It dawned on me that maybe she was trying to tell me something, so I didn't do anything. I just stood there, staring right back at her, and thought about the whole thing. I wondered why she might drop a dumbbell right after picking it up. So I walked over to look at her more closely."

Beth's voice broke a little, and I could hear her take a deep breath before she continued. "When I looked in her mouth, I was so glad I believed her and that I hadn't yelled at her or tried to make her pick it up. Somehow, she had broken off one of her teeth, and the nerve was exposed. Picking up that dumbbell must have hurt like hell. We got the tooth fixed, and she went back into training and did great. Now, every time Bella needs to tell me something, she stops and stares at me, and I know she's telling me something important. It's made our whole relationship better—I really trust my dog now."

A GIFT OF LIGHT

Accepting the dog's gift of complete honesty is not easy. It requires that we understand our own feelings and that we can make the distinction between what we project onto our dogs and what movie is actually showing at their theater. Learning to accept an animal's honesty is very literally an act of trust, one sometimes made difficult by our human experiences. This has been a difficult process for me—my experience in life has not been one where trust is unfailingly honored, and I've not always been trustworthy. Without question, my experience with the human capacity for deceit influenced my relationships with animals. If trust and honesty are not a part of everyday life, an atmosphere of suspicion develops. Though we may not be fully aware of it, though we may think that we step outside of it in our relationships with animals, distrust begins to color all in ways we did not intend, a deadly gas creeping through the cracks of our self-knowledge.

Very early on in my career, when I was eighteen, I was bitten by a young dog. She was an impulse buy from a pet store by people who did not understand exactly how much was involved in raising a very active and determined puppy. Faced with no leadership and plenty of energy, the dog had quickly learned that she could shape the world to her liking with a well-timed show of teeth and a fierce growl. Puffed up with pride and armed with what was appallingly inadequate knowledge, I viewed her behavior as a deliberate defiance of my "authority." (Does anyone have less authority than someone who even thinks in those terms?) In retrospect, I can see that my lack of honesty with myself was the driving force; I was not yet able to admit to myself how little I really knew about dogs and dog training. I was also emotionally suspicious, having not yet matured enough to resolve some deeply affecting experiences that had taught me how untrustworthy some people could be. As a result, I was not able to fully trust animals as well, though I was unaware at the time that my "authoritarian" response to the dog was a clear sign of my own fearful distrust. Just as I triumphantly managed to squash the "defiant" dog into a rough resemblance of the desired down position, she told me precisely what she thought of my stupidity and rudeness: She sank her teeth deep into my wrist. I don't remember precisely what my response was, but I do remember bleeding copiously in the client's bathroom and trying to explain to the very upset family what had happened. I've apologized many times in my mind to that dog for concluding the disaster by labeling her stubborn, dominant and difficult. She was the only honest one in that whole scenario.

I replayed that fiasco many times in my head—it was a horrible situation that I did not want to repeat. I did not mind the bite, and I value the scars as tangible reminders that I am capable of great stupidity. What I could not shake was the look in the dog's eyes. Over and over, she warned me, absolutely honest in her communications; but faced with someone who would not hear her, she clearly felt she had no other choice but to bite me in order to communicate with me. I also remembered the horrified look on the client's faces. In one brief moment created out of my arrogance and ignorance, they had seen their young dog turn into a fierce beast capable of biting and drawing blood. This was not a bad dog; this was just an untrained dog. My glib assignment of blame to the dog was unfair, and I knew it. Much later, I was willing to accept the truth that can be found in a dog's eyes, the sometimes unwelcome but valuable truth about my own behavior. In that moment, I began to understand that a dog's absolute honesty is a gift of light on the darker corners of my soul.

There's another twist that complicates the issue of honesty. Though we can trust that what the dog tells us is an honest communication, *the dog expects the same from us.* And that can present some interesting dilemmas. Firmly fixed in their canine perspective, dogs assume that our communications to them are like theirs to us—honest, straightforward and meaningful. In this, dogs are very much like young children, unable to see us except as we are in relationship to them.

My all-time favorite comment on what this really means on a day-to-day basis came from one of my clients. She was trying to figure out how to solve some minor problems with her three dogs, and as the conversation went on, it became apparent that one of the underlying problems was her inconsistency in her communications with the dogs. Trying to help her understand why it was important that she be consistent in what she said and did, I mentioned that dogs didn't understand how or why it was that she came home each day in a variety of moods. They didn't see her as a hardworking saleswoman with a pain in the ass for a boss. They only saw her as the head of their family group and, as such, paid great attention to what she said and did. They always told her the truth and expected that she also meant what she said. There was a long pause on her end of the phone, and then a gasp as the full meaning of what I said sunk in. "Oh no!" she wailed. "You mean they believe everything I say?"

The answer, of course, was yes—dogs do believe what we say. They have no other way of interpreting our communications. The blessing of being able to trust that what our dogs say is what they really mean is not without cost; in return for their trustworthiness, dogs expect no less from us.

Understanding that a dog's responses are always honest ones is easy to accept intellectually. Bringing that understanding to bear in the moments of day-to-day life is something else altogether, particularly since so many of our daily interactions are dishonest or only partially trustworthy simply because they are interactions with other humans. Even if we practice what we preach, it takes a long time for our belief in a dog's honesty to sink deep into our bones. As J. Allen Boone discovered, it is possible to open yourself to new ways of seeing and conversing with animals, but to do so requires that we work to resolve the stumbling blocks within ourselves. When we clear away the blinders we have placed on our own eyes, we see standing before us animals who offer us the amazing gift of honesty in their communications with us. Accepting this gift opens a new world of possibility in our relationships with our dogs.

NOW IS A GOOD TIME

Dogs offer us another gift that, like their truthfulness, is a double-edged sword: the gift of immediacy. What they have to say is said honestly and in the very moment it needs to be said. In their immediacy, dogs are like young children. Whether unhappy or ecstatic, they don't wait for weeks to tell you about it. (And like honesty, this isn't out of choice—it's just the way it is with dogs.) What a dog feels, he tells you. Right then. Not a few hours later, or a year. From the moment you even think about putting on your shoes, grabbing a coat and reaching for the leash, the dog tells you how thrilled he is that you're going for a walk together. At every step of the walk, the dog tells you how much fun he's having, and how very glad he is to be with you. One of the great pleasures of being with dogs is their spontaneous expression of what they are feeling. A dog never needs to say "I may not tell you enough but . . ." That's a phrase humans need, especially adult humans.

You would think in a society that wants instant gratification and immediate feedback, this quality of immediacy would be welcomed. But immediacy requires an equal response. This is not always convenient. No matter what else may be going on, you cannot tell a sobbing two-year-old to stop crying and promise her a thoughtful discussion later about balloons and their tendency to drift away once the string is released from a small hand. The loss is now, and the upset child needs attention now. No mother dog ever told her puppies: "You just wait until your father gets home" or "We'll discuss this later." Whatever needs to be dealt with is dealt with at the moment the need arises.

Dogs do not understand delayed responses—it's just not part of their world, though it certainly is part of human experience. To be successful in communicating with dogs, therefore, we need to really understand what that means in a practical, daily sense, and not just in theory. In canine culture, responses are as immediate as the communication that prompted the response.

There are benefits to delayed responses, such as allowing us to gather our thoughts, deal with our own emotions and not act impulsively or hurtfully. But most of us have learned that delayed responses can also be hurtful or at the very least surprising. Few things are as destructive to a relationship as long-held resentments or hurt unexpressed, sometimes stewing and festering for years before erupting in painful and shocking ways that can do serious damage far beyond the scope of the original cause.

In our relationships with dogs, delayed responses to a dog's actions can create very serious problems. With a human friend, we might simmer slowly for a few hours before pointing out that something they did or said hurt or upset us; a discussion at that point can be helpful, since our human friend is able to go back in time and understand that it is the past being discussed. But we cannot do this with a dog—yelling at a dog who chewed up your best loafers hours or even minutes before you walked through the door and discovered the dastardly deed is not only useless but very confusing and even frightening for the dog.

Dogs draw very straight lines when connecting the dots in life. Faced with a place mat meant to entertain bored children at a diner, a dog would not bother to search out the convoluted path from Start to Finish—they'd just draw a line that went directly from one to the other. In terms of our relationships with them, dogs believe that however it is we are acting, whatever it is we are doing is directly connected to that moment and to their own behavior in that moment. Thus the dog who merrily greets his returning owner and is promptly yelled at or met with an angry face does not think, "Oh, I'll bet she's not happy I ate those new Nikes a few hours ago!" The dog may simply tiptoe away, unsure of what provoked your (to him) inexplicable wrath. Or he may draw a straight line from Angry Owner to Greeting, and assume that you are angry that he's approaching you. In contrast, expressing your displeasure when you actually catch the dog in the act of chewing on your new sneakers allows him to do a little simple dog math (if you do this, this happens) and reach the proper conclusion: Shoes do not constitute an appropriate food group.

There's a lot to recommend an approach to life where everything happens in real time, so to speak. Imagine having a friend let you know at the very instant things between you went out of balance. We trust our closest friends to tell us that there's a bit of toilet paper stuck to our shoe or some spinach in our teeth. The world would be a far different place if our trusted intimates could also help us maintain more than our physical decorum. It would be good to have someone let you know that your emotional zipper needs adjusting, but such friends are rare. Coupled with the understanding that your friend would always be truthful, this would provide an amazing freedom in which to develop a profound relationship. Dogs do let us know our mental flies have come undone, though we don't always care to hear the message.

You can't talk about it later when a dog tells you something is wrong. Right there, in that moment, when things have slid off balance, when communication is most essential (but also most often missing), the dog needs an answer, a resolution to the conflict. Without ego, a dog stands before you without caring about who is watching or what they might think of you or him. He doesn't care that the clock is running or that the competition is lost or that the neighbors are looking on. He only cares about what is happening between you and him, and more than anything, he wants it to be right again. This does not feel good, this anxiety, this fear, this strange behavior from someone he trusts, someone he depends upon to lead the dance. And so he tells you in every way he can, his eyes troubled, "Something is wrong." To hear him, we need to quiet the roar of our ego and silence the critical voices eagerly reminding us that the clock is ticking, that people are watching, that we look like fools, that we do not belong here, that we are failures. When we hush our own minds, we can hear the pure sweet sound of a dog urging us to make this right. Now. And when we learn to do this with our dogs, it spills over to other relationships. When we hush the noise in our own minds, we remember that life is short and that the connections with those we love are precious; to live most fully, we need to address disconnections and distance between us and those we care about as quickly as we can. As our dogs remind us every day, now is always the best time to make things right. Like his honesty, a dog's immediacy is a double-edged sword that cuts both ways. Incapable of deceit, unable to understand the future, the dog lives in the now and expects that we will meet him there.

I once heard a psychologist discussing parent/child relationships. She pointed out that one of the greatest gifts any parent could give a child was simply to be genuinely glad when the child came into the room. Thinking about this, I realized that this is the gift our dogs give us over and over. If I step out to pick a few sprigs of parsley from the herb bed just at the edge of our front steps, I return to cheerful greetings and wagging tails. My dogs are glad to see me though I was gone only a moment. I thought about my own son and wondered how many times he had seen a clear welcome on my face when he came into view. With shame and regret, I thought of how many times I had greeted him or John or anyone else I loved with less than gladness.

Looked at one way, it is easy to sneer at the dog's glad greetings as the product of a dim memory or a simple mind. But I know my dogs have very good memories and that they are intelligent beings. I'm not willing to discount this gift of immediacy; it grounds me in the reality of here and now. And I'm definitely not willing to dismiss the gladness in my dogs' eyes when they greet me. If Robert Frost was right, and home is the place where they have to take you in, then may home always contain a dog who loves you so you are sure of one glad greeting at least.

10

What I Really Meant to Say Was . . .

*The greatest problem in communication is the illusion that
it has been accomplished.*

Daniel W. Davenport

Though I'm sure somewhere in the Dog Trainer's Ten Commandments there is a warning against the sin of coveting thy client's pup, I just couldn't help myself. Truth be told, I coveted Dodger, an eight-month-old mixed breed with astounding eyes and considerable intelligence. His owner Jennifer told me that Dodger was "hyper," an awfully vague description that further questioning proved to mean he was easily excited at certain times, such as when she went to unhook him from his dog run and bring him into the house. She was also concerned that he was possibly aggressive, since in his excitement he frequently grabbed her hands and legs with his mouth. In the last two weeks, Jennifer had found herself not even wanting to bring the dog into the house. She was afraid and upset that the family companion she had hoped for was slowly turning into an unmanageable monster who weighed sixty pounds and was still growing. She knew Dodger wasn't stupid or mean. In fact, he had done very well in training class, quickly catching on to every new exercise and working well for her at home once she had him calmed down and on leash. But his increasingly fierce behavior deeply worried her.

As we talked, I turned Dodger loose in the room, watching him as he explored. After a few minutes, he had thoroughly investigated the room and, finding it rather dull, returned to sit next to Jennifer, following the conversation with his remarkably intelligent eyes. Each time his name was mentioned, his ears perked up slightly and his tail wagged, but when nothing more was directed his way, he resumed his post as attentive listener. A few more minutes passed and, now growing bored, Dodger decided to leap up and visually confirm what his nose had already told him: There was some particularly delicious food on the table. As he placed his front paws on the table's edge, Jennifer scolded, "Dodger!"

Instantly the dog's head swiveled toward her, alert, ears up, tail wagging. I noted how responsive this dog was, and how willing he was to forego the attraction of food for an interaction with his owner. "Dodger, get off!" Dodger's tail wagged harder, but his front feet stayed right where they were. Pushing back her chair, Jennifer reached for the dog, trying to push him off. In Dodger's eyes, there was an unmistakably gleeful light. Rolling his head back and to one side, he responded with a paw slap toward Jennifer, his tongue lolling goofily out of the side of his mouth. She shoved him again, and again the dog waved his leg at her, slapping a big paw down onto her forearm. She moved closer, trying to grab him gently by the collar, and as she did this, Dodger grabbed her arm in his jaws. Now able to dislodge him from the table edge, Jennifer found herself half kneeling in a wrestling match with the puppy, who alternated between wrapping his paws around her arms and grabbing at her with a wide-open mouth. The entire time, Jennifer was keeping up a string of increasingly louder and more breathless commands: "Off! Dodger, sit. Stop that. Off! Sit. *Sit!*" Finally, Jennifer was free and sat back in her chair looking flustered and exasperated. Dodger stood watching her hopefully, his tail wagging happily. "Do you see what I mean? That's what happens."

Knowing that the scene would be repeated, I quickly told Jennifer that the next time the dog did that, she should sit still and say nothing. I would handle it. Before I could say another word, Dodger heard an imaginary bell signaling Round Two and, with a gleeful look directed at Jennifer, put his front feet on the table again. Immediately, I gasped as if shocked beyond all belief, and Dodger, surprised, dropped back to the floor. The moment his feet hit the ground, I quietly told him he was a good dog. He wagged his tail in agreement. For a few seconds, he looked back and forth between me and Jennifer, puzzled by the silence. Then the bright idea crossed his mind: He could start the party again by putting his feet on the table! Once again, paws on the table, another horrified gasp from me, followed by silence. This time, he kept his feet on the table, turning his head to look at Jennifer and then me. Clearly written in Dodger's expression was puzzlement—this was not working the way he had thought it might.

Another idea flashed into his mind, and he noisily slapped both paws on the table edge, looking at us for reaction to this. Disappointed when we did not move or speak, he sighed and settled back to the floor. Instantly, I told him he was a genius, something he already knew but enjoyed hearing anyway. Tail wagging, he immediately leaped up on the table but, hearing my gasp, froze. He stared at my face for a long moment, and then, in slow motion, he sank back to sitting on the floor, his eyes never leaving my face. The instant all four feet were on the floor, I praised him. "I've got it now!" was written all over his face as he came to bury his head in my lap for some much-deserved loving before he voluntarily lay down with a satisfied sigh. I gave him a chew toy, and he settled down to amusing himself quietly.

Jennifer was speechless. Her "hyper" puppy was lying quietly at our feet, and I had never once touched him, nor had he tried to "attack" me. Dodger was not aggressive, or even hyper. He was simply responding to Jennifer's communications. To his doggy mind, her shoving and breathless verbalizations were an invitation to play. He quite correctly read the gentleness and lack of threat in her behavior, as I had when the first wrestling match occurred. (If she had been angry or threatening, I would have intervened on behalf of both woman and dog.) Like many dogs, Dodger enjoyed wrestling games with people, since they mimic the often-fierce play dogs use with each other. As he would do with another puppy or dog, Dodger had slapped her with his paws and grabbed her hands and arms, but very gently. Far from dissuading him, Jennifer's attempt to push him away was an enjoyable activity, a game for the dog. What Jennifer intended to convey was "No, don't do that!" But only her *words* said that, and only to someone who understood English, which Dodger did not. All of her actions invited play, and the puppy was glad to oblige. As the old joke notes, "Ah, your lips are saying no but the rest of you is saying yes, yes, yes!"

What was missing from the conversation was any clear way for Dodger to understand what Jennifer really was trying to tell him. Though without question her tone of voice was disapproving, nothing else in her communication gave the puppy the idea that he was wrong. A fair canine interpretation of this whole message might be that the "disapproval" in her tone of voice was nothing more than mock growling, part and parcel of canine play. Dogs interpret messages in context, weighing all signals together to arrive at their interpretation. The clear delight in Dodger's goofy, playful expression was a tip-off that he found the entire process quite enjoyable.

When Jennifer understood how her actions were sending the opposite of what she meant to say, she was able to use her body like a switch to turn Dodger on or off depending on what he was doing. If she did not like what he was doing, she verbally indicated her "shock" with a dramatic gasp or her displeasure with a short, curt phrase and absolute stillness in her body, messages Dodger understood quite clearly. From his canine perspective, there was no invitation to play in those gestures. Dodger quickly figured out which behaviors resulted in Jennifer shutting down and disengaging from him, and which behaviors earned him her attention and praise. (Simple dog math: If you do this, this happens.)

The language of Dog is not unlike our own human language. It is filled with nuance and subtleties, the sum of which—examined within a given context—provide a total communication. Like our dogs, we can communicate volumes without uttering a word, though doing so with great clarity requires awareness of our own bodies and the subtle meanings behind gestures. Ask any man about the Look and you'll be talking to someone who understands that when a woman's eyes get sharp and narrowed and the corners of her mouth grow a bit tight, there's been a shift in the winds and wise men ought to take heed. (All those mirrors at the perfume and makeup counters? They're just for perfecting the Look, and those smiling salesladies are actually instructors; the Look requires diligent practice to master.)

Even if the technology were possible, there would be no point in Dog Radio. Though verbal communications are part of the dog's language, it is rare that dogs communicate *solely* through verbalization. To the best of my knowledge, communications that take place between dogs who are not in visual contact are limited to simple phrases. For the dog talking to another dog, purely verbal communications are not terribly precise or useful for sending complex messages. In canine language, verbal communications without the accompanying visual cues are useful only for transmitting simple messages: "Where are you?" "Hey, look, someone's here!" "Go away!" "I'm hurt." "I'm lonely." A rough analogy might be what we could communicate using a brief telegram—a crude message lacking nuance or complex themes.

In reasonable weather, our back door stays open so that the dogs can come and go as they please into the large fenced yard. Often, while we watch TV, one dog will slip out without the others noticing (or perhaps they simply don't care), and while investigating the yard, will discover a deer tiptoeing past in the field or hear the coyotes singing up on the ridge behind the farm. The alarm is then sounded, a long, strung-out series of *woo-woo-woo-woo-woo*s mixed with a few definitive woofs, a vocalization meant to alert the others in the pack that something's afoot but at a distance, not an immediate threat. (This is different from the very specific, brusque warning barks that warn someone approaching the house that they'd best have an invitation.) The reaction from the pack is an electrified response, and all dogs leap to their feet and shoot out the door to investigate. Once outside, they too can look and listen and smell and know what the alarm-sounding dog was talking about.

The dog understands communications from us as a whole picture that includes all of our nonverbal messages as well as our spoken ones. Far beyond learning what exact words and phrases mean, dogs listen carefully to the whole picture of what we are telling them. The canine language is an elegant and precise one, where context and congruity— and not the spoken word—reign supreme. What sets a skilled trainer apart from the average (and often frustrated) dog owner is the congruity and clarity of their communications with the dog. This does not mean that they say "Sit" or "Heel" with better elocution. The difference is that the message they send is clear, with total congruity in their tone of voice and their whole being—mind, body and spirit.

Endless books primly advise us that dogs don't really understand what we're saying. While it is true that a dog does not learn the meaning of words in the sense that he can use them correctly in a sentence, he does certainly learn the names of things. There are those who snicker as they point out that a dog could learn to sit when he hears "frump" and point to this as proof of the dog's stupidity. Of course, if these folks were learning another language and their teacher decided to teach them how to say "Your mother is a pig" when what the folks thought they were learning was "Thank you very much!" . . . You get the point. Dogs quite agreeably work hard on figuring out what we mean by the torrent of words that pour forth from our mouths every day—and they wisely discard most of those words as meaningless to them. In the end, even the most brilliant of dogs are working with a crude vocabulary not unlike a tourist in a foreign land. And just like the tourists, dogs learn the words and phrases that have the most meaning for them: "Where is the toilet?" or "I need a drink." (Granted, only dogs would actually link these two phrases into one meaningful question.) Looked at in a certain light, this points to a very practical intelligence at work that probably prevents dogs from dying of boredom or going mad in the face of our seemingly endless babble.

Countless authors of dog-training books as well as trainers themselves urge dog owners to remember that their tone of voice is all-important. If we view dogs as non-English-speaking guests in our world, then it's easy to understand how important tone of voice can be. Depending on my mood, I find the whole tone-of-voice advice bit hysterically funny or deeply sad because it reveals an underlying truth: We're in need of being reminded how to speak to our dogs. Why does this advice about the tone of voice even need to be said? Isn't tone of voice important in all our conversations, at least the ones in which we are addressing someone we love? I doubt most of us would appreciate having our friends and family come up and bellow "I love you!" in a belligerent tone. If we snarl "Give me the salt," our loved ones might understandably take offense, though they still might pass the salt. I haven't seen any child-raising books that feel the need to urge mothers to use soft, loving tones with their babies—"After thorough study of the vocalization patterns of maternal behavior in a wide variety of cultures, it appears that babies prefer not to be shouted at for any reason." Nor have I seen any dating advice that tells a man that he'll get further with a woman if he refrains from shouting in her ear and slapping her on the back like one of his buddies down at the bar. If we want to be successful in our relationships, we shape our conversations to reflect the love and respect we feel for the other.

Unless we've lost all basic civility (been to Long Island at rush hour?), unless we no longer care about the person or the relationship, unless we have lost control of our own feelings, we don't interact with others that we care about in harsh, demanding tones, ordering them about in peremptory ways. And we certainly don't like it when we're addressed that way; it is not a loving or even a respectful way of conducting conversation. One clear warning sign that trouble is brewing in a relationship is the way in which we communicate. We no longer speak with love or patience or respect in our voices. We grow shrill, angry, demanding, dismissive, impatient; we don't listen. (And we may get the same in return.) If we love our dogs, if we respect them, if we view ourselves as being in a relationship with them and not just as being their drill sergeants or keepers, then our verbal communications to them need to be as loving and respectful as to any human. This seems to me to be at the very least simple common courtesy. Within a loving relationship, it is more than that—it is a critical ingredient without which we may not succeed. And when we lose our way, when we find ourselves shouting at our dogs or treating them in ways we would resent for ourselves, we need to hush so we can hear the echoes of fear or anger in our own voices.

Of course tone of voice matters. In the tone of our voice, regardless of the words we use, there is a world of information. Dismay, anger, happiness, alarm, frustration, fear, sadness, surprise, encouragement, confusion, warning, urgency, approval—all these and so much more can be communicated just in the tone of voice. Our voices can be marvelous tools of communication, allowing our dogs to hear clearly what we are trying to say. But focusing on our tone of voice without also learning to control the rest of our bodies is pointless at best, and terribly confusing to the dog. Dogs just don't buy the "do what I say and ignore what I do" garbage humans hand each other. It is the whole message of voice and body that tells a dog what is really being communicated. Although we humans pride ourselves on our linguistic skills and often believe that we communicate mostly through a verbal/written language, the truth is that we're not all that different from dogs and other animals. Nonverbal signals comprise an amazingly high percentage of human communication. Some researchers estimate as much as 80 percent of our communication is contained in our gestures and body language.

I think it is worth remembering that some of the most moving human experiences are the moments of inarticulate emotion, where words fail us or seem only something to fumble with while we search in vain for some new means to express what it is we feel. At such times, we may resort to precisely those silent gestures animals use—a head pressed against a friend, a hand laid quietly on a shoulder or leg, a body gently folded around the contours of someone's grief and pain. We proudly claim language as that which sets us apart from animals, and yet, when language fails us as it often does in the face of profoundly moving experiences, the animal quality of pure gesture is all that we have left. To my way of thinking, it is not a sad commentary on animals that they do not have a verbal or written language by which to express their feelings, be that love or sympathy or joy or grief. It is, I think, a rather telling note that when we are most deeply moved, we return to the pure eloquence of communication that animals use all along. We are, sometimes, most eloquent when we are dumb.

READING BETWEEN THE LINES

Fortunately for us, our dogs are masters at reading us like books, though it's obvious they're sometimes hard-pressed to follow the plot. They're also terribly good at reading between the lines. Our reliance on verbal communication coupled with a lack of awareness of how our bodies also contribute to what is being said leads straight to what dogs must consider very confusing conversations. "Come here," we tell the dog who has slipped his lead. Assuming he correctly understands the phrase, the words register but are balanced by everything else he hears and sees: the anxiety in our voice (we fear he may run out into the road), the tension in our bodies as we lean forward toward him (a gesture that serves to push the dog away from us), the shift in our breathing (telling him something is alarming us, though he is unable to relate that to his actions), all the tiny signs of our growing frustration. Taken as a whole picture, this tense, anxious and possibly angry person grabbing for him contradicts the verbal direction to "Come here." If the messages we send are not under our full control or awareness, we may be very surprised at the response we get from our dogs.

When in doubt, dogs disregard words and believe our actions. If I cheerfully tell my dogs that they are very bad dogs indeed, they laugh. If I put a different inflection on it, speaking sternly, frowning fiercely, my dogs still laugh. They live with me, and accustomed to my dramatic moments, thoroughly educated in the art of living with a lunatic, they know that I'm as full of play growls as they are, and they recognize my mock warnings as just that—make-believe. Only when a stern tone of voice is matched with the hard eyes, tight jaw, tense muscles and very still posture of an angry me do they take me seriously. A dog who did not know me well might easily mistake my mock warning for a real one, just as we often mistakenly interpret gestures or words of someone we do not know well.

Before we open our mouths, even though we've opened our mouths and long after we've opened our mouths, dogs are busy trying to understand the *whole* message. And they can only understand any of our messages as they are understood filtered through the canine point of view. What we say in actual words might read back nicely on a courtroom transcript where all but the most violent outbursts go unnoted. A stenographer does not make notations such as "sounded tense" or "in an annoyed tone" or "sarcastic." In my experience, when people report to themselves or a trainer what was said in a situation with a dog, it is common for that report to be in roughly the same format as a courtroom transcript—all the subtleties and inflections are missing except for the really dramatic ones. But the dog takes far better notes than any court stenographer, mostly because he has a holistic recording device: the canine brain. Nuances of gesture and voice are strictly and accurately noted. Let's look at a typical scene from the human "transcript" point of view, and then from the dog's holistic recording device.

Scene: It is a quiet house. A dog lies dozing at his owner's feet while she reads a book. The doorbell rings, startling the owner. The dog is instantly up and trotting to the door, where he begins to bark. The owner quickly follows. She attempts to quiet the dog and get him to sit so she can open the door. She's eager to sign for this month's delivery of *Doggy Digest*, an edible magazine meant to be chewed by the dog after the owner has devoured the fascinating articles on "Fleas Flee" and "Top Ten Ways to Tell If Your Dog Is an Alien." Here's the transcript as our drama unfolds:

Doorbell rings.
DOG: Bark, bark, bark, bark, bark . . . (*Continues even while owner speaks*)
OWNER: Quiet.
DOG: Bark, bark, bark, bark, bark . . .
OWNER: Quiet. Quiet.
DOG: Bark, bark, bark, bark . . . (*Deliveryman asks if he should come back some other time*) growl, growl . . .
OWNER: (*to deliveryman*) No, wait. (*Raises voice to be heard*) I said wait, please. Just wait a minute while I get the dog under control. (*Addresses dog*) Quiet. Quiet. Quiet. Hush.
DOG: Bark, bark, bark, bark . . .
OWNER: Quiet. Sit. Quiet. I said Sit. Sit. Sit. I mean it—sit.
DOG: Bark, bark, bark. Yelp! (*Owner has grabbed his collar*) Grrrr . . .
OWNER: Sit. Sit. Quiet. (*Adds shake of collar to emphasize her point, and pulls him up*)
DOG: Bark, bark, bark . . . (*Sits*) bark, bark, bark . . .

Now, let's replay that scene told from the dog's point of view: Doorbell rings. At the instant the dog hears the doorbell, he's thrilled. Doorbells mean it's time to play "What's behind door number one?" *Could be that nice kid from next door wanting to play; he can really throw a ball. Might be that nice guy that always has dog biscuits in his pocket when he comes to stare at the electric meter. Got to go check—could be an intruder who needs to be chased away from the door. There's that guy that comes every day and pushes strange papers through the slot in the door. He's easy to chase away: just a few barks, works every time.* As the dog is getting up to respond to the doorbell, he hears a slight intake of breath from his lady. She is slightly startled by the bell, and the dog notices this. *Aha, that caught her off guard too!* As he trots toward the door, he begins barking, announcing that the visitor might or might not be welcome, but either way, he's on duty to check all passes. Behind him, the dog is pleased to note, his lady is also hustling. *Not much of a watchdog, but at least she tries.* He increases his barking to assure her that he's got it covered, and as usual, she chimes right in herself. *Strange, he thinks to himself. Human barks are strange. You think they'd know that single-syllable woofs are easier to say—never could get my mouth around the Q sound—but hey, each to his own. Man, she's revved today! She's barking like a fool puppy, all breathless and high-pitched!* The man says something, and the dog sees the woman get more frantic in her actions and sounds. *Oh, boy! That really got her going. Wonder what he said to get her all riled up like that? She's barking at him, she's barking at me, and she's moving around quick like— heck, if she had a tail she'd probably be wagging it too. Her barking's getting louder, and—damn, here it comes—as always, she's forgetting about the guy out there and turning on me. Barking right at me, like I'm the intruder! Ow!* He wishes she'd be more careful when she grabs that collar. Twisting it like that really smarts. He growls a little to warn her to watch what she's grabbing. Crazy lady—now she's shaking his collar a bit, and pulling him up off his hind legs. *Better sit down—when she gets like this, there's no telling what's next. But wait. There's still that guy at the door. Bark, bark, bark . . .*

A different impression could be made on the dog if instead of joining him in his barking—as he is most likely to interpret our excited vocalizations and quick movements—we moved slowly, quietly and with an air of calm assurance. The sum total of our communication in the above scenario is not one of authority but one of excitement and arousal that equals his own and may egg the dog on—precisely what we hoped to avoid in the first place.

Arrogantly (though we may not intentionally be so), we insist that regardless of the conflicts and mixed messages of our communications, dogs somehow sort out what we mean and then obey. One training approach would be to punish the dog's actions even though they are in response to our actual communication. But that would hardly be fair— dogs, like us, are not living in a vacuum. They are responding to the world around them and, when interacting with us, to the messages they receive. One of my cardinal rules for dog training is that if I see a dog acting inappropriately, my response is to look carefully at the person on the other end of the leash. Quite often, the answer for the dog's behavior can be found there in mixed or unintentional signals from the handler.

We are often imprecise or conflicted or careless in our communications, yet we expect our dogs to figure out what we mean and act accordingly. Faced with confusing or mixed messages, dogs do their best to figure out what is meant. Confused, they also often give up and simply do whatever suits them, an intelligent response to a situation where no one appears able to tell them clearly why or why not something should be done. Just like us, until notified otherwise, dogs shape their world to their best advantage. They're not being deliberately bad or trying to "get away with" something. They're simply responding to a lack of clear information and taking advantage of opportunities that present themselves. We may find this quite annoying, particularly if we're unaware that we are being confusing or sending conflicting messages. But think of this as tax loopholes. In the face of unclear tax regulations, humans often shape their interpretation of the rules to best benefit themselves. (When in doubt, do you send the IRS extra money?) Of course, we always have the fear of the IRS lurking in the back of our minds. For the dogs, sometimes *we* are the IRS, stepping in after the fact to sternly say, "That's not what you're allowed to do." Like many a puzzled taxpayer, dogs might justifiably respond, "Well, then why didn't you make that clear in a way I could understand?"

When we fully appreciate the exquisite attention our dogs offer us, we realize we have to clean up our act; we, and not our dogs, are most often to blame for miscommunications. Faced with an audience that is listening very hard (unless we have systematically though inadvertently taught them to pay us no mind), failures of communications rest squarely on our shoulders.

To understand our dogs, we need to learn to look for the whole picture and listen for the whole message the dog is trying to send. We do this for our human friends, but understanding the vast world of nuance and gesture in human communication is something we've been working on for a lifetime with countless people around us. We've been practicing with humans for a very long time, and still most of us have not yet mastered the communication style of more than a few close intimates.

Given that most of us have but a handful of dogs in a lifetime, it is not surprising that we are often less than fluent in Dog. With limited opportunities to practice and only so many native speakers of the language to learn from, our ability to communicate successfully with our dogs and understand what they are trying to tell us will not come "naturally." Like any foreign language, Dog takes time and practice to master. But this is joyful work, this exploration into another being's world, and the rewards are countless. We need not be perfect, but we do need to deeply want to know more and then some.

My niece Hannah's dream of a dog of her own came true when she was nine years old and her family adopted Ben, a nine-year-old Labrador. A true gentleman in his manners and heart, Ben was the perfect first dog for a family of five despite his considerable size and, as Hannah noted wryly, his "goobers" of saliva whenever it was hot or he was watching people eat. In the first few weeks of Ben's arrival, there were many phone calls back and forth to Aunt Suzanne as my sister and her family integrated this dog into their busy home. Of all the wonderful things that were reported to me, my favorite remains Hannah's enthusiastic description to her mother of all the subtle ways she had learned to understand Ben. She described how she knew the difference between Ben's needing to go out *now* and a need that could wait a bit if necessary. His woofs and barks conveyed a world of information to Hannah, and she understood his playful growl and the more serious "Someone's at the door" woof of warning. In vivid detail, Hannah could pinpoint the slight shifts in the shape or expression in Ben's eyes, the lift or droop of his ears, the lift of his tail or the madly delighted wiggle of his whole body. "I know what he's saying, Mom, I really do. I'm knowing this dog!"

And there, in a child's pure knowledge and love, is the only magic any of us need to understand what our dogs tell us in so many ways, even when we are not listening. Hannah's joy and curiosity, her complete willingness to study Ben with careful, loving eyes and to trust what Ben told her—without rationalizing or intellectualizing—is what made "knowing this dog" possible. To hear what our dogs say, we need to listen with a child's heart, knowing past our minds, knowing with our hearts. But for many adults, this is a struggle; we have to learn how to climb down out of our minds and listen. If we don't understand that we are holding our hands over our own eyes, if we assign magical powers to those we see who apparently can communicate, if we think this is a skill granted by the gods to only a few, then we will be forever in search of Dr. Doolittle or someone like him. But the truth is, all of us can learn to talk to the animals, and best of all, perhaps most important, we can learn to hear what they have to say to us.

11

TAKE ME TO YOUR LEADER

The leader who exercises power with honor will work from the inside out, starting with himself.

BLAINE LEE, *THE POWER PRINCIPLE*

IT HAD BEEN A LONG DAY AT DOG-TRAINING CAMP, and Carson and I were both tuckered out after hours of learning about dogs, practicing obedience and a long swim in the lake. Joining some other campers in the lounge, we settled down to play a board game. Understandably not thinking much of the hard floor, Carson stepped up onto the couch, settling herself behind me as I perched on the edge of a cushion.

"You shouldn't let her do that," another camper warned me. I was surprised—I had thought it pretty clear that clean dogs were allowed on the camp's rugged furniture. "Oh, I know they said it was all right, but you still shouldn't let her do that. She's trying to top your scent."

For all the world, Carson looked like a dog trying to take a nap. If she was topping my scent, whatever that meant, it would be hard to distinguish that behavior from sleeping. Seeing that I was confused, the woman explained further. "You should never allow dogs on furniture or in your bed. That's how they end up dominant. You know, alpha, top dog. When you let her put her scent on top of yours, you're letting her be the boss." The woman looked somewhere between horrified and disgusted that I didn't understand these basics of dog behavior. But she persisted. "I'm not making this up. Wolves live in packs, you know, and the alpha is the top wolf. And dogs have packs too, and they need an alpha. If you let your dogs on the furniture, they think they're alpha. But you should be the alpha. Otherwise, your dogs won't listen to you. They won't respect you."

"Are you saying that if I let a dog on furniture I'll be unable to control them?" She nodded, evidently glad that I was catching on. "But if I can tell the dog to get off the furniture or out of my bed and they listen to me, isn't that enough? Wouldn't that show respect?" She hesitated. I turned to Carson and quietly asked her to get off the couch. Half asleep, Carson got up and moved to the floor. "I think she's just sharing the couch, but she's fine with giving it up if I ask. Isn't that the point here?"

"I guess so," she replied slowly. "I suppose you might just be lucky—she's a nice dog. You might be able to get away with it with one dog, like her, but if you had a pack of dogs like I do, you'd understand how important it was."

I apologized to Carson and invited her back up on the couch. She looked at me as if I had lost my mind, hopped back up and settled down with a sigh. I didn't have the heart to tell the well-meaning woman that the other six dogs at home were equally nice, that they all get off the couch when I ask, and that most of them sleep in my bed every night. I just smiled, patted my nice dog gratefully, and turned my attention to the game. While we played, Carson stayed comfortably tucked up against my back, looking like she was asleep but possibly hard at work topping my scent.

Though her advice was filled with all-too-common misinformation about what constitutes the behavior of leadership, the well-intentioned woman was right about one thing. Unlike our human friendships, our relationships with our dogs include an obligation to provide leadership. Leadership is as important to dogs as food, water, shelter and love. It is, so to speak, the emotional air they breathe. If we are uncomfortable with issues of power, if we think that being humane means not setting clear rules for our dogs, we may ultimately be guilty of great cruelty. We may work diligently to provide the finest food and veterinary attention and do everything in our power to make their lives comfortable in countless ways. But we still may not fully meet our dogs' needs. If we fail to provide leadership, we have failed our dogs. At the heart of many dog behavior problems lies a lack of appropriate leadership. Humans are not put to sleep for failing to provide leadership for their dogs; countless dogs have lost their lives for want of it.

SOME ANIMALS *ARE* MORE EQUAL THAN OTHERS

The dog's need for leadership and our obligation to both honor and provide for this need has nothing to do with the whole dominion-over-the-animals approach brought to us courtesy of Judeo-Christian ideology. It has nothing to do with viewing the human race as superior and animals as inferior. This is not a matter of belief, though I've had more than one client earnestly tell me, "I don't believe in setting rules for others." Unfortunately for the dogs of such folks, the emotional response and "beliefs" have nothing to do with what the dog needs. If we agree to share a life with a dog, then we are obligated—if we are honest and compassionate people—to embrace and honor all that means. And in this case, we must accept that the canine's deep need for leadership springs from the realities of canine culture, of life as a social animal. The moment we put on the collar, we have entered into a covenant that promises a dog that we will provide for his needs. All of them.

Dogs, like all social animals including humans, live within a complex hierarchy of power and would readily agree with George Orwell that "some animals are more equal than others." Whether or not we are comfortable with this notion, most of us can—though perhaps reluctantly—admit that an equal distribution of power is neither possible nor realistic in any social group, human or otherwise. Whether we like it or not, we understand that some people in the world have more power than we do, and others have less. It is a basic truth of social animals. As the old saying goes, not everyone can be a chief. Dogs expect someone will be.

Our biases and beliefs about notions of power may bring us directly into conflict with our dogs, who have a thoroughly canine perspective on the matter. Most of the rules we have for our dogs' behavior are not set so that we can live our lives as petty bureaucrats, exercising power over another living being. The rules we set and the leadership we provide are precisely what keeps our dogs safe while also ensuring that the dog has the greatest possible freedom and enjoyment of his life.

Adaptable and adept as the dog is, he still must act in accordance with his canine core, which both defines and limits how far the assimilation into human culture can go. While a dog can adapt to life as a pampered pet in Peoria or life with Australian Aborigines, the dog's expectations and need for leadership do not change, though it is safe to say that the more "unnatural" and civilized his existence, the greater his need for leadership may be simply because such a lifestyle inevitably results in the dog bumping up against an increasing number of rules regarding his behavior. In the northern Sahara, the nomadic Tuareg people do not believe in tying up their treasured hounds; then again, they don't need to—rush hour might consist of a few camels or an occasional motor vehicle. Such dogs also live within a more predictable, stable society. The more complex world of suburbia with its multitude of people and dogs and flux creates greater potential for conflict and confrontation (with neighbors, other dogs, vehicles, etc.), and the urban dog faces greater challenges yet. And more potential conflict and challenges means more rules, which require more guidance and leadership from us in order for the dog to remain safe and a welcome member of society.

When we fail our dogs as their leaders, we may, without ever meaning to, deny them the fullness of life and sharply limit the degree of intimacy possible between our dogs and ourselves. All dog trainers have a steady stream of clients who, though they dearly love their dogs, cannot adequately control a dog's behavior in certain situations, whether that is walking in the park, in the presence of other dogs, when guests visit, when a squirrel dashes past, etc. As a result, the dog is not free to be a part of many excursions or events, even if the dog's human family would like to include him. The limits thus placed on the relationship are precisely what troubles these folks—they want to be able to enjoy being with their dog and have their dog enjoy his life with few, if any, limitations. They are also unhappily aware that the quality of the relationship in these difficult moments is not what they want. These problems do not rest solely on a failure of leadership; proper training and socialization are also critical to develop the dog's ability to deal with the complexities of a life shared with people. But training and socialization alone do not and cannot compensate for a lack of appropriate leadership, especially in moments of conflict or confrontation.

We would not hesitate to answer our dogs' need for food, shelter and love, but we sometimes find ourselves uncomfortable with answering our dogs' need for leadership in their lives. But the covenant of the collar obliges us to shape our own behavior in order to provide that leadership in ways that are meaningful and satisfying to the dog.

Where Do I Fit In?

The dog's need for leadership and a clear definition of his status, particularly within his core family group or the blended human/canine "pack," is hard wired into his brain. In their third week of life, puppies are already beginning the lifelong work of understanding where they fit in the social hierarchy. By week five, the wrestling matches that may appear as simply play to the naïve eye are actually explorations of status among the puppies, who work relentlessly at determining their status relative to their littermates in every possible situation. If allowed to interact with adult dogs as they should be, puppies also receive messages about their social status beyond that established between littermates. And once they have left their litter and moved on to their own lives, the testing continues.

Whether the dog's family consists of a "pack" made up of one dog and one person, or a more complex social group made of many dogs and/or many people, the questions each dog asks are still "Who's in charge? What are the rules? Where do I fit in?" Whether the dog comes into your home as a puppy or as an older dog, the questions are still the same. It's startling to realize that even at the tender age of eight weeks old, the puppy has been working on these questions for nearly five weeks. In each situation, with each person and/or dog he meets, the dog asks the same questions. By way of answers to his questions, the dog is looking for particular behaviors from us that indicate high status and leadership: control of or undisputed access to resources, control or direction of others' behavior and proactive intervention. Dogs arrive in this world understanding Donald McGannon's comment that "leadership is action, not position." While they need us to provide leadership, we are not always automatically given respect or the high-status leadership role simply because we walk upright and have opposable thumbs, though for some dogs, that's good enough. Our opposable thumbs may be impressive (at least in our own minds), but most dogs need more, and they watch us carefully, taking notes on who acts in ways they understand to be high status.

A few years ago, actress Winona Ryder appeared on a talk show, and in the course of conversation, she revealed a bit about her childhood and what it was like growing up in a remote, safe area with liberal parents who set only vague rules, such as a curfew that required her to come home at least a few nights a week! When asked by the show's host if she liked having such a loosely structured childhood, Winona paused for a moment, then shook her head. "No," she said, "I didn't really like it. You know the old saying that square parents raise round kids? Well, I had round parents and I wanted more square in my life." The pure geometry of her description caught my attention, and glancing down at the dogs scattered at my feet, I wondered what "shape" I was as a pack leader—round or square or something in between? Further, what were the shapes my dogs expected or needed from my leadership, both individually and as a pack? Some dogs do beautifully under even a "round" laissez-faire approach to leadership; others see it as a loophole to be exploited to their best advantage. (Sounds just like human beings, doesn't it?) Like Winona Ryder, our dogs may need more "square" or clearly defined leadership than we are offering; the definitions of status are blurred and thus confusing to dogs. In their behavior, they let us know whether our approach is working or not. Regardless of your personal leadership style and your dog's individual personality, there is no one correct approach to providing leadership, no more than there is only one effective way to manage or lead people, be an effective parent or have a solid marriage. As the corporate world would ask, what does the bottom line say?

To assess the bottom line in your relationship with your dog—the effectiveness and appropriateness of your leadership style—there are only two basic questions to be answered: First, do you have undisputed access to the resources your dog considers important? In other words, if you ask, does your dog willingly surrender to you anything he considers valuable? Second, in times of excitement, importance or conflict, does your dog yield to your direction of his behavior? It doesn't matter how beautifully trained your dog may be when all is quiet and calm; it does matter how your dog responds to you out on the street, at the vet's

office, when the doorbell rings or guests come and go, when a cat dashes past or another dog passes, etc. If you answer no or "only sometimes"
to either or both of these questions, then those are areas that your dog's
behavior is pointing to as problems that need to be worked out.
Resolution needs to occur at the foundation, at the primary level of leadership and respect.

A good friend of mine was bemoaning how annoying her dogs' behavior had become. Despite countless hours of training throughout their
lives, each of her three dogs had started acting in less-than-desirable
ways. One was bolting out the front door at any opportunity, another was
apparently stone deaf to any command that didn't quite suit him, and
another had merely smiled without apology when caught in the act of
standing on the kitchen table and eating butter. "What is wrong with
my dogs?" Karen asked. I assured her there was nothing wrong with her
dogs. They were simply acting like dogs and pointing out in ways she
didn't appreciate that her leadership of the pack was slipping. She admitted that she'd thought about that. With a demanding job and three children, Karen was pulled in countless directions to act as mother,
employee, manager, wife, daughter, and leader for her dogs. Sometimes,
overwhelmed and tired, Karen acted in ways her dogs perceived as less
than worthy of their respect. In her next statement, Karen neatly
summed up the difficulty at the heart of the issue: "You know, if I could
just stay home and be nothing but a dog leader all day, I'd be a great
leader!" Couldn't we all?

Every one of your interactions with a dog is one that the dog takes seriously as your answers to his questions. Let me repeat that—*every* interaction with a dog is one that the dog takes seriously. He has no other way
of interpreting his world. The dog's world does not contain careless interactions. In every interaction with another dog or person, a dog says what
he means. This is a good and delightful thing, and one of the finer aspects
of life with dogs. Would that all we loved were as meaningful in their
communications with us! But this cuts both ways—unfailingly honest
in what he says and does, the dog assumes everyone around him is doing
the same. All day. Every day.

Top Ten Ways to Lead with Style!

With so many demands on our time and energies, honoring our commitment to any of our relationships is not always easy. Lurking under our hectic attempts to find time for the relationships we value is a pitfall that unfortunately traps many of us: the tendency toward compartmentalization, which in turn leads to simplification. I think of this tendency to simplify as the *Cosmo* approach, a journalistic style made famous by such *Cosmopolitan* magazine articles as "Ten Easy Tips to Become a Red Hot Lover!" The intent of the *Cosmo* approach may be to encourage us to remember that we can enhance the quality of our lives by taking just a few extra minutes or giving a bit more attention to something. That's just nifty when we're being offered recipes for Snow Pea Surprise or Make Ahead Cream of Kidney Soup. However, when the *Cosmo* approach is applied to relationships, the unfortunate result is that lovely, complicated aspects of our lives are reduced to bulleted lists and simplified advice.

Whether it's being a great lover, a better parent or a terrific dog owner, we all know that relationships are not layer cakes. There are no recipes that can be followed step by step to create a profound, intimate relationship. The deep connections we seek, whether with a life partner or a child or a friend or a dog, require far more than a few minutes a day to develop. "Look honey, I've got ten minutes for you, and right now, I'm ready to be your mom. So, let's do it!" Under such conditions, it is doubtful that we could provide anything even vaguely resembling the ongoing guidance and leadership children need, never mind develop a profound connection. We are not parents in short, intensely focused sessions where we "train" the children, but rather parenting is the sum of our actions in every interaction with our children.

Yet more than one dog-training book takes a *Cosmo* approach to our relationships with our dogs, offering promises that you can have a well-behaved dog in just five or ten minutes a day, or that in one month, your dog can learn everything you'd like him to know. A truthfully titled book on dog training might be *Your New Puppy and the Next Two Years You'll Spend Helping Him Become a Wonderful Dog*. The book would probably not sell, though false promises that you can have anything you want without much effort certainly do. It is true that you can train a dog to *do something* in just a few minutes a day. Dog owners everywhere faithfully grab their leash and collar, the homework sheets from obedience school, and head out to the backyard or neighborhood park to "train the dog." Thus it is dogs learn to sit, stay and heel, and other niceties. But they may also be learning that outside of this dedicated training time, there is a lack of leadership in their daily lives.

Leadership and training are not synonymous, and to the detriment of our relationship with our dogs, we sometimes confuse the two. Training has to do with what the dog knows how to do—specific actions or activities. Leadership is the foundation for the dog's understanding of how his world is organized, providing him with information about his relative status, directing his actions as necessary and setting the limits on his behavior as well as setting the tone for how important situations will be handled. If we mistake training for leadership, we will find ourselves bewildered by some of the things our dogs do. A dog may graduate at the top of his obedience class and still growl at someone who tells him to get off the bed. It is quite possible to have a dog that is highly trained and obeys a multitude of commands and even wins countless awards and ribbons but who still has no real respect for you. It is also quite possible to have a dog with very little if any formal training but deep respect for his people.

How can this be? We all know that there can be a world of difference between a polite, respectful child and a child who knows a lot of stuff. Just because a child has learned his alphabet, can tie his own shoes, and knows his name, address and phone number, this is not a guarantee that he has respect for his parents or others. He may also speak French, be an algebra whiz, have a good grasp of American history, be a great tennis player and a talented violinist—and still be as rude as hell. No matter how wonderfully our dogs perform in class or in the backyard, even if they graduate as the valedictorian of their obedience class, if we fail to provide the leadership they need in every interaction, all we have is a dog who knows *stuff.* And some of that stuff may include the fact that we're not really calling the tune on the dance of man and dog.

In a world where it sometimes seems that there is never enough time, dogs remind us that now is the only moment we have—and the only

one we need. In each interaction, we always have the time to act in careless ways that are devoid of leadership or guidance; we also have the
same time to provide our dogs with what they may need in that moment.
When we consciously choose to create the event of quality with our
dogs, we discover that being aware and fully present when we turn our
attention to another requires no more time than a hasty, incomplete
connection. As ever, a small investment of our full selves reaps rewards
without measure.

The Dynamics of Status

Raise the question of leadership, and you'll inevitably hear the words
dominant and *submissive*. Like all labels, the terms *dominance* and *submission* are not terribly informative, though they may describe the far
ends of a particular behavioral spectrum, just as *night* and *day* describe
the presence or absence of the sun. But does the word *night* really tell
us much at all? To an Alaskan, a summer night is largely a glory of light.
In more temperate climates, where the sun's departure defines the night,
there are still endless variations on what a night might be: moonless,
moonlit, cloudy, clear, cold, stormy and endless combinations of these
and other aspects of night. If I would have you understand what a particular night is really like, I need to describe in detail what I am experiencing. The more detail, the more specific a night I can describe.

To label a dog as dominant or submissive tells me very little. The beautiful shadings of what is possible along that vast spectrum of behavioral
possibilities are lost, neatly obscured by the clumsy, crude labels. Labels
also have the unpleasant bonus of shaping our view of the dog in rather
rigid ways, leaving us unable to see the real, complex dog in front of us.
We may see nothing more of that dog than fits neatly in the label's frame.
If we are unable to detail the intricacies of how our dogs express themselves in a particular moment, if we cannot define the subtleties of gesture, then we also cannot deeply, intimately know an individual dog; we
will be able to go so far and no further. At deep levels, intimacy is built
on knowledge so complex that it defies labeling or explanation to someone outside the relationship. The more fully we understand our dogs as

individuals, the less willing we are to sum up the loveliness of an individual with a label.

Dominant and *submissive* are useful terms only when we're trying to give a rough sense of typical *reactions*. If a conflict arises, will the dog respond in a confident, assertive way, or will he typically yield? Generally speaking, a more dominant animal has greater self-confidence and is willing to push for things to go the way he'd like them to *if it's something he cares about*. When attempts are made to direct and control his behavior, the more dominant animal asks (rather persistently) "Why?"— and he expects a damn good answer. Lacking a satisfactory answer, his confidence is turned toward shaping the world to suit him. Such dogs are often labeled stubborn, hardheaded, independent, even difficult to train, though the truth is they simply expect a very good answer to their questions and are willing to work—even fight—for what they want.

A more submissive animal lacks the assertiveness to push for what he wants if it means he has to confront anyone to achieve it, and in the face of a conflict, is willing to go along with what someone else has in mind. For these dogs, their question (if raised at all) of "Why?" can sometimes be answered with "Because I told you to." These dogs are often called smart, easy, soft, trainable, though the truth is that they are simply by nature much more willing to go along with our game plan than make a case for what they might prefer.

Within the context of a relationship, I'm not sure that *dominant* or *submissive* have any place at all—do you describe any other of your friends in such terms? I have friends I might describe as determined, fearless, happy-go-lucky, pushovers, prickly, unflappable or any host of other descriptions that are informative in a general way. But I don't describe my human friends as dominant or submissive. Increasingly, I keep stretching myself to find new ways to describe my canine friends and to do so in ways that accurately reflect their behavior as well as my feelings about them. This is an acknowledgment that the words we choose have great power to shape our actions. If I describe a dog to you as "confident, persistent, intelligent, intensely aware of others' feelings and intentions," you'll have one picture in your mind and act accordingly. But I doubt that it's the same one created by this description: "He's dominant." With the first description, you might ask about the shadings and range or degree of what I've described—just how confident or persistent is he? Intelligent in what way or compared to who? If I describe another dog as "agreeable, disinterested in confrontation, easygoing," the picture in your mind and your response to that dog is much different than if I tell you a dog is submissive.

Along the continuum between dominance and submission lies a whole world of possibilities, and to my mind, the term *status*—fluid, dynamic, contextual—is a better way of looking at the complex realities of how dogs interact with us and other people and animals. Status is a dynamic, fluid quality that can shift based on the situation and the context and may be quite specific to a particular relationship. For example, a mother driving her child down the road might well be seen to be the higher-status member of that pair; the child, appropriately, defers to her greater control of resources and is willing to accept her control and direction of his behavior. (All right, it's a very young child. . . .) When Mom is pulled over for a speeding ticket, her status shifts. Relative to the police officer, she assumes a position of lower status; she is deferential to him if she's smart, and assuming she's not interested in a high-speed chase through three counties ending in a standoff at the local mini-mart, she'll accept his control and direction of her behavior. Dropping the kid off at school where unbeknownst to her he's the king of his class and even the teacher gives him her milk money, Mom then proceeds to work, where she is middle management and has status higher than those under her supervision but less status than her superiors. In the evening, she drives home alone. We cannot determine her status in that moment, because just like our dogs, no one is dominant or submissive, high status or lower status *except in relationship to someone else*. In this simple truth, the complexity of social hierarchies can be seen: It all depends on where you are, what you're doing and who you're with. In the absence of another, status is meaningless. A billionaire on a deserted island is just a lonely man.

An understanding of relative status is critical to the dog's understanding of his world because the very organization of his daily life and behavior hinges on the answer. In trying to sort out the relative status of his home pack, the dog is trying to figure out whose rules he must obey and for whom he can set rules. Like anyone, the dog does not wish to annoy or threaten more powerful beings; that way lies conflict, possible physical confrontation and maybe even bodily harm.

Dogs learn that it is foolish and possibly quite painful to annoy or challenge those who are more powerful. On the other hand, it's both possible and probably safe to take greater liberties with or simply ignore someone who has less status than you. But without an accurate assessment of relative status, the dog is not sure how best to behave in any given situation. This is not a comfortable position for the dog, no more than similar situations are for us. Many dogs I have worked with were anxious, confused and even angry in the absence of clear leadership. Loving our dogs is not enough, just as loving anyone is not enough. Knowing that our dogs need a clear delineation of their relative status, we must honor their need and provide leadership. However, thumping our chests—or more literally, thumping the dogs—is not necessary; leadership is not a clenched fist but a guiding hand. As Dwight D. Eisenhower noted, "You do not lead by hitting people over the head. That's assault, not leadership."

I AM ALPHA—HEAR ME ROAR!

If there's a single word I could remove from the language of dog lovers and particularly dog trainers, it's this: *alpha*. A Greek word meaning *first*, *alpha* has seen a lot of duty, mostly serving as the righteous rationale in the ongoing war between man and dog. Like the cross waved by the Crusaders as justification for a staggering list of atrocities committed on non-Christian peoples, the idea that we are acting as alpha has served as justification for a fair amount of unfairness and downright cruelty to dogs. Lurking behind the battle cry of dog training—"I can't let him get away with that!"—is our fear that if we do let the dog get away with x, y or z, we will lose our status as top dogs.

Borrowed from the language of animal behavior studies of social animals, alpha is used to indicate the top-ranking animal in a particular social group, or the top-ranking male and the top-ranking female. To be sure, all social animals have a hierarchy of power, popularly known as "the pecking order," a term that originally arose from Thorleif Schjelderup-

Ebbe's 1935 research in poultry behavior. This model for describing a social hierarchy is much like a ladder. At the very top rung is the highest-ranking animal; the lowest rung is occupied by the lowest-ranking member, and the other members are assigned positions somewhere in-between, with some animals below and some animals ranking above them.

The problem with this strict model is that while easily understood, it's also vastly overly simplified. Real life with real animals is not rigidly linear, but a beautiful and fluid weave of understanding and reciprocity among the various members; authority is often not absolute but rather highly situational. Discussing wild wolf behavior in *The Wolf*, wolf expert David Mech offers his observation that the government of the pack is neither autocratic nor democratic. While at times the leader does unquestionably guide the behavior of all pack members, this is usually in a time of crisis or conflict. At other times, all pack members have influence on the behavior of all other pack members, including the leader.

In trying to observe and understand how wolves interact with wolves, and how dogs interact with dogs, we have made a very serious mistake in modeling our own behavior after that exhibited by *captive* animals. It should be noted that the behavior of captive wolves, like the behavior of all captive social species including humans, is far more rigidly delineated than that of animals with normal, natural life situations. Drawing conclusions or guidance for our own behavior from the behavior of captive wild animals is a very poor springboard for understanding what is natural and right to a species. And we forget that dogs are not wolves, nor do they think that we are, and they're fully aware that we're not dogs either. While we can take a good deal of guidance from how dogs handle issues of leadership with other dogs, the truth is that we still have to find the balance unique to a dog/human relationship.

We have a vastly oversimplified and wildly inaccurate set of rules of how to be a leader of canines. Some of the "how to be a top dog" advice found in the popular dog literature is purely nonsensical, some is based on poorly understood truth, and some is nothing short of strangely twisted interpretations of what dogs really do with dogs. In the end, our clumsy extrapolations result in a rather autocratic approach to dogs, as evidenced by the sad reality that there's a whole lot of *nevers* involved. For example, "Never let your dog go ahead of you through doorways or on stairways." I'm a bit confused on how to apply this consistently. Just how you get a dog into the car while following this rule is a mystery to me—are you supposed to get in first and then invite the dog to join you?

"Never let your dog eat before you do." This advice might work well when you and your dog are sharing a deer carcass. After all, wouldn't you rather have the really choice bits for yourself? I mean, if you let the dog go first, he'll eat all the delicious intestinal contents before you get a shot at them. I usually feed my dogs before I eat because it seems kinder and because I don't need to make them drool and watch me eat in order to provide them with effective leadership. If a person needed to deny me a shot at the donuts in order to prove how powerful they were, chances are good there were some other issues they needed to work out with me and with their own notions of what constitutes effective leadership. If we actually look to wild wolf behavior for some clues on how best to handle the "Who eats first?" question, we learn that if there's plenty to be had (as there might be with a moose carcass), all get to eat with no rank pulled by anyone. If there are young puppies, they often get first dibs, with Mom and other pack members literally regurgitating a hot meal for the kids. If pickings are slim, whoever can get hold of and keep the food is the winner; obviously, higher-ranking animals win this particular hand more often than lower-ranking members. For dogs whose owners insist on eating before their canine pals do, I wonder if some dim genetic memory stirs up a bit of anxiety that there's not much available in the pantry? Do puppies who are not fed first wonder if they've landed in a dysfunctional pack that doesn't understand the importance of feeding the kids first?

The list goes on and on: Never let your dog sleep in your bed or get up on the furniture. Never let your dog have free access to toys or bones. Never pet your dog when he asks you to. Never go over to your dog to give him attention; make him come to you. (Strange advice this, particularly since a direct approach to another animal is a high status maneuver.) And one of my favorites—take your dog's "kills" away from him. Huh? In fact, I understand this one pretty well. Banni once tried to sneak through the door with a possum he'd caught. Head down, he positioned himself in the middle of the whole gang of dogs waiting to get in, but I noticed something odd about him, which turned out to be a possum in his jaws. So I took his kill away from him. Actually, I just told him to drop it, which was a good thing since it was doing what possums do— just playing dead. Banni dropped it, and when I told him, "Let's go," he picked it up again, and when I said, "Drop it" he did; and when I told him, "Let's go," he picked it up again. We went around like this for a while, which just goes to show it is not easy to take a dog's kill (even a live one) away from him unless you remember to add "Leave it" between "Drop it" and "Let's go." I offer this helpful hint for those who feel the need, as I did, to discourage dogs from bringing home their own pets or eating their kills on the couch.

All of the simplistic *never* advice contains the implied but unspoken phrase of dire warning "or your dog will become alpha." This is as silly as saying if you let children run and play, you will never have control over them. The truth is that if you don't have control over the children in the first place, then when they do run and play and get terribly excited, you won't be able to control them in that situation. If you can't tell your dog to get off the furniture or out of your bed, it's not because a comfortable couch has eroded the dog's respect for you. Particular actions in and of themselves are not usually the problem when it comes to leadership issues. The lack of respect we have earned from our dogs is the problem. Our failure to provide appropriate leadership is to blame, not the comfy chairs. No matter how many of them you may have.

People love to substitute rules and formulas for understanding of complex issues. I don't know why, and I doubt that dogs have a clue either. I suspect it's because rules make complex issues seem easier to understand. In the initial stages of learning anything, having some basic rules helps us feel less lost and gives our rudderless flailings something akin to direction. Within the context of a loving relationship, I find such rules offensive, and deadening to all involved. One tip-off that a relationship has not achieved a high degree of intimacy is the need for strictly adhered to rules. Reliance upon rules reveals our desire for quick, easy fixes and our unwillingness to do the work necessary to gain the understanding of our dogs and the respect *from* our dogs that makes such rules unnecessary. Learning to become fluent in Dog has to extend past mere theoretical understanding into a shift in our behavior so that we are truly communicating in ways that make sense to the dog.

When two living beings are involved, a soulful approach requires, perhaps even demands, that we remain open and attentive to the reality of what is happening dynamically between the two; anything less is life lived by rote, not by feel. In the long run, the very beauty that complexity makes possible is denied and made unavailable within the confines of rules; the dynamic quality of a connection bound only by mutual agreement and understanding, not by rules, is lost. Following a list of rules, our hearts are not free to dance in response to another—we are only dully plodding along in an imitation waltz. We cannot help but be disappointed with what rules create within a relationship: a static unsatisfying version of the real thing that neither broadens nor warms our soul.

12

LEADERSHIP IS ACTION

*One of the tests of leadership is the ability to recognize a problem
before it becomes an emergency.*

ARNOLD GLASGOW

I'VE YET TO MEET ANYONE WHO SAID, "I hoped this dog would take over
my household and he has. Praise be!" Instead, there's been a steady parade
of bewildered clients who find themselves unable to control the dog
they love very much, who are frustrated by the dog's behavior and
unhappily aware that something has gone quite wrong. Without ever
intending to, and simply because they don't understand the dog's perspective on leadership, owners have abdicated. In the absence of clear,
consistent leadership, dogs do what dogs do—the best they can and in
a way that suits them.

In every interaction with their family and with other dogs and people they meet, dogs are getting answers to their questions about who's
really in charge. And they're taking very, very good notes. Dogs are always
just being who they are—dogs and nothing else—and if they fail to
respect/obey/cooperate, chances are good that they are reacting to a
perceived void. Remember just how honest dogs are? Well, here's where
that honesty may come back to bite us in the butt—sometimes, quite
literally! The respect dogs accord us is precisely and exactly the respect
we have earned. According to *their* scorecard—according to the expectations every canine brings to a social interaction.

On casual examination, having a dog who mistakenly believes he's
in charge of his own little fiefdom seems relatively harmless. So what if
the dog is "spoiled" or out of control? (The smaller the dog, the less like-

ly anyone is to be concerned about a dog's lack of respect for people; a "spoiled" dog with paws the size of dinner plates tends to get attention.) But having created a four-legged Napoleon is not merely a matter of annoying visiting guests. While the concept of a dog believing that he is the emperor of his own little empire may seem amusing, this kind of confusion can be very dangerous.

There's a very serious problem with a dog who believes he is the highest-status animal in his family. According to proper canine protocol, the dog who believes that he has the right to set the rules for how others will behave is also entitled to enforce those rules. This can put us in direct conflict with our dogs and create some very ugly situations where both parties are feeling righteously entitled to their behavior. If we act in what he considers unacceptable ways, he'll let us know in purely canine fashion, dealing with us precisely as he would deal with a bratty pup. Displeased, a dog will not write a nasty letter or call you up to complain; he will, however, growl, snap, snarl or bite. I've worked with countless dogs who were led to believe that they ruled the world or at least their small corner of it and then were labeled "aggressive" by their angry, scared and bewildered owners. Some of these dogs ended up dead, victims of the lack of understanding from the people who claimed to love them yet did not set rules for their behavior.

Generally speaking, our dogs do not want to be in conflict with us, though they often find themselves in that unhappy position. This is usually not because dogs desire to thwart us, thumb their noses at us or deliberately defy us, though they are capable of doing all three. They are usually acting in good faith, and though we may not like it, are giving us accurate feedback on our leadership and the degree of training and socialization they have received. If we lead the dog to believe he's the one in charge, he is.

Though many training approaches emphasize "deranking" the dog or taking him down a few pegs socially speaking, the truth is this: The *dog* does not need to be "deranked" so much as the *people* need to learn to act like people worth listening to. The emphasis is on the wrong end of the leash; the failure rests with the two-leggeds, not the dogs, though it is certainly easier to blame the dog than accept the responsibility for our behavior. Insubordination is very often a charge leveled at inferiors by incompetent leaders. When we take the responsibility to shift our own behavior so that we become people that dogs want to be with and respect, dogs act accordingly. On a daily basis, dogs remind us of the truth that to get respect, you have to act in ways that deserve respect.

THE BEIGE RUG SYNDROME

Try this sometime: Rush into a crowded room and announce that no one, and you mean no one, is to touch the jellied calves' brains on the kitchen counter. (Humans only—dogs will be dashing off to check it out.) What you'll get is happy agreement that yes indeed, the calves' brains are safe. Tell the same crowd that there are thousand-dollar bills, the keys to new cars and also a lot of Belgian chocolate all stacked knee-deep in the kitchen, and you may find they require a bit more convincing to leave it all untouched. Why? Because cash and cars and chocolate probably matter to them, and jellied calves' brains probably do not.

Tell a dog to sit in the middle of the kitchen on a quiet afternoon, and you'll most likely get compliance. Ask that same dog to sit while cats dash past or other dogs are playing or when there's a knock at the door, and you may find it's quite a different story. If we cannot control the dog in situations of great importance to him, we may find ourselves in deep trouble when the food-crazy dog mugs the neighbor's toddler for a graham cracker or chases a bicyclist or attacks a visitor. Despite Buddy's love of food, we need to be able to tell the dog to leave the toddler's snack alone. No matter how thrilling the chase may be, Giselle needs to watch quietly (though perhaps with wagging tail and a gleam in her eye) as the Tour de France zooms past. And regardless of what Fluffy thinks of Uncle Dominick's aftershave, the dog needs to take his cues as to who is and is not a welcome guest from you. The more important something is to the dog, the more important it may be that we have the dog's respect, that we have earned the right to control the dog's behavior or impulses. If something is important to the dog, he's going to be willing to push for it; it's easy to control anyone's behavior if they don't care about something.

Unfortunately, we sometimes respond to and attempt to direct only the behaviors that infringe on what *we* consider important or just important at that moment. We might ignore a dog who jumps on us when we are wearing old jeans and a T-shirt, but suddenly consider that behavior worthy of our full attention if we are wearing an expensive suit. We forget that the dog is carefully taking notes on our response to what *he* considers important as well as noting what appears (based on our behavior) to be important to us. This can lead to some interesting situations. Dog trainers the world over are familiar with (although sometimes helpless in the face of) the Beige Rug Syndrome.

Those dog owners suffering from this particular syndrome inevitably have *(a)* an expensive, and usually fairly new, beige rug; and *(b)* a dog that they cannot control in many settings. Despite their inability to walk the dog down the street without incident or control him when guests appear, there is one guarantee—the dog has been taught to never, ever, for any reason, set foot on the beige rug. Students would earnestly assure me that their dog unfailingly abided by this rule, but I didn't believe that anyone with so little ability to direct a dog's behavior could actually have achieved this. One day, visiting a student for an in-home consultation, I watched in amazement as we strolled into the living room (where the beige rug was) and the dog stopped dead in his tracks as if an invisible force field barred him from the room. Bemused, since the woman's chief complaint was that she didn't seem to be able to control her dog, I asked how she had managed to teach her dog to stay off the rug.

"Oh that?" She airily waved her hand. "It was easy. First I blocked him from even getting in there, and then I'd leave the gate open only when I was around to watch him. After a while, I could sit in here and we'd practice having him stay out there. Every time he even thought about it, I just warned him to get out. I've saved up a long time for this rug, and while I love my dog, he's got the rest of the house to be with us. I don't want his muddy feet or dog hair in this room." It really mattered to her that the rug stay clean, and so she was willing to work diligently, ever alert to even a vague hint that the dog was headed that way. I asked if she waited till he was actually on the rug before she acted. "Oh, no. I could see if he was just thinking about it, and that's when I'd remind him or tell him no."

She was amazed when I pointed out that she had proven herself to be a very good dog trainer by *(a)* dealing with intent and not the actual action whenever possible; *(b)* setting rules that she absolutely reinforced no matter how much the dog wanted to be in the living room and no matter what else she was doing; *(c)* creating a situation where the dog could not make a mistake (putting up a gate) when she could not supervise him; and *(d)* deliberately training him while she could and would keep a close eye on him. I pointed out that if she applied those same successful techniques to everything else she tried to teach him, she'd probably do very well indeed. "You mean, treat everything he does like it's really important that he learn it, like staying off the rug?" I nodded and she grew thoughtful. "Well, that makes a lot of sense!" She and her dog went on to have a very nice relationship.

Unfortunately for our dogs, they often receive mixed or inadvertent messages about their own status, and ours relative to them. How then do you know if your dog is simply well loved and indulged but not dangerously misinformed about his status? A quick gauge of how the dog may be interpreting your behavior can be had in the answer to one simple question: When there's a conflict (either between you and the dog or something external to the relationship), will your dog accept your direction and control of his behavior? It doesn't matter how beautifully the dog responds to commands or behaves in peaceful moments. What counts is the dog's willingness to accept direction from you when *he* sees the situation as important—in other words, when canine protocol says that a high-status family member should be the one to make the decisions.

If you make a list of the situations in which you find your dog's behavior frustrating, embarrassing or uncontrollable, you will also have created the list of situations the dog finds very important to him. This does not always mean that such situations are ones the dog finds pleasurable, but rather that in those settings, the dog is highly aroused, whether that's feeling protective, angry, irritated, excited, anxious, afraid, defensive, predatory, ecstatic or in pain. At these "important" times, the dog most desperately needs clear leadership and guidance, just as the people you love need you most not in the easy and peaceful times but when the currents of complex, perhaps overwhelming emotions make it difficult to keep their heads clear. But the level of trust in a relationship that allows us to step in and provide guidance and support and direction must preexist the moment of crisis. If you've not established this relationship in various and sundry ways in everyday life and in less critical circumstances, chances are better than good the dog will disregard your attempts to control or direct his behavior.

Put Down That Pickled Okra!

Much training advice deals with controlling the dog's resources as a way of establishing leadership. At its core, this is sound advice. Among dogs, the privilege of high status is evidenced in access to and control of resources. What exactly is a resource? Ask me, and I might say pickled okra. The mere thought of the stuff makes most folks gag, but there are those among us who love it. I'm one of the few, the strange, the okra lovers. When a Southern friend sent me a case of pickled okra, I opened it with glee and then snarled at my husband, "This is mine." Throwing up his hands and backing away from the box, John was quick to assure me that if I fell off the face of the Earth that night, he'd not touch my pickled okra. It's not a matter of how deeply he respects me, or how much he wishes to avoid any confrontation—after all, nothing short of absolute blissful harmony is the key to our marriage. (Yep, just like the flying green pigs that are the hallmark of our farm.) His assurance was based on this little fact: He hates pickled okra. While I view it as a valuable resource to be guarded, he has no interest in it at all.

Obvious resources are food, toys, bones, chews (pig ears, cow hooves, rawhides, etc.), treats, even water—or the *expectation* of any of these. A dog may guard an empty food bowl not because he's hallucinating that it's filled with food, but because the bowl represents an expectation of food. Visitors to our house who don't know that a certain cabinet contains dog treats are startled to find many large dogs jostling each other for position when that cabinet is opened. To the dogs, the cabinet represents an expectation of treats. Although it also contains the potatoes and onions and other nondog items that the guest was actually seeking, the dogs know that each time that cabinet is opened, there is the *poten-*

tial for treats. Thus, being nearest the cabinet and the person opening it serves as a resource for our dogs, just as an empty food bowl may be viewed by other dogs as a valuable resource. Less-obvious resources may be attention, access in or out of the home or certain rooms, sleeping areas (whether dog beds or the human bed), freedom, solitude, perches (either in laps or on furniture) or viewpoints (such as a window or door), specific furniture, proximity to a person or activity, a particular position near a door, fence or gate.

Blanket statements about what constitutes a resource ignore the importance of understanding each dog as an individual. What one dog finds valuable may be of no interest whatsoever to another dog or to a person. Like beauty, a resource is only a resource in the eyes of the beholder. I once sold a puppy named Ellie to a woman who had a beautifully appointed home full of fine antiques and collectibles. As is my habit, I tucked in something familiar and comfortable from home alongside the food, toys and papers that accompany any puppy. In this case, I grabbed an old mattress cover that the puppies had been sleeping on. Though torn and stained, it was clean, and perfect puppy bedding, soft and warm but only a few uses away from a one-way trip to the dump. It would, I figured, ease Ellie's transition from our home to her new life. Unfortunately, Ellie's owner and I underestimated how attached the puppy would become to her "blankie."

At first, her owner didn't mind, keeping the mattress cover in the puppy's crate, thinking that eventually she'd discard it and replace it with something more attractive. One night, she dragged the tattered cover out and replaced it with an expensive, thick pad. Ellie considered this with interest, and then, picking up her beloved puppyhood blankie, dragged it onto the beautiful new pad. Every time her owner tried to discard the weary mattress cover, Ellie fretted and paced and hunted down the garbage bag or can where it had been tossed, and, relenting, her owner would return Ellie's treasured blankie to her. It became an embarrassment when she was entertaining guests. At a certain point in the party, her lovely dog would trot upstairs and reappear, proudly dragging behind her for presentation to the bemused guests her most beloved treasure: the sad skeleton of a very elderly mattress pad. In the end, the woman found a way to make both herself and her dog happy with a splendid bed custom-made for Ellie. Though beautiful on the outside, it suited Ellie just fine—tucked inside it was her beloved blankie.

I now send puppies home with items that offer a more timeless appeal than a grubby mattress pad, but when I think of what may constitute a valuable resource for any dog, I remember Ellie and her blankie. To understand our dogs, we need to step into their world and understand what they consider valuable and important resources. If the balance of power has gone askew between human and dog, an understanding of what constitutes valuable resources for the dog enables us to wisely use their value to help us earn the dog's respect and restore a healthier balance to the relationship.

The problem with dogs and resources is not how much access the dog has to things he finds enjoyable or pleasant. Sleeping in bed, hopping up on the furniture, having a wealth of toys and bones and chewies, being petted, and so on—none of these resources cause a dog to lose his mind or become a canine Napoleon. Like so much of dog training, we're looking at the wrong end of the leash. (Maybe what the world needs is a bumper sticker that reminds us "Toys don't spoil puppies. People spoil puppies.") The important question is this: Do *you* have access, free and uncontested, to anything that the dog considers a resource? When a dog begins to set rules about resources, this is an unmistakable sign that your leadership may be lacking in some way. And it is a sign that should be taken very, very seriously, because having set rules, a dog will enforce them in very canine ways, just as he would with another dog: with growls, snarls, snaps and even bites.

MINE, ALL MINE

My friend Kathryn called one night to pick my brain about a brewing problem between her two dogs. Though they lived quite peacefully together most of the time, Meiske, an elderly but still feisty mixed breed, had begun snarling at Flink, a younger, very active Kelpie, an Australian herding breed. When Kathryn was cooking, Meiske stationed herself between the kitchen door and Kathryn's work area. Kathryn's house is quite small, so from that position, Meiske was no farther than five feet from Kathryn or the door, allowing her to keep an eye on any tidbits that might be tossed her way and to effectively block Flink from entering the room. Initially, Meiske had simply crowded near Kathryn, growling at Flink only if he tried to move closer. As time went on, Meiske began making new rules, eventually insisting that Flink not even set foot in the kitchen. Flink was torn between his respect for Meiske and his desire to be near Kathryn and the food, but Meiske's persistence and consistency paid off; he waited in the next room.

Kathryn could not understand what was happening between these two dogs who had lived peacefully together since Flink's arrival as a pup several years before. Was there some shift in the pack order? she wondered. Was this a dominance issue? Was Flink somehow challenging Meiske in ways Kathryn could not detect? Of considerable concern was the age and size difference. Though she found it hard to believe that the problem could escalate to a serious fight and injuries, Kathryn knew that if Meiske attacked Flink, the younger, stronger dog was easily capable of hurting the old girl or maybe even killing her.

Hoping for some insight from me into these dog-to-dog interactions, she was quite surprised when my answer was that instead of examining her dogs' behavior, she needed to look to her own. Specifically, she needed to start acting like a leader. As a leader, she needed to remind Meiske that while being in the kitchen was a valuable resource, it wasn't a resource that was Meiske's to defend. (A human parallel might be two children squabbling over their dad's wallet. It doesn't matter which kid sets the rules or what they are: "You can't hold it, you can only touch it." The real story comes clear when Dad walks in and claims his wallet. Neither child has the right to control that particular asset.) This was something that Kathryn, as the high-status family member, controlled; access to resources was strictly at her discretion, not the dogs'. The solution was quite simple. Anytime Meiske acted in ways that indicated she was the one who controlled a particular resource, Kathryn was to gently but unmistakably show the dog that she was not the one entitled to make those rules.

When Meiske growled at Flink in the kitchen, she was quietly escorted from the kitchen. Naturally, Meiske viewed this as a temporary blip in Kathryn's mind and tried to reenter the kitchen many times. Each time, Kathryn made it clear that she was not welcome. A bit disgruntled and bewildered by these new rules, Meiske eventually got the message and lay quietly watching from the doorway. In this subtle, nonconfrontational way, Kathryn could clearly communicate in a way that Meiske could understand: "My kitchen. Not yours. Dogs enter here because I say they can." Though not thrilled with this new development, Meiske watched from outside as Flink made himself comfortable in the kitchen. After a few minutes of this, Kathryn called Meiske into the kitchen, asking her to sit, which the dog happily did. She gave each dog a treat, patted them briefly and turned to her cooking. For a few minutes, peace reigned, but then, as Flink moved to settle himself nearer to Kathryn, a growl was heard. Calmly, Kathryn escorted Meiske from the room, and the whole cycle began again.

In just one evening of consistency from Kathryn, Meiske understood that as much as she valued being in the kitchen with Kathryn, she was not the one who set the rules about this resource. In fact, if she acted in anything but tolerant ways that included Flink, the resource she valued so much was unavailable to her. Without raising her voice, without having to use any physical force, Kathryn made her point in a way that made perfect sense to the dog. And Meiske demonstrated that this was understood and valid for her. (Had it not made sense, Meiske's behavior would not have shifted and might even have gotten worse, a common canine response to being confused by unclear or invalid messages.) The message was clear: Not yours. Mine. And importantly, mine to share with you *if* you act in ways I find acceptable. Sharing a resource with a lower-status animal is typical only of very high ranking animals.

While initially Kathryn felt like many owners—uncomfortable with such an approach, feeling that it smacked of dictatorship and perhaps even an ugly level of control—she learned to let the dogs tell her whether or not this approach was one that made sense to them. When we let our emotional interpretations of our actions override the reality of what the dog's behavior tells us is working (or not working) for him, we have stepped out of a relationship and into something that exists only in our own minds. Most of us, at one time or another, have been in human relationships where another person refused to see or understand our behavior and instead assigned their own interpretation or value system to the situation. It is maddening at best, and at some level is an act of self-centeredness that neatly excludes us and shapes the world according to the other's beliefs.

LET'S MAKE A TRADE!

While high status is revealed in the control or access to resources and in leadership activities, guarding food or other possessions is a slightly different story. Here an understanding of canine culture and "dog law" is important to keep us from making mistakes we do not intend to make.

Faced with the question of how to entertain three six-week-old puppies who appear to be nothing but biting and chewing machines (all right, in their spare time they are eating, peeing and pooping machines as well), we've rummaged through the freezer to come up with perfectly sized puppy bones. Raw beef bones, they are just right for small, eager jaws and provide a bit of nutrition as well, as the pups use their sharp teeth to strip bits of meat and fat from the bones. For the sake of uninterrupted chewing time, we've blocked the adult dogs from the puppy pen for a few hours. When I wander out to see how the puppies are faring, I open the gate, and immediately, all the adults leap over the low barrier that keeps the puppies where we want them. With wriggles of delight, the puppies abandon their bones and dash to greet their elders.

I warn the adults to leave the bones alone, and they do, but in their sidelong glances at and casual passes near the bones they make it clear that they're keeping a close eye on the little treasures in case I either change my mind or forget. The initial excitement of reunion over, the puppies return to their bones. I watch as puppy Bird grabs one, drawing two-year-old Bee's attention. Nose down, clearly intent on the bone, Bee approaches Bird, who deftly spins away, keeping her prize out of reach. After just two or three determined avoidance spins, Bee lets the puppy wander off, watching with a soft expression and wagging tail as Bird struggles to carry a bone easily as big as her head.

As Bird demonstrated, even very young puppies are granted the right to exercise one of the most respected laws of canine society: possession.

No matter how low-ranking the dog, if he has something in his mouth or immediate vicinity, he has a right to defend it *if he wants to*. Wolf expert David Mech has observed this same behavior in wild wolves, something he calls the "ownership zone" around the wolf's mouth. To be fair with our dogs, we need to remember this when working with them so that they learn to voluntarily give up possessions if asked; should we forget, we might get a response from the dog that surprises or upsets us but equally shocks the dog in the rudeness of our own behavior!

Generally speaking, the higher the dog's status, the larger the zone around him that constitutes "vicinity." Very high ranking dogs might place something quite a distance from their paws and still have it "in their possession." This was a particularly favorite sport of my dog Bear, who would make a big show of some prize to puppies who needed to learn a lesson or two about respecting this most basic canine law. With much drama, Bear would lie down, deliberately placing the object as far from his paws as the reach of his head and neck allowed. Depending on how sophisticated the puppies were socially, Bear might simply just wait for a puppy to show interest, never taking his eyes off the youngster and quick to warn the puppy at the first hint that the puppy was thinking about snatching the bone. A more advanced pup might be given the very casual act, in which Bear appeared quite uninterested in the bone though he was actually keeping tabs on the pup in his peripheral vision. Attempts by the pup to grab the object in this setting were often met with more dramatic vocalizations and fierce air snaps.

Lower-ranking dogs might need to have it directly under their chin or actually in their mouth for the possession to be recognized. Bird, for example, would not have dared to put her bone down in Bee's presence—at most, she would have put the bone on the ground and then hovered directly over it. Generally speaking, there is an inverse relationship between the distance at which a dog feels the need to protect a possession and his level of confidence. A deeply confident dog might not even glance up as you walk directly past him while he's working on a delicious bone, while a much less confident dog might start anxiously growling the moment you enter the room or look his way. (Note: Appropriately handled from early puppyhood, a dog should not feel anxious or worried about his possessions, at least in regard to people.

But this requires deliberate and systematic desensitization such as offered in Dr. Ian Dunbar's program, *Sirius Puppy Training*.)

While Bee, a young adult, could have snatched the bone from the twelve-pound puppy, her response to Bird was the same as it would have been if her older brother Grizzly had had a bone—interested investigation, evidence of "Boy, I'd like that" but also respectful acknowledgment of "No, sorry, this is mine!" even when it was given by a six-week-old puppy. This is not to say that possession gives the possessor undisputed rights to keep his prize, whatever it may be. A high-status dog can use his status to intimidate another dog into dropping a possession or walking away from food by using nothing more than a look. At one house we lived in, there was an old in-ground pool, perfect for the dogs, who greatly enjoyed retrieving balls and bumpers by diving off the side to swim in fierce competition to be the first to get there. Our oldest male at the time, Banni, decided that in his old age, he didn't have a prayer of beating the youngsters to the ball, and after a while, he adopted a new strategy. We'd throw in a ball and he'd watch as the young dogs launched themselves with exuberant splashes, eager to beat each other to the toys. While they exhausted themselves swimming hard, Banni would walk over to the stairs—the only exit from the pool—and wait. In order to get out of the pool, they had to pass him, and at that point, he'd exert his status with a pointed stare; reluctantly, they'd drop the ball or bumper, and it was his. Sometimes, a dog would turn his head away from Banni and try to sneak past. This worked some of the time, especially if there were several dogs approaching at once with balls. Some dogs would deliberately swim around for a while, waiting for someone else to be the sacrificial lamb at the stairs, and then, while Banni was occupied with that dog, they would dash by and out of the pool.

With something in his possession, a low-ranking dog may defend it even against higher-status dogs. Even at the tender age of six weeks, Bird included a low growl with her evasive maneuvers to let Bee know that she meant to keep her bone. Other than being a fascinating glimpse into dog behavior, what does this mean for us in our relationships with our dogs? It points to the reality that status alone is insufficient for our dogs to willingly surrender objects, whether food or toys. Even with a dog who respects you as the high-status family member, the natural inclination to simply pick up the object and evade you is a perfectly natural, reasonable and *not disrespectful* response. From the dog's perspective, he is within his rights to do so. Our attempts to either wrest the object from his jaws or to intimidate him into giving it up may, understandably, be met with a fully canine response of growls and warnings. We're not acting like leaders or high-status family members; we're just acting rudely.

Understanding that in a dog's world, possession is nine-tenths of the law leads us to choose a different approach in teaching the dog to voluntarily surrender anything in his possession. Whenever we are able to gain voluntary compliance from another, we sidestep the potentially thorny moments of conflict and possible confrontation. We already apply this principle in our human relationships—forcing someone to accede to your demands may, in the short run, result in "success" if you're willing to view success as simply the achievement of your goals. But compelling another's cooperation has long-term effects; you may have won the battle but lost the war and possibly damaged the relationship. Voluntary actions leave dignity intact, and for any social animal, the value and importance of "saving face" should not be underestimated. Forced compliance can lead to a spiraling effect: A dog who has a bit of garbage wrestled from his mouth may give it up—that time. Next time, however, he may be even quicker to defend his prize and, now aware that *you're* willing to engage in a physical confrontation, be prepared to fight back. At the first sign of any interest on your part, the dog may growl or run off. This can quickly escalate to a nasty cycle with emotions and frustrations running high on both sides.

There's a need to both respect the value of what the dog considers important and to balance that with the practical reality that like children, dogs sometimes need to be kept safe from some of the things they may find, steal or be given that may not be good for them. The easiest approach is to teach the dog that voluntarily surrendering any items to you is a good and profitable thing. One way to teach this is to set up specific training sessions where you systematically ask the dog to "trade" what he has in his mouth for a particularly yummy treat in your hand. When he releases the item, you quietly pick it up while simultaneously popping the treat in his mouth. Then, and this is the critical part, *you return his treasure to him*. Repeated over and over with every item you can think of, the dog learns that surrendering his treasure earns him a treat as well as the return of his possessions. Sometimes you can have your cake and eat it too!

Working with a dog from a local animal shelter, I was amused by his attempts to both retain a stuffed toy banana and eat the proffered liver in my hand. For a good minute or more, the dog tried every possibility he could imagine to shift the banana in his mouth to make room for the liver, but when that didn't work, he finally dropped the toy and reached for the treat. Since his behavior indicated he was quite anxious about losing the rare opportunity to play with a toy (shelter dogs often lead terribly deprived lives, since keeping them alive takes priority over the niceties of toys and play time), I did not reach for the dropped toy with my hand, but instead moved quietly and stepped on it with a foot. Had I reached directly for the toy, the dog might have felt the need to gulp the treat and then desperately lunge for his precious toy.

Instead of reaching for the toy, I tossed another treat past him, so that he had to turn away from me and hunt briefly for the liver. This gave me time to take advantage of a loophole in the canine possession law—if you voluntarily turn your attention away from an object and another dog swoops in and takes it, that's fair. Puppies and determined young dogs learn to patiently wait as close as another dog will allow, watching and waiting for that moment when something draws the possessor's attention away. Once the attention is truly shifted to something else, they make their move, looking very much like a runner stealing a base. I've not seen a normal dog chase down the one who successfully took the possession under these conditions (though I have seen them chase a dog who tried a snatch from right under the owner's watchful eye!) but the ritual of "It's mine!" and "Give it up!" can and often does start all over again.

Though the dog noticed that I had the toy in my possession as he turned back to me, it had been accomplished "fairly" according to his canine perspective and without ever making him feel threatened. Best of all, from his point of view, I returned it to him with a smile. After a few minutes of practice, the dog was agreeable to giving me the toy by placing it in my hand in return for a treat. He had learned to trust that I would keep my word and wanted to just momentarily trade one for the other; trading with me did not mean the loss of his toy.

Eventually, over time, I would have gone a step further and occasionally begun to keep the item I had traded for, but would have returned to him another toy or suitable treasure so that the notion of "if you give me this, I'll give you that, and then you'll get a toy back" was firmly in place. Finally, I would have worked with the dog so that even without a specific trade in mind, he would volunteer whatever he had for my interested examination. I love how dogs watch me with great curiosity as I peer at the item and even sniff it; some look just a wee bit concerned if I am too enthusiastic about their prize, while others wag their tail in agreement that it is indeed wonderful! What I want and work for is the dog to wait patiently for me to return the item, which I do within a few seconds, usually telling them, "That's really very special! Thank you!"

Practiced in calm, nonconfrontational settings, teaching a dog to trade is preparation for the day when you will not be able to return his treasure—say, an expensive shoe or a chicken bone. When Bee as a teenage dog pranced into the living room with an entire stick of butter, I had to merely inquire with happy curiosity, "Well, well, what have you got?" and she trotted directly to me, pleased as punch to hand over her loot. Though I did not return the butter, I was quick to tell her how pleased I was that she had let me have it, and together, we ran to the kitchen to find a tasty reward. I then made quite sure that I quickly located a suitable toy and played with her briefly. Butter safely retrieved, Bee happily settled down with the toy, and all ended pleasantly with no upset feelings on either side.

While undisputed access to resources is a key act of leadership, we need to also remember that from the dog's point of view, even a small puppy has the right to keep what is actually in their mouth. Understanding this cardinal law of canine behavior, we can find ways to encourage our dogs to cooperate with us in ways that will keep them safe and not damage the relationship, as might happen when we act in ways that make no sense from a canine perspective.

13

WHOSE COUCH IS IT, ANYWAY?

*If I can listen to what he tells me, if I can understand how it seems to him, if
I can sense the emotional flavor which it has for him, then I will be releasing
the portent forces of change within him.*

CARL ROGERS

THE AFGHAN BITCH, OPAL, WAS LOVELY, and her adoptive owner Mary
Anne was delighted with this quiet, well-behaved dog. Opal's background was unknown—a rescue group had discovered her in an animal
shelter and had fostered her until Mary Anne adopted her. All was fine
until the day Mary Anne entered the living room to find Opal on the
couch. This was not a problem in and of itself—dogs were quite welcome
to share the furniture. A longtime hound owner, Mary Anne knew that
most hounds possess a gene that unerringly directs them to the nearest
(and softest) cushion in any situation. What surprised her was the deep
growling that arose from Opal when Mary Anne approached the couch.
Though taken aback, Mary Anne moved closer, motioning with her hand
as she told Opal to get off the sofa. The growl grew more intense, and
when Mary Anne reached for the dog, meaning only to gently guide her
on to the floor, long jaws snapped at the air near her hand. Not sure
what to do, Mary Anne retreated from the room, unwilling to be bitten. As she stood staring out the kitchen window while she thought
about this ugly turn of events, Opal trotted into the room, tail wagging.
The dog seemed fine, as loving and friendly as ever, and Mary Anne put
the behavior down as perhaps a leftover from the dog's mysterious past
or maybe even just an off day. Perhaps, she told herself, she had startled
the dog or woken her from a dream. Quite a few days passed before the

situation repeated itself. This time Opal began growling as soon as Mary Anne entered the room. This time Mary Anne was concerned enough to call for help.

When I met Opal, the aloof yet soulful Afghan gaze sent me flying back in my memories to my own Afghan many years ago. She was surprisingly assured in my living room, which was filled with the scents of my own dogs. A warning bark from behind my office door (Carson notifying all interested that she was on duty) merited only a mildly interested glance from the hound, who calmly curled up between Mary Anne and me. Though quiet and friendly, Opal was also quite confident, something Mary Anne did not fully recognize. "The poor thing—I feel so bad for her. How could anyone give up such a beautiful dog?" She gazed down at Opal with a pitying smile. "I guess maybe this aggression comes from being abused?"

When problem behaviors arise, kindhearted owners sometimes blame the dog's history, as Mary Anne did, believing that the problem was a result of prior abuse. Like Mary Anne, many owners who have rescued or adopted a dog also hold the image of the "poor thing" so clearly in their minds that they cannot see the reality of the dog standing before them. Opal's assured greeting of me and her total relaxation on what was decidedly the home turf of many large, strange dogs revealed a dog with a fairly high degree of confidence. Having sympathy for a dog's past experiences is a good thing, and understanding a dog's background can provide important clues. And in cases of extreme abuse or neglect, there may be gaps or holes that can be only roughly patched, never fully overcome; scars sometimes remain in body and spirit. But we must always keep our eyes open to really see our dogs as they are, not lock them in their past or carry for them the emotional baggage that they have discarded.

If good, reliable information is available, understanding the past is helpful in that it may point to reasons why certain behaviors or attitudes are more difficult to change. Far too often, however, well-meaning people such as Mary Anne "hallucinate" the dog's past. While abusive pasts certainly do exist for many dogs, it does the dog very little good if we interpret his behavior through that particular filter. No relationship thrives if one of us is busy hallucinating what the other's reality might be; intimacy is not founded on supposition but on knowledge of how the world seems through another pair of eyes. In trying to know another, we may guess, but then need ways to ask if we have guessed correctly, "Is this so for you?" If we can't create a way to ask the dog in some way whether our guess is correct or not, we are indulging in kindhearted hallucination.

I often remind clients that if they had simply found the dog on the street, they would have no clue as to the dog's past, no rationalizations or excuses for why a dog acted in a particular way. The only assessment they could make is the one that needs to be made: What, if any, of the dog's behaviors offer evidence that the dog needs to learn better ways of coping with his life so that fear, anxiety, uncertainty or even anger can be minimized or eliminated? Having made such an assessment, it's time to get to work on making positive changes. As a Zen saying asks, "This being the case, how then shall I proceed?" Undesirable or unproductive behavior—whatever its source—always needs to be resolved.

Mary Anne's kindheartedness had also played a key role in leading the dog to the unfortunate conclusion that she, Opal, was actually the highest-ranking member of the household. Eager to make the dog feel secure and loved, Mary Anne had thoughtfully provided for Opal's every need. If Opal nudged her hand, Mary Anne showered her with attention, trying to make up for the sad circumstances she imagined in Opal's past. Should Opal cast a glance toward her food bowl, Mary Anne was quick to provide a treat. A slight restlessness on Opal's part resulted in Mary Anne leaping up to take the hound outside or even for a leisurely walk. While all of this loving care was provided with nothing but the very best intentions, it backfired. To the canine mind, certain privileges such as access to resources and the right to elicit/demand attention are associated with high status. When Mary Anne lovingly delivered valuable resources like food and fun (walks) at Opal's request, the hound interpreted this as proof that she was a high-ranking dog. When Mary Anne responded to Opal's desire for petting, this just underlined the message. To top it all off, Mary Anne's gestures toward the dog looked even to my noncanine eye to be quite deferential: slow, almost hesitant, quick to freeze or withdraw at any sign from Opal. Although I knew Mary Anne was intending only to act in gentle, nonthreatening ways, Opal was viewing their interactions quite differently from her thoroughly canine perspective. After a period of months of receiving these inadvertent messages regarding her status, Opal felt quite well within her rights as the top-ranking family member to tell others that she did not wish to be disturbed while on the couch. Rule setting was her high status privilege, and she intended to enforce her edicts in fully canine ways with growls, snarls, and even bites.

The conflict between human and dog occurs when we don't realize that what we consider loving acts of caretaking may be interpreted by the dog as deference to him and our agreement that he is the one in control of resources. We intend to send the message "You are loved and cared for, your needs will be met." The dog may hear "Your wish is my command." It takes no imagination or even an understanding of dogs to see how quickly this can become a serious problem. A message that twists in the space between speaker and listener is always problematic, particularly when we do not take care to note whether the message that lands is shaped precisely as it was when it left our lips.

As we discussed all this, Mary Anne was surprised to learn how different Opal's canine perspective was from her own. She understood how Opal might have come to the wrong conclusion, but frowning, she said, "What I don't understand is this. All my life, I've had dogs, many of them dogs I rescued from the local shelter, and I've treated all of them just like I've treated Opal. None of them ever growled at me or seemed to think they were in charge. I see your point, but it doesn't make sense when I look at all the dogs I've had."

Mary Anne's conclusion was understandable and quite common. A woman I dealt with at a seminar had a similar response based on her experience. She'd had Cocker Spaniels her entire life, had treated them all with the same approach and had never had anything but compliant, well-mannered dogs who were a delight—until her last dog, a hotshot puppy she had chosen specifically as her next competition dog because of his gung ho attitude and athletic ability. This dog had both delighted her with his lightning-fast mind and dismayed her with his often-problematic behavior. When I pointed out that Mr. HotShot needed a more crisply defined leadership, she found that hard to swallow—her particular style of leadership had been very successful for a long time with many other dogs.

What Mary Anne and the Cocker Spaniel lover were overlooking is that while a dog is a dog is a dog, every dog is a different dog. Anyone who has raised more than one child or had more than one meaningful friendship understands that successful relationships of any kind require that we adapt our particular style to the needs and responses of the other. To stand rigidly in our preferred patterns and insist that all others bend to suit us is hardly an effective approach in any relationship. To then blame the other when conflicts arise is selfishness of a very high order, and denies the importance of the other's needs. Within a loving relationship, even when we are in a leadership role (perhaps especially in that case), we must always consider what the other's behavior tells us about our own. The bottom line for the Cocker's owner was that the approach that had worked beautifully with a twenty-year lineup of Cocker Spaniels was evidently not sufficient leadership for a particularly bold, confident pup. Mary Anne's previous dogs may not have been as assured as Opal, and possibly not even interested in being a high-ranking dog.

Contrary to popular belief, not all dogs are alpha wannabes just waiting for the humans to slip up so they can take over the household if not the country and perhaps the world. What all dogs *are* willing to do is shape their world as best they can to suit them. The Cocker lover's previous dogs may have thought their world was just dandy, so going with the flow was pleasant and easy. If life is good, why rock the boat? (As politicians know, a well-fed and entertained citizenry rarely causes problems.) For whatever reason—different experience or personalities—Mary Anne's other dogs evidently had been happy to go along with her gentle style. Opal, on the other hand saw the world differently and was comfortable in a high-status role. Her particular personality was actually quite strong and assured—rude dogs she encountered received little more than a haughty stare, and people she did not care for she dismissed by looking through and not at them, as if they did not even exist. It's fair to say that her personality was one that was more sensitive and alert to nuances of leadership. From Opal's point of view, Mary Anne's attentive care to her every need had shown that Mary Anne was very trainable and compliant; in other words, lower-status. This has nothing to do with love—Opal clearly loved Mary Anne and vice versa. But love and leadership are two different issues in a dog's mind, and loving though she was, Opal was setting rules about the couch.

Resolving the problem required that Mary Anne establish in Opal's mind that she was worthy of the hound's respect. "Am I going to have to yell at her or jerk her around? Because I'm not going to do that," Mary Anne warned me. She was relieved to know that the most effective techniques were also humane, nonpunitive and nonconfrontational. As Opal had already demonstrated, in situations where respect for a person is limited, any confrontation or use of force may be perceived by the dog as an attack by a subordinate and may result in a completely canine response.

Earning a dog's respect can be accomplished by making it clear that the valued resources come through you—and only after a doggy "please" has been heard. When a dog walks directly to us and places his ball or toy in our lap, he is saying "Play with me." And he's not including any form of "please." Envision your dog as a rude child who walks up, slams a board game down in front of us and demands that you play with them—*now*. We would find such behavior unacceptable, and to remind the child that there are more appropriate and respectful ways of interacting with others, we might set conditions: "I'll play with you after you've taken out the garbage." Or, "You may leave the room, and come back and try asking me again, but this time in a nice way, with 'please' and 'thank you' included." Even young children can learn not to just point at something and expect it to be handed to them; wise parents teach children to say "please" as a condition for cooperating with their requests.

Person or pup, politeness counts. For example, a low-status dog who wishes to engage a higher-status dog in play needs to offer deferential behaviors while shaping the request to come play. Play bows, licking at the mouth, lowered body posture, groveling—all these are gestures of great respect and deference, and to the canine mind, part and parcel of a polite conversation. If we fail to keep our end of the bargain by acting like a high-status animal who will insist on politeness, then the dog may interpret our response to his request as proof that his status is greater than ours. And we really don't have a right to be shocked if our dogs tell us that we've been acting like lowly puppies unworthy of their respect.

Mary Anne had already taught Opal to sit and lie down on command, so these basics were going to be the dog's way of saying "please." At mealtimes or when giving out a treat, Mary Anne would ask Opal to sit or lie down (both of which she already knew how to do), giving the dog perhaps three seconds to comply. If Opal ignored her, Mary Anne would put the bowl back on the counter and turn away for five or ten seconds, then try again. If after three requests the dog was still ignoring her, Mary Anne would put the food in a cabinet or the refrigerator and leave the kitchen without saying a word, and go read a book or stare out the window for a few minutes. Then she'd try again. Only when Opal sat or lay down within the desired time frame would Mary Anne deliver the food. A similar routine was instituted for going outside. Opal would have to sit or lie down before the door was opened. Petting, no matter how winningly solicited, would happen only after Opal sat or lay down as requested, and was to be kept quite brief. Mary Anne was quick to point out that this was going to be very difficult, as it is for many owners. She was relieved to know that once she had earned Opal's respect and shifted the balance of power in the house, such restricted petting might no longer be necessary. But it was critical to helping Opal see Mary Anne in a new light. As time went on, Mary Anne would gradually begin to expect Opal to respond promptly to the first request and do more than just sit in order to earn attention.

The second part of the program was teaching Opal to get on and off furniture on request. Armed with some tasty treats, we began working on this in my living room. I offered Opal a treat or two to be sure she knew what delicious goodies I had to offer. Stepping away from the couch where Opal had curled up beside me while Mary Anne and I talked, I called the dog to me, rewarding her with several treats and praise. I stepped back to the couch and, patting the cushions, invited Opal to "get comfy" (a phrase chosen by Mary Anne.) Opal hopped up, and giving her a treat, I told her with enthusiasm what a genius she was. Showing her a treat, I tossed it on the floor, and as she prepared to get off the couch, I told her, "Off." Back and forth we went, practicing what "get comfy" and "off" meant. Opal found this a very agreeable game, and soon was hopping off at a quiet request in anticipation of a reward. After a brief rest for Opal and a review of the technique for Mary Anne, it was Mary Anne's turn to work with her dog. To her delight, Opal was as responsive and eager to cooperate as she had been with me. "Why does this work so well?" she asked as she and Opal settled down for a break. "Is it just because she knows this isn't her couch?"

The difference was not the particular couch, but the dog's emotional state. In my living room, Opal was relaxed, did not feel threatened and was thus in a pleasant state of mind. When Mary Anne had stepped into the living room at home, the dog had warned her to back off. At that point, a possible confrontation was brewing in Opal's mind. Mary Anne's initial attempt to simply force Opal off the couch, however gently, had just increased the dog's arousal. Believing herself to be the top-ranking dog, Opal had viewed Mary Anne's action as one of insubordination and had dealt with this in a very canine way: more dramatic growling and a warning snap. In my living room, nothing had happened to shift Opal from a relaxed state of mind. If I had felt the need to show Opal who was boss by forcibly removing her from the couch, the situation could have changed very quickly.

From Opal's point of view, she was not getting off the couch because I was "making" her; she was *voluntarily* moving in order to get to the treat I had tossed on the floor. In any training situation (in fact, in any relationship) gaining voluntary cooperation neatly sidesteps challenges to status. If the queen of England agrees to play checkers with you, her agreement makes status unimportant. But if you're going to try to force the queen of England to play with you, you'd best be someone she takes directives from with a smile. The underlying problem that created the whole couch incident was one of leadership and status; challenging a dog's status does not resolve the underlying problem, which needs to be addressed more universally. No threat perceived, no confrontation brewing, no challenges to her status, so Opal remained calm, cooperative and enjoyed the interaction.

Opal was relaxed and interested in this "game," not defending a valuable resource. At home, Mary Anne would not wait until Opal was on the couch and already in a defensive, confrontational mood, but deliberately take the dog into the living room to play the "get comfy/off" game, and do this quite a few times each day. Finding ways to carefully and gently revisit areas where emotions can run high is far more productive than a head-on confrontation during moments of great intensity. Identifying what the problem is allows us to step back and find a more loving, compassionate approach to working toward a resolution that suits all involved without hurt feelings or wounded pride.

Like many dogs, Opal was not being a bad dog. She was simply being a dog, responding to what she believed to be the rules and power structure in the household. Changing the rules and shifting the balance of power to a more appropriate one where Mary Anne and all other humans had higher status than Opal was going to take some time. But Mary Anne was willing to do what was necessary, and she welcomed a chance to work in nonconfrontational ways that would keep her safe while also earning Opal's respect. In the weeks that followed, faced with new rules, Opal found herself in some disconcerting situations. The first time Opal flatly ignored a third request to lie down before getting her meal, Mary Anne put her food bowl in the refrigerator and walked away. Opal was dumbfounded. She walked after Mary Anne, nudging her as if to say, "Excuse me? Did you forget something?" As planned, Mary Anne calmly ignored Opal for a few minutes before giving her another chance. This time, Mary Anne's request was met with a prompt response and a distinct look of relief when Opal was given her food. After a month of persistently and consistently applied new rules, Opal and Mary Anne had rebalanced their relationship in a more appropriate way, with Mary Anne acting much more like someone worthy of a dog's respect. Though still the luxury loving hound, Opal no longer viewed the couch as hers, and at a quiet request, would leave when anyone asked.

Opal and Mary Anne had work to do before they could find a comfortable balance in their relationship. There was a period of discomfort, one that is typical of relationships where problem areas have been highlighted and are the focus of attention and energy. Mary Anne reported that initially a great deal of what she did with Opal felt artificial. Although her previous approach had felt more "natural" to Mary Anne, Opal's behavior had pointed unmistakably to the fact that it was not an approach that worked for the dog. I encouraged Mary Anne to think of her feelings of awkwardness as akin to learning a new dance—at first, the steps feel strange, unfamiliar and moving smoothly is not possible. But with time and practice, your feet learn just where to go without the need for forced attention to the steps; then the joy of the dance returns. Despite feeling faintly false, Mary Anne persisted, encouraged by how much better she felt about Opal and their relationship. Beyond her own growing satisfaction with the connection that this approach made possible, she also watched Opal for confirmation that this new approach was working for the dog as well. After all, no matter what a trainer or a book or a veterinarian or any other source of advice might say, the final arbiters of whether or not an approach is working have to be the two involved in the relationship.

14

I'll Go First—This May Be Dangerous

Leadership should be born out of the understanding of the needs
of those who would be affected by it.
MARIAN ANDERSON

FLIPPING THROUGH CHANNELS IN A HOTEL ROOM one night, I chanced
upon a spaghetti Western that was so broadly painted in its stereotypes
that it was amusing. In one scene, the poor farm family is tending to
chores (all, miraculously, requiring the actors to be conveniently grouped
right in front of the old homestead) when up rode the Bad Guy, a neigh-
boring rancher who was foreclosing on their land. The young girl instantly fled behind her mother's billowing skirt, and the young man of the
family bristled, ready to take on the Bad Guy using, I suppose, his bare
ten-year-old hands. Dropping his shovel, the man of the family strode
forward and, sweeping his family behind him with one powerful gesture,
placed himself unmistakably as the front line of defense against whatever might be threatening his beloveds. Though it was a hackneyed scene,
I was struck by the message contained in that gesture, and by the act of
leadership displayed in the man's stepping forward: "You'll have to come
through me first."

This particular gesture of stepping forward into the line of fire, so to
speak, is one that dogs understand and employ among themselves. Walk
as a stranger into a room containing a bitch's puppies, and you may find
yourself face-to-face with a watchful (if not downright wrathful)
momma. Dogs with strong guarding/protective instincts will automat-

ically step forward to place themselves between a perceived threat and their people, a gesture that is most welcome when we find ourselves in frightening situations. On several occasions, my dogs have had need to step into the line of fire in the face of very real threats; when they stood growling between me and a threatening stranger on a dark street, my relief was boundless.

Apart from control of or access to resources and the control or direction of behavior, there is a third component of leadership in the dog's world: proactive intervention. Rarely addressed in most training books, it is nonetheless critically important to the dog's perception of his own safety both within the home family group and out in the larger context of the world. Proactive intervention is something that most of us already understand and employ in our daily lives. Simply put, it means being alert to and willing to respond to any potential threats toward the ones we love, especially those more vulnerable than ourselves. No sane parent would allow anyone to come up to a child and begin slapping them around or even verbally harassing them. An appropriate protective response would be to quite literally put the child behind you, placing yourself directly between the threat and the child. In the simple act of stepping forward, you are establishing yourself as the one in charge and saying, though you may not utter a word, "You'll have to come through me first."

HE JUST WANTS TO SAY "HI!"

Sadly, many dogs find themselves lacking the protective intervention of alert leadership. It is both unfortunate and shocking how many dogs presented to me as "dog aggressive" were actually feeling vulnerable and unprotected. In the majority of cases I've seen, the "aggressive" dog had been minding his own business and was often sitting or lying quietly at his owner's side when—either playfully or with more evil intent—the rude dog ran up, ran into, jumped on or attacked him. Inevitably, as the owners who have allowed their dogs to act rudely retreat from the situation, there are comments made about "that aggressive dog" (meaning the dog whose space had been invaded) and the classic comment, usually said in hurt tones, "He just wanted to say 'hi!'"

We would think very little of a parent who allowed a child to leap onto strangers while the parent did nothing more than smile and note, "He's a very friendly child." But dog owners frequently allow their dogs to act in equally rude ways, dashing up to other dogs and even leaping on them, and triggering defensive responses. Handlers of such dogs may not realize that they may be endangering their dog as well as putting other dogs and people in a difficult and unpleasant situation. Believing that their dogs are incapable of aggression, and not realizing that being rude is a form of aggression, they see only the growls or snarls of the dog who is on the receiving end of the rudeness.

My experience has been that it is owners of breeds considered "nonaggressive" that cause the most problems in dog-to-dog interactions. This is not because these people are more careless or less intelligent than other dog owners. The problem arises simply from a complete lack of awareness that their dog is rude. To the owners of nonaggressive breeds, there doesn't appear to be any thought that rudeness can take many forms. Anyone can recognize that a dog lunging and snarling is being rude. Far too few folks recognize that simply getting into another's dog space—however sweetly and quietly—is just as rude in the world of dogs. Owners of rude dogs do not perceive their dogs' actions as rude; they see only "friendliness." Thus the classic line, "He just wanted to say 'hi!'"

Alarmed, embarrassed and upset by their dog's aggressive display, owners are often unable to take careful stock of what triggered the unhappy event. Here's a real letter from a concerned owner:

> Cream is a sweet dog, good with commands, wonderful with people and children. She has regular dog pals that she plays with almost daily—they wrestle, play bite, and run around together. She's fine with dogs who are calm, but she has one problem: she hates young, hyper dogs. If a dog starts jumping all over Cream, Cream gets aggressive—starts to growl, shows some teeth, and if the dog doesn't take the hint after a few seconds, Cream will "attack" the dog. She only displays this aggressive behavior with young, hyper dogs.

Let's change this a little to read: "Maggie is fine with people who are calm and well behaved, and interacts with them appropriately. She's also endlessly patient with and kind to children, even bratty ones. But when loud, obnoxious teenagers begin shoving her around, she's really weird—she starts telling them to leave her alone. When they won't stop, she screams at them. What can we do with Maggie? Her behavior has us stumped."

Suddenly, the story seems quite different, and the dog's behavior far from puzzling. To label a dog like Cream aggressive is as senseless as labeling a woman as a cranky bitch because she slapped the face of a stranger who fondled her. And since these dogs are often roundly punished by their horrified owners (often on the advice of trainers who do not understand dog behavior), the dog finds himself in a terrible situation. Not only is the dog left open to the assault of the rude dog in the first place, but then he is also attacked (punished) by his owner. Little wonder that these dogs can become hyperalert to dogs who exhibit no sense of respecting the personal space of others or dogs who are excited and out of control. Some dogs can begin to set considerably large safety zones around them, compensating for the lack of protection available from the handler. In the absence of clear leadership that offers proactive intervention, these "aggressive" dogs often feel that they have no other option but to act defensively on their own behalf. And for that, they are often harshly punished, banned from classes and deeply misunderstood by the very people who should have been the ones to offer loving, alert protection—the proactive intervention of leadership.

Though these same owners would not let a stranger come up and begin kicking or yelling at their dog, they sometimes make no move to protect them from the rudeness of other dogs and the people who allow their dogs to behave rudely. This is not because they are unfeeling or careless. They may be laboring under the assumption that whatever dogs do is "natural" and that they ought not to interfere. They may be convinced, especially after being repeatedly told, that their dog (who may be offering a fully appropriate and normal response) is "aggressive" or "vicious," and feel terribly guilty about their dog's behavior. Even handlers who realize that their dogs have had their personal space infringed on will find little support from other people who have a limited understanding of aggression and who thus interpret anything that seems even mildly threatening in a simplistic, often inaccurate way.

For dogs who have problems with other dogs getting into their personal space, or dogs who lack confidence about meeting new people and/or other dogs, the simple act of the handler stepping forward is a profound one. What this gesture tells the dog is "I see the threat, and I will protect you." In other words, what the dog sees in our action is an assurance that we are willing to act as a leader should, an assurance that relieves or at least minimizes the dog's need to act in his own self-defense. By its very nature, the simple act of a human stepping forward with intent and confidence can make another dog intent on getting your dog to back off or slow down. And if it does not have that effect, it does at least position you to do something before your dog can be contacted rudely or possibly attacked. Though there are usually other failures in leadership that added to the dog's anxiety that he was unprotected, teaching handlers to make this simple gesture has brought many a worried dog much needed relief and a feeling of security.

Trust within a relationship is built on the belief that our behavior will be noticed and responded to, if not necessarily always fully understood. In my experience, dogs whose owners recognize, acknowledge and act on early signs of discomfort have deep trust in their owners' ability to protect them in almost any situation. To my way of thinking, a critical part of the relationships I have with my animals and anyone I love is this promise: "I will protect you." And to the best of my abilities, I do not violate this promise in any way. To keep that promise, I must be vigilant and willing to step into harm's way on their behalf. Not merely when the people and other dogs around me are cooperative and polite. Not when it's convenient or pleasant for me to do so. To be a dog's protector, to champion his rights at all times even when it means stepping up and speaking out on his behalf, this is a true gift of loving leadership.

KNOCK IT OFF—NOW!

Another aspect of proactive intervention involves defusing of potential conflicts. Leadership requires that we remain alert to the interactions between other family members and, if we deem it necessary, end run a brewing confrontation. My mother had a particularly keen eye for how her four children could find ways to irritate each other, and if she saw a brawl taking shape, she would intervene in various ways. At times, she simply redirected us, setting us to tasks that would occupy our attention and, preferably, remove us from each other's company for a while. At other times, lacking any way to distract us, she would resort to clear warnings: "Knock it off. Right now."

In the same fashion, our role as our dogs' leader requires us to be alert to possible conflicts, reading the subtle gestures that flash from dog to dog. As pack leader, my dog Vali was remarkably skilled at assessing whether two dogs might be having a grumbly but civil discussion and when a more serious argument was taking shape. From her preferred perch on the couch, I could see her look up and watch the dogs in question. Sometimes, she just sighed and looked away, and at those times, the squabbling dogs would resolve the problem without needing intervention—a sharp bark or unhappy grumble, and it was over. At other times, however, she saw something else, and would get up from the couch and walk directly to the would-be combatants, placing herself directly in between the two dogs. She would stand quietly, turning her head first to one and then the other, and wait until each had gone their separate way. Crisis averted, she'd return to the couch and her nap.

As dogs do with other dogs, human leaders of dogs need to learn to read the subtle signs that point to problems that are brewing, and step in proactively. This can be tiring, as it requires a great deal of attention, particularly when the potential for conflict is high: unknown dogs being mixed together for the first time, the excitement of a class or show situation, new additions to an established group, the presence of high-value resources (toys, bones, food, attention), when visitors arrive, etc. In stable groups, the degree of attention required is minimal, with more attention (and intervention if necessary) brought to bear only at the moments where potential conflict arises. By and large, dogs are a peaceful bunch who would much rather party than parry, but prevention is always better than cure. Recognizing the moments where excitement or emotions may run a bit higher or hotter than usual, the wise leader helps maintain peace by setting the tone.

Those dealing with multiple-dog households have a bit more on their plate, especially since our very human tendency is to want to place blame on one dog or feel sorry for the (perceived) underdog. Since we often do not read the relative status of the two dogs or the situation correctly (usually because we're not seeing it from the canine point of view), it's often best to take the approach that wise human mothers take: Neither party to the conflict is upheld, but both participants are reminded to behave themselves. As my mother often said, "I don't care who started it. Both of you go to your room." Sometimes, I just tell the dogs involved to knock it off, and they will cease their squabbling without any other intervention. At other times, I might need to underline my message by telling both dogs to lie down and stay for a few minutes, a technique that also allows them to calm down.

Sometimes, one dog simply won't let it go, or both are unwilling to back down. Or mysteriously, dogs will enter that strange war zone where the conflicts between the combatants are unfathomable to a nonparticipant but recognized by parents the world over by the classic wail arising from the backseat: "Mom—she's looking at me like that again!" What the particular look may be and what response it's exciting in the victim are far beyond any mortal adult's comprehension. But to the two children involved, this is more than just a way to pass time on long car rides—it's a genuine conflict. Dogs have similar conflicts, though they are rarely triggered by boring road trips (during which dogs usually have enough sense to just sleep or stick their heads out the window). Watch for eye contact—even across a very long distance—as a possible trigger for the doggy version of teenagers on a school bus making faces at passing cars. Bored dogs sometimes entertain themselves by playing head games using nothing more than eye contact to get a rise out of other dogs. Dogs who do this have the same unerring instinct as kids who play this game, and they are able to choose their victims with great success. They do not pick on confident, assured dogs or people. Instead, they target the unsure, the immature or the downright frightened, and are thus guaranteed of a fascinating response. Countless owners have found themselves terribly surprised when their dog erupts in a barking or snarling frenzy toward another dog who, as is often said, "didn't do anything but look at him!" The opposite is also true—it is possible to find yourself shocked when your dog is the target of another dog's seemingly inexplicable annoyance. As a rule of thumb, unless engaged in a game or posing a challenge, dogs don't maintain eye contact with each other. Appropriate leadership includes watching what our dogs are watching and making sure that rude staring contests are not going on, just as responsible parents would not allow their children to engage in such foolishly rude behavior.

It always cracks me up when people visit and watch the interactions between my dogs. They seem to think we're living on the set of a nature documentary and that I've been given a copy of the script. And if things heat up to a mild grumble, the questions fly hot and fast: "Why did they do that? What does that mean? Why is he growling at her?" They're shocked when I sometimes answer that I have no idea what the hell the dogs are saying to each other. Though it's nice to have an understanding of what caused the problem, sometimes we just have to accept "Mom, she's looking at me like that again!" Like the wise parent who then blindfolds the kids or leaves the troublemaker at the next rest stop, we need to just trust the conflict is real though mysterious and deal with the participants appropriately. A mom routine is usually appropriate—I'll escort both dogs to their crates or separate them for a brief time-out.

Our dogs rely on our leadership to provide them with protection. Maintaining an awareness of what is happening around and to a loved one is a tremendous gift of our attention. All of us long for a living, breathing guardian angel who watches out for us. This is something dogs have traditionally offered mankind; it seems only fair to reciprocate with loving, protective awareness of our own, at least for the dog at our side.

KEEPING THE COVENANT

We may be very uncomfortable with the concepts of power, status and leadership within the context of our relationships with our dogs. And yet, no matter how unwilling we may be to think in such terms, it does not alter the reality that dogs perceive their world in these terms. If we fail to give full weight to the importance of benevolent, reliable and evenhanded leadership in a dog's life, we will fail our dogs. If we cannot come to grips with our own emotional responses to issues of power, our dogs will have to deal with the uncertainty and anxiety that many dogs experience when they lack appropriate leadership.

Facing inconsistent or ineffective leadership, dogs will not interpret this as a momentary lapse or as the actions of a stressed human trying to fulfill far too many roles. Dogs will not understand that our inability to sort out our own feelings may be blocking us from acting as they need us to act. What dogs believe when faced with inadequate or shifting leadership is that change is in the wind. Should a leader grow old, incompetent, weak or be disabled in some way, the natural progression of canine society is for the role of leadership to be filled by someone more qualified and willing to take on the job. Someone must be in charge, preferably someone strong and sure and competent, and shifts in the behavior of a group's leader point to the potential need for some other member of the group to step up and take over that position of authority. Our behavior—whether we intend it to be or not—may serve as a marker that the pack's hierarchy is up for review and restructuring: "Seeking qualified leader for small, intimate pack. Benevolent management skills a must."

This uncertainty about who is in charge can make dogs quite anxious, as any of us are in the face of uncertain but impending changes. And it can also make dogs behave in interesting (though often disconcerting, puzzling or even frightening) ways as they attempt to redefine their world and how their position in it may be shifting. A shake-up in the structure of the dog's family group is no less disconcerting and upsetting to a dog than an equivalent change is for us within our human families and groups. Following the death of our longtime pack leader, our dogs had to recast the pack order among themselves. Though the steadiness of what John and I were able to provide in terms of leadership helped ease their stress, the old dog's death left a hole in more than just our hearts—she left a gap that required the dogs to reestablish their status relative to each other.

We need not be heavy-handed dictators or anxious bureaucrats who feel the need to enforce every subsection of every rule and regulation. We do need to ask our dogs if perhaps they need more from us, or if they need us to offer guidance with a lighter hand or with a crisper style.

How do we ask them? We watch how it is they go through their days, noting where it is we feel that we cannot control or direct them, when it is that they ignore us or threaten us, or how it is that we accommodate them in order to prevent a confrontation or "trouble." If we can honestly assess where freedom and joy are limited by a dog's behavior, where our relationship feels strained, then we have identified the areas that need work. In trying to provide leadership for our dogs, we may need to undertake an internal journey to examine our own feelings about the issues of power and status, finding the balance that uniquely exists between one person and one dog.

We may stuff our heads with theoretical understanding, but our dogs will remain unimpressed by anything but action. And without fail, lest our dogs pay for our failures with their lives, we must act. Love, after all, is an action, not a feeling, and leadership must spring from loving guidance. The German philosopher Goethe summed it up beautifully: "Knowing is not enough; we must apply. Willing is not enough; we must do."

From moment to moment, in even the smallest of our actions, our dogs will read the answers to their lifelong questions: "Who's in charge? What are the rules? Where do I fit in?" In each moment, we offer our answers. If our heads are filled with notions of alpha wolves and rules, if we are shying away from our own feelings about authority and status and leadership, we may miss the many beautiful and gentle ways that we can answer our dogs with what they want and need to hear from us.

15

MY, WHAT BIG TEETH YOU HAVE!

Fear makes the wolf bigger than he is.
GERMAN PROVERB

WHEN LITTLE RED RIDING HOOD NOTICES that Grandmother has eyes much larger than remembered, her concern is quickly assuaged with a smooth assurance that it's simply "all the better to see you, my dear!" Puzzled by Grandmother's unusually large, oddly shaped ears, the dim-witted child is convinced with a smiling explanation—"All the better to hear you, my dear." But even dear, dull-minded Red can't help but notice the fangs, the collection of dental stalagmites and stalactites gleaming white and sharp, and at that moment she comes to understand that maybe the hairs on Grandma's chin aren't just personal hygiene choices. Something is very wrong, and while little Miss Hood is slow enough on the uptake to qualify as fit prey for any alert predator, even she knows that fangs usually don't spell fun.

Within the context of the dog/human relationship, aggression is a topic that brings to mind J. R. R. Tolkien's wise advice: "It does not do to leave a live dragon out of your calculations if you live near him." The dragon, in this case, is not the possibility that our dogs may rise up against us in violent ways without warning or cause. Though the dog's potential for aggression is very real and to be respected, normal, healthy dogs do not suddenly go berserk or "turn on their owners" or act aggressively without reason. Instead, the dragon lurks in the form of our lack of understanding.

Many aspects of our relationships with our dogs parallel our human relationships or are so similar that in many situations we might safely cross out the word *dog* and substitute *child*, *lover* or *friend* and still be appropriately guided as to what a loving action or response might be. When a dog snarls or growls or snaps or bites, we find ourselves in a strange land where we are not quite sure how to move safely. Quite sensibly, we may find ourselves afraid in the presence of throaty grumbles and bared teeth. Whether this is an archetypal response to a predatory threat or just a commonsense desire to keep our skin intact, it doesn't change the fact that few of us look upon a growling or biting dog with equanimity.

Our lack of understanding about what lies behind our dogs' growls, snarls, snaps and bites can create very serious problems within our relationships with our dogs. Where understanding is absent or incomplete, fear slides in to fill the gaps between what we know, and we live in an uncomfortable place where we cannot distinguish threat from invitation. Unable to understand the behaviors that may frighten, threaten and possibly hurt us, we remain unable to understand the dog himself. The dog unfortunately bears the brunt of our misunderstanding and fear; when in doubt, we tend to assume the worst. At the very least, we may find ourselves bewildered and frightened by a dog's aggressive behavior, and confused as to how best to respond. Frustrated, we may end up simply managing the unwanted behavior instead of working toward a resolution. At the other end of the spectrum, a dog may end up dead, his epitaph simply—and quite possibly inaccurately—just this: "He was aggressive."

The ancient Celtic tale of the dog Gelert is one that bears repeating. A knight's hunting hound, Gelert, was prized for his skill as a ruthless killer of wolves, yet also a faithful and kind companion to the knight and his family. The story tells of the wolf who has crept into the child's room, and the fierce battle between the loyal hound and the wolf. In their struggle, the baby's cradle is overturned, the child unhurt but hidden under the bedding. Wolf and dog lock in mortal combat, and blood flows freely. At last, in a dim corner of the room, the hound manages to kill the wolf. Hearing the sounds of a struggle, guards and the child's nurse rush in to find Gelert standing alone in the middle of the room, covered in blood. Surveying the scene, not noticing the dead wolf's body hidden in the shadows, not looking beneath the bedclothes of the toppled cradle, all present leap to the conclusion that Gelert has killed and eaten the child. Stunned and furious, the grieving knight orders that the dog be killed on the spot. It is only after the dog is dead that the child is discovered alive and well. The wolf's body bears grim testament to the loyalty of the dog and the fears and faithlessness of men.

Aggression is a heavily loaded word, conjuring up various images depending upon the mind of the speaker and of the listener, and it is not particularly descriptive or informative. Labeling a behavior as simply "aggressive" tells us nothing about the situation and the motivation behind the behavior. "That dog is aggressive" might mean that given the opportunity, he would rip your throat out. It might as easily mean that the dog growls when someone tries to clip his nails, or barks wildly at other dogs on the street, or fiercely defends a car from threats such as people walking past with shopping carts, or that he has killed a squirrel, or that he has bitten someone breaking into his house. These and other behaviors are often labeled as aggressive, but they are not all the same, nor should they be handled in the same way.

So, why do dogs act aggressively? No matter how fearsome we may find their behavior, we can find some relief in the knowledge that dogs act aggressively for the same basic reasons we do: fear, pain, irritation, anger, protection of territory (in humans, this is known as war), protection of family (usually puppies are being guarded, though bitches experiencing false pregnancy may protect completely imaginary or substitute puppies, such as toys; dogs can and do protect other family members of whatever species), self defense, protection of possessions and resources, sexual conflict, social status, hunger. And like humans, dogs can act aggressively in abnormal ways due to biochemical imbalances, various diseases, genetic defects, psychological and/or physical abuse, drugs or chemicals, and for reasons science cannot explain. Like their human counterparts, such abnormal dogs are rare but can be extremely dangerous.

Having already established that dogs act as they do for a reason (whether a good reason or not, whether the reason is one we can understand or even vaguely apprehend), it's safe to say that any behavior we might care to tar with the broad brush of "aggression" has a reason behind it. In cases of aggressive human behavior, the situation in which the crime is committed along with the motivation or intent behind the criminal act all are weighed in society's final determination of just how serious a particular act may be. (Keep in mind that in human society self-defense is a justifiable motivation for something as terrible as murder.) As with all behavior, the context in which the behavior occurs is critically important to our understanding of what prompted the growl, snap or snarl. If we are unable to place the "aggression" within its proper context, we will undoubtedly view it from just one perspective—ours, and from that limited and often fearful perspective, we will undoubtedly be wrong.

At the root of all aggressive behavior (*not* predatory behavior) is this simple truth: There is a problem, a conflict on some level—physical, mental or emotional. If we can keep that uppermost in our minds when dealing with aggression issues, then we pull away the mystical shroud of aggression as something only experts can understand. Though expert help may be needed to resolve an aggression issue, all of us are capable of imaginatively projecting ourselves into the dog's point of view and perhaps understanding how he might be perceiving a conflict. Whether that conflict or problem is crystal clear to you is another story, but as previously discussed, dogs can be counted on to tell you their truth at the moment. If a dog is acting in any way that seems aggressive, he has a reason. Normal, healthy dogs don't tend to go tilting at windmills or fighting nonexistent battles. Not even Boxers shadowbox. Illness, pain, biochemical disorders, seizure disorders and disease can make dogs act aggressively in abnormal ways. (The first step in dealing with any aggressive behavior is a thorough physical examination to rule out these possible causes. Yet even in such cases, the aggressive behavior is an important message that something is wrong.)

THAT KIND OF DOG

When dealing with aggression in any form, we need to tread carefully, alert for the stumbling blocks of our own (often false) assumptions. If we truly seek to understand a dog's behavior, then we cannot ever forget that all dogs are dogs. To the extent that we have a sanitized view of our dogs, we will inevitably be shocked, horrified and gravely disappointed by our dogs when they act in doglike ways. I've met many bewildered dog owners who told me, "I couldn't believe Duke could (choose one or more: bark, growl, snarl, snap, bite, attack, kill)! I didn't think he was that kind of dog." I'm not sure just what "that kind of dog" might be. *All* dogs are the same kind of dogs—dogs who can bark, growl, snarl, snap and bite.

Every dog—regardless of parentage, pedigree or personality—possesses the full repertoire of normal canine behavior. I've never met a dog incapable of growling, barking, snarling, snapping or biting. *These are all normal dog behaviors*, and an integral part of canine communications. (Ironically, these same behaviors serve to prevent serious violence between dogs!) The difference from dog to dog has to do with the dog's individual personality, his social experience, his genetics, his upbringing, his health, sex, age, diet and the situation. The only difference between individual dogs and the larger groups of individual breeds is the readiness with which various behaviors can be triggered and the extent to which a dog will carry his aggression. Dogs created to guard may be more quickly triggered to act in aggressive ways than dogs bred to work as bird dogs or as ladies' companions. But this does not guarantee that guarding or working breeds will bite or that lapdogs and retrievers won't. A familiar parallel can be found in our understanding that men are most likely to act violently, though women are certainly equally capable of the same behavior. And while adults are more likely to be dangerous than are children, the truth remains that children are capable of dangerous—even deadly—behavior. To point to any individual dog or breed or group of breeds and make assumptions is about as helpful to your relationship with a dog as an evaluation of violent domestic crime statistics will be to your marriage.

Folks who've bought the whitewash job that certain dogs or breeds are nonaggressive are invariably shocked when their dog, who did not read the propaganda, acts in a way that proves that Aunt Tilly's lapdog is as capable of snarls, snaps, growls and bites as a street dog in the Bronx. Konrad Lorenz wrote of looking out his window onto a grisly scene of bloodied snow where two dogs had caught a deer and savagely torn it apart. He turns and looks at his four-year-old granddaughter asleep before the fireplace, peacefully snuggled up with his large dogs—the same two dogs who had killed the deer. A dog is a dog is a dog.

We want to believe in the Lassie myth, to focus only on the dog's gentle, forgiving, loving nature. Of all the rocks on which we may stub our emotional toes, this is a big one. We do not want to think that the dog lying at our feet is a predator and a powerful one at that. It may be that we'd prefer that the people and animals we love most dearly have no dark, ugly side; we idealize them with this simple "Oh, he'd never do that!" or "She's just not that kind of person." In any relationship, such sanitized, idealized views of another being does not lead to deeper understanding or a more intense connection but to the inevitable disappointment that occurs when we are unable to embrace both the potential for both light and the dark contained in all of us. This is not to say that all dogs will sooner or later act in aggressive ways, no more than all humans will eventually harm another person. The dark potential that lurks within each of us needs to be recognized, and our relationships shaped to encourage the joyful lightness of being, not trigger the ugly possibilities.

Poisonous Puppies

Myths and misconceptions about dogs and their capacity for violence are widespread, and some contain a grain of truth at best but, like most tales of terror, are created from a lack of understanding that leads to fear. I was once carrying a ten-week-old German Shepherd puppy through a crowded flea market. Very tired after a busy morning of meeting people and taking in the sights, he was glad to lie in my arms as we made our way back to the car. A man approached, and in response, the puppy's tail wagged madly against me. "Is he friendly?" he asked, and assured that the puppy was, he reached out to pet him. The tuckered-out puppy mustered enough strength to lean toward the man and cover his face with kisses while the man told me about his own dogs and how much he loved them. "What kind of dog is this, anyhow?" he inquired between sweet coos directed at the pup. Informed it was a baby German Shepherd, he reared back as if the puppy had become a cobra. "Whoa! They're venomous when they grow up, aren't they?"

Though admittedly I'd never heard anyone label a dog venomous before or since my flea market encounter, I've heard many other variations on the theme. As *everyone* knows, some dogs eventually grow up and turn on their owners. According to popular wisdom, some breeds are inherently vicious; others are baby killers. These and other falsehoods do not serve dogs or us well; when they lurk in the back of our thoughts, it takes only a spark of misunderstanding for our fears to catch fire. While nearly everyone you meet can tell you tales of biting dogs and deadly attacks, the truth is that as a species, dogs do amazingly well in trying to live with humans. In fact, they do a better job of peacefully living with humans than humans do.

To be quite fair, when we look at the subject of aggressive behavior in our dogs, we ought to consider our own behavior. In his seminars, veterinarian and dog behavior expert Dr. Ian Dunbar leads the audience through a simple exercise designed to increase their appreciation for the degree of "aggression" that is present in our human society. He first asks how many audience members have ever been angry or had an argument with someone; naturally, all hands are raised. He asks how many have ever been angry enough to raise their voice or even yell at another human (the equivalent of a dog growling or barking)—again, all hands go up. How many have ever gotten so angry that they have physically contacted another person in anger? A few less hands go up. Finally, Dunbar asks who has ever seriously hurt another person, sending them to the hospital. No hands go up. His point, of course, is that obviously humans are argumentative, and there's a fair degree of "aggressive" behavior among the average group of human beings. And yet, only rarely does that "aggression" escalate beyond clear expression of anger, fear, irritation or the defense of property or self. Damaging attacks on others and murder are, fortunately, quite rare—even among humans. The same is true of dogs. Just as human society has rules and taboos that prevent us from seriously injuring or killing each other, thus enabling us to live in relative peace, our dogs also have normal inhibitions of aggression.

With the exception of rare individuals and the breeds specifically bred for fighting, the average dog doesn't enjoy arguments or altercations or fisticuffs any more than the average human being does. Being angry, defensive or afraid are not pleasant states of being for dog or man; dogs are wise enough to try to avoid or quickly resolve encounters and situations that create these uncomfortable feelings as much as possible, though the same cannot always be said of humans. While capable of "murder," dogs rarely fully employ their considerable aggressive potential and, like us, restrain and inhibit their actions so that communication is clear with a minimum of damage (if any).

To put the matter into the proper perspective, Dr. Dunbar points out in his 1998 video, *Dog Aggression: Biting*, that more children are killed each year by their parents than by dogs. Dunbar offers these upsetting statistics: In the United States, roughly two thousand children die every year at the hands of their own parents, but less than a dozen are killed by dogs. And yet people don't look at children and whisper, "Be careful. Parents can turn on you." (Perhaps they should.) Thousands of children are severely injured or killed in automobile crashes each year, and yet, as Dr. Dunbar notes, we don't ban Fords or Hondas or any other vehicle.

While dog bites and attacks are a serious problem that should not be ignored, our sometimes knee-jerk reactions to any behavior that we think even smacks faintly of aggression reveals a terrible lack of knowledge about dogs and aggressive behavior. History teaches us that what we fear and do not understand does not fare well at the hands of man. Dogs are no exception.

What Is Aggression?

What constitutes aggression? Operating strictly from the viewpoint of the dog/human relationship, the easiest definition of aggression is probably this: Behavior that threatens, alarms or actually harms us. While the academics and behaviorists who just fainted are being revived, let's think about this. I'm perfectly well aware that my definition of what constitutes aggression may be highly unsatisfactory to behaviorists and trainers. But it seems to me that working from within the only context in which behavior will be interpreted—that of a relationship—defining aggression as any behavior that threatens, alarms or harms another is fair. Feeling threatened or scared is hardly conducive to intimacy.

We need to allow for the possibility (on both sides) that an innocent behavior could be misinterpreted and though not meant to, still have the result of being threatening or frightening. Some of this has to do with the differences between dogs and people—direct eye contact is considered a challenge dog to dog, but a sign of interest and attentiveness in the Western world. (In other human cultures, however, direct eye contact is considered rude.) On an individual basis, any gesture may be misinterpreted depending on the individual's experience (or lack of). For example, a person leaning over to greet a dog may seem a kind, nonaggressive behavior to us, though from a fearful dog's point of view this well-intentioned gesture could be interpreted as a terrifying threat. Equally so, dogs find themselves bewildered by our frightened or angry responses to their behaviors that were not meant to threaten or scare us, such as dogs growling in play or rumbling with nearly inexpressible pleasure or even the delightful "smile" which to the naïve eye may appear as a fearsome snarl. One of our friends has taken literally years to understand that if one of our dogs lying near her offers a warning growl to another dog, the growl is not meant for her, though never once in all these years have any of our animals threatened her in any way.

Lumped under the general umbrella term of *aggression* is a very wide range of behaviors, from confident threats of bodily harm to fearful reactions meant to create an opening for escape and/or to scare off whatever is scaring the dog. But among the general dog-owning public, "aggression" usually consists of these basic elements: barking, growling, snarling, snapping, lunging toward a person or other animal, biting and any combination or variation of the above. Unfortunately for dogs, these same behaviors can also be used in nonaggressive behavior, though our poor grasp of canine language often leaves us unable to make the necessary distinctions.

Social animals ourselves, we know that disagreements, dislikes and even noisy but relative harmless fighting are part of life, though not necessarily enjoyable, productive or desirable. With sufficient experience and knowledge, we are able to place the behavior of other people in its proper context and perspective. A person who raises her voice in anger or slams a door in pure frustration during an argument is not assumed to be on a nonstop course to committing murder. And yet, a dog who growls at his owners may be considered just a step away from "turning on them." A dog who engages in a noisy squabble with other dogs is often described as "trying to kill them." Somehow, we've gotten it into our minds that there is an inexorable progression from a low growl to full-blown canine murder.

Because we may fearfully assume that a growl inevitably progresses to a bite, and bites may progress to a fatal attack (an especially common fear when the aggressive behavior is directed at another dog), we are quick to react to *anything* we perceive as aggression. Unable to distinguish a grumble of annoyance from a serious threat, we simply attempt to quash *all* behaviors we find upsetting, regardless of the cause, regardless of the value these communications have for us and for other animals. In doing this, we not only block ourselves from understanding and from improving our relationships with our dogs, but we also set unreasonable expectations for our dogs' behavior. I've known people who truly expected that their dogs never growl, that their dogs never have arguments, that their dogs like and happily get along with every other dog and person they meet—in other words, somehow get through life in ways a saint would be hard-pressed to match. Who among us could even begin to meet such expectations? I'd fail within an hour flat some days.

Under the broad category of aggression are many behaviors. The key word here is *behavior,* which is communication. Whether a dog is wagging his tail or biting your arm, he's communicating. We're just not always thrilled to be on the receiving end of the less-pleasant communications dogs might send our way. Appreciating growls, snaps or even bites as meaningful communication requires a willingness to recognize and deal with the fear that quite naturally arises within us. Our fear in the face of a dog's aggressive behavior may be disguised as anger—"How dare you!" or "You're not going to get away with that!" Left unrecognized and unresolved, our fear can provoke us to react to the dog's behavior in ways that may not be best for the dog, ourselves and the relationship. If we interpret a dog's aggressive communication as a challenge to our authority and we don't understand that our own fear is what drives that response, we may feel quite justified in responding with what amounts to aggression of our own. If you're interested in proving to your dog that you're bigger and tougher than he is, an aggressive response of your own may be the way to go. If you're interested in a trusting relationship, you need to understand aggression in any form for what it is: a meaningful and very important communication.

READ MY LIPS

Recently, a trainer was demonstrating for me just how "aggressive" a small dog was. While the dog was looking away, she stepped up and, hovering over him like his personal weather front, tapped him lightly on the butt. With great slow deliberation, the dog turned his head to look up at her, his head still, eyes hard and fixed on her face. She tapped again, and the dog laid one ear back, slitted his eyes a bit and slightly wrinkled the lip nearest the trainer. She tapped again, and this time the dog growled softly and more dramatically lifted his lip so that the bottom tip of his teeth could be seen. "See what I mean?" she asked. When I asked her why she had ignored the first two warnings that the dog had kindly given her before actually escalating to a growl and a show of teeth, she looked at me blankly. She had quite literally seen nothing from the dog in the way of warning until his teeth were visible; through her own lack of awareness, she forced the dog to make his meaning very clear.

To the best of their ability, normal dogs actually try to minimize aggression in their lives, using eloquent, subtle communications that escalate only as necessary to make their point. Just like humans, dogs communicate their feelings in a progressive way, starting with subtle signs of fear, anger, pain or irritation and slowly escalating the communication to the point where it is heeded or a confrontation is inevitable.

Beyond these obvious gestures, there is an entire world of more subtle gestures that dogs use to indicate their state of mind. In a normal, healthy dog, the first sign that something's gone awry is not a full-blown attack. Instead the dog uses other ways to communicate—body posture, speed and direction of head and eye movements, the position of ears and tail and even the whiskers. Tiny alterations in breathing, the expression of the eyes, or even the angle of the dog's head can communicate volumes to another dog or to a human who is paying attention and understands what it is being said.

"Ah, how mysterious this all is," we may think, and despair of ever being able to understand what our dogs are telling us. But if we do that, we are forgetting that we've learned to read precisely such subtleties in the people around us: A mere glance from an annoyed mother is sometimes sufficient to silence a child; a look held just a fraction too long may signal a flirtation; a mere tightening of the lips or jaw warns us of irritation in another. Learning to read a dog's warning signals requires practice and an awareness of the early, less-obvious signs that a dog is moving out of a relaxed and balanced state of being.

Normal, healthy dogs follow proper canine protocol of progressive communications, which may also be looked at as warnings. Since dogs act aggressively only in response to a perceived conflict, the aggressive behaviors we observe are warnings that the dog is feeling pressured in some way. Oblivious to multiple and (from the dog's point of view) fair warnings, we may blunder along until at last the dog finds the level of communication that gets our attention. Though meant to warn us, these subtle gestures are not always effective signals due to the rather poor reception on our mental TV sets. Since we've not seen or have disregarded the many warnings that preceded the growl or the snap or the bite, we're shocked; questioned, we report, "All of sudden, he just went nuts." If the dog could be interviewed, his version would be quite different: "I warned her and I warned her and then I warned her some more. Finally, I did what I had to do to get through to her."

Let's look at a human parallel for a moment. You're standing in line at the movie theater, aware of the people around you but happily anticipating the showing of the classic *Old Yeller*. The line moves forward a few feet, and as it comes to a halt once again, you realize that the person standing behind you is standing too close for your comfort. You step slightly away from him, using the crowded space as best you can. To your annoyance, you realize that the person is still close behind you. Throwing an irritated glance over your shoulder, you huff quietly but audibly. (Both behaviors are subtle but meaningful and unmistakable expressions of irritation.) Suddenly, there's hot breath on your neck— the fool is actually leaning forward to make contact with you. With slitted eyes and an icy demeanor, you turn and say with a slow, deliberate growl, "Leave me alone." (Again, your combined body posture and vocalizations clearly delineate your growing annoyance.) For a second, you think about stepping out of line and moving away, but this thought irritates you further—you've been waiting in line for half an hour, you want to see the movie and you are not about to give it up because of some idiot with no manners. When two hands slide around your waist and pull you into a tight embrace, you're indignant and alarmed. Pulling away, you raise your voice: "Leave me alone!" (Your struggle and protest are very clear communications.) To your shock, the person pays no attention to your outburst or your struggles but holds you even tighter. Furious, you twist around and slap him hard. Surprised, he lets go of you and staring at you in wounded amazement asks, "What did you do that for?"

A greater intensity of connection is possible when we understand the other's warning signals. If we can't understand when we are being warned, then we cannot make choices about our own behavior, or work to shift the underlying problems that necessitated a warning. A friend's slowly tightening jaw tells us that we may be treading on delicate ground, but if we do not notice or understand it as a warning signal, we may blunder along until at last she's truly upset and screaming at us. In a healthy relationship, such warnings *do not* mean that we veer off never to return to the subject or situation that prompted such a warning; avoiding problems never serves to deepen intimacy and trust. A gentle, loving and compassionate approach to sensitive or troublesome issues can turn a potential conflict into an opportunity for growth, increased trust and a deeper relationship. A friend's tight jaw points to a problem that needs to be addressed; heeding her warning signal allows us to carefully, lovingly and respectfully find a way back to the issue in another way or at another time so that we can further explore what may be wrong.

Complicating matters for both dogs and humans is this little twist: Dogs vary considerably in their warning signals. More precisely, dogs, regardless of breed, use the same basic signals in their communications. A dog from Outer Mongolia could speak to and understand a dog from Brooklyn without too much difficulty. (Dogs never will need the UN, which is probably a good thing for all involved. The Dachshunds might not support a peacekeeping action in a Boxer rebellion.) The *speed* of the warning signals and the *progression* from mild irritation to more serious phrases can vary greatly, just as some humans have a very long fuse and some are grenades with the pin pulled. Some dogs are as slow and deliberate in their communication style as a senator bent on a filibuster; other dogs are more volatile, shifting from vaguely annoyed to really ticked off in just a few seconds. I've known dogs who sent long, involved telegrams of warning, even lengthy volumes, as if Tolstoy had come back as a dog and was working out *War and Peace* in a new language. I've also known dogs whose warning signals might be aptly characterized as canine haiku, dense with meaning and very brief.

For a lovely time, I shared my life with the usual complement of German Shepherds as well as a Labrador mix, a Shetland Sheepdog and a Scottish Deerhound. Consequently, the puppies born in those years learned all kinds of accents even before leaving home. This was not an entirely painless process. Apparently, Deerhounds speak with a particularly spare voice true to their Scottish heritage, wasting no words as it were. German Shepherds, on the other hand, like to spin long, drawn-out Gothic tales full of dire warnings meant to impress puppies (or maybe just bore them) with the importance of respecting your elders. A dramatic people, Shepherds employ a considerable range of vocalizations and facial expressions, ranging from "the Look" to a full, snarling, teeth-bared warning that if ignored, results in nothing more than snapping in the puppy's direction. The puppies—roughly six weeks old—were merrily toddling around the house, learning good manners (i.e., annoying everyone) and being tolerated with good grace. Fred, the Deerhound, had wisely retreated to a couch to lie watching the merriment from a puppy-free zone. One bright little chap decided that if being up there was good enough for Uncle Fred, by golly it was good enough for him. Getting his front paws on the cushion's edge, he began his struggle to climb up and join his big pal. Seeing this, Fred drew himself up so that he was sitting and leaning against the back cushions, all feet well out of the puppy's reach. But persistence pays, and the puppy, delighted with his success, wriggled over to share his joy.

Accustomed to his German relatives' long-winded speeches, the puppy did not notice the first sign of Fred's irritation: a quiet glare directed down his long, mustached nose at the beast frolicking at his feet. He also missed the next warning sign: one eyebrow (the one nearest the puppy) was raised. Unfortunately, he didn't notice the final warning: both eyebrows raised and "the Look." Since this appeared to be a rather dim-witted pup, Fred made his annoyance crystal clear by leaning down and roaring at the pup though touching him with nothing more than hot breath. Tumbling off the couch, the puppy began screaming as if invisible hands were pulling his intestines out through his nostrils one inch at a time. The other dogs didn't even bat an eye, and the puppy's mother simply glanced up as if to check that he was not being carried off by an eagle or something that required her intervention. Since puppies learn by doing, each of that litter had to learn firsthand just how quietly Uncle Fred muttered, "Go away, you little pest." Eventually, all puppies left for their new homes, wiser and fluent in both in their native tongue, Sturm and Drang, and the elegant but rather spare Hound.

I do not think dogs understand that we are often completely *unaware* of the more subtle signs. After all, they are using what they know to be very clear language, their native tongue, and the only one they know. The dogs are operating under the assumption that we *do* see and understand these signals, just as we speak with the assumption that we are heard (an assumption that can be proven false if we are dealing with someone who is deaf or who speaks another language or is simply not even in the room). In my experience, dogs (like us) may interpret our lack of appropriate response as their communications being heard but *disregarded*. This is a critical distinction. If we believe someone has not heard us or perhaps doesn't understand what we have meant, our reaction is quite different than if we believe they are deliberately disregarding us. Things can get very ugly quickly when we feel disregarded or deliberately ignored instead of simply not heard or misunderstood. Dogs are no different in this respect. Like us, a dog's response varies according to his own personality and experience, the situation and the other person involved. Some dogs patiently try to make their message very, very clear without resorting to even vaguely aggressive behavior; some dogs quickly march up the irritation scale and escalate the communication to one that is heeded. Flashing pearly whites tend to get most folks' attention, and not just because they're a pretty color.

I can only imagine how maddening we humans must be for dogs, masters of nuance and gesture in their communications. I suspect that dogs must view us as rather dim though nice, and I do know that they sometimes take great care to exaggerate their signals to us, just as we talk in slow, exaggerated ways to children or the confused. Regretfully, dogs sometimes learn that their subtle warnings go unheeded but that snarls and snaps get our attention.

AGGRESSION CAN HURT

One of the greatest gifts I ever received from another trainer was the experience of taking a bite from a well-trained dog. "You do not need to fear dogs, but you must always respect how powerful they are," he told me. "You should feel this power for yourself, because you'll never forget it." Setting me in the appropriate position, my left arm protected by a steel-lined, heavily padded sleeve, he brought in one of his Schutzhund dogs. (Schutzhund is a sport that tests the dog's ability to work in three areas: tracking, obedience and protection [or "bitework" as it is casually known]. Correctly done, this sport offers a challenge to test the dog's intelligence, trainability and character.) When the dog saw the sleeve, his eyes grew intense and he began barking in keen anticipation of this game he knew so well and loved. Instructing me to keep the protected left arm foremost toward the dog, the trainer released the dog with a quiet command.

As it does in such moments, time became a wondrous taffy of slow motion, stretching the minutes so that I could see everything clearly. I remember being awed at how effortlessly the dog covered the distance between us in two bounds, his dark eyes intent on the sleeve as if nothing else in the world existed. If I had somehow been beamed aboard a spaceship leaving only the sleeve hanging in midair, I doubt the dog would have noticed. Although I trusted this trainer and knew this was a friendly, stable dog with excellent training, I could not stop the fear that rose in my throat as the dog launched, jaws open and airborne, directly at me.

The pure force of the dog sinking his teeth into the padded sleeve rocked me back and spun me slightly sideways, and then we were locked in a dance eerily symbolic of predator and prey. Unshakable as death, though with a joyful light in his eyes that I pray the Grim Reaper does not possess, the dog hung by his jaws, his hind feet barely touching the ground. Had I been taller than I am, the dog would have been suspended in midair—and that would have made no difference whatsoever to him.

"See if you can get him off your arm," the trainer suggested with the hint of a smile. More than a few times in a life shared with animals, I've been handed vivid reminders that humans are, for all intents and purposes, fairly puny physical beings and that only the workings of a few ounces of gray matter allow us to survive in this world. This was one of those times. I tried my best to shake that dog off that sleeve or even disturb his grip. Years of working in stables had left me quite strong for my size, but not so much as a tooth shifted even though I nearly wrenched my arm out of its socket trying.

As the shock of the impact passed, and the sharp fear that had risen in me subsided, I could see that for the dog, this was a game, a fierce one that was a bit frightening for a new two-legged player, but a game nonetheless. His expression, I noted with interest, was not any different from my own dog's expression when struggling to pull a large branch from the creek or pitting his strength against mine in a game of tug-of-war. There was nothing angry or deadly in this dog's eyes but rather a blissful excitement, a look I have seen in many dogs' eyes when they moved with passion to answer a challenge of their skill. And through it all, I could feel the steel lining of the sleeve being compressed against my flesh like massive surrogate jaws at work on the dog's behalf.

Having made his point about the awesome power of the dog, the trainer gave a command, and instantly the dog released the sleeve. As he trotted toward his handler, the dog threw a wistful, reluctant glance over his shoulder at me, or more accurately at the sleeve. And that was the second most amazing thing I learned that day: that it was possible to work with a dog so that all his power and skill might be directed on behalf of a puny two-legged who despite physical limitations could find a way to crawl inside a dog's mind and turn it to his own purposes. What was possible was both thrilling and sobering.

I do not intend in any way to discount how frightening or dangerous a dog can be. Only a deeply ignorant fool would discount or belittle the dog's capacity for inflicting damage. I've been on the receiving end of bites, heard very deep growls uttered from very big dogs whose lips were just inches from my throat. At age fourteen, I watched helplessly as our family dog tore through my nine-year-old sister's face and bit off half her ear. I have experienced firsthand what a dog is capable of doing. Nor do I intend to offer false assurance to the reader that a dog's growl or snap or bite is simply a communication and "natural" and thus not of any great concern. As discussed later, aggression—like all behavior—is communication, and needs to be understood as such. **Any aggressive behavior is a very serious warning that must be heeded and promptly attended to, using qualified professional assistance as quickly as possible.** The damage that a dog can do in just seconds is staggering—and potentially fatal—and we are fools if we ignore the warnings our dogs give us. Believe the dog when he tells you something is wrong, and move quickly to get help so that you can make things right. Sadly, people find many reasons to avoid addressing a dog's dangerous behavior: embarrassment, denial, shame, anger and a seriously misguided belief that "he'll grow out of it." Promptly heeding the message that something is wrong is an act of loving responsibility in any relationship.

Make no mistake about it: For all the inhibitions and peacekeeping intentions at work in canine culture, dogs are staggeringly powerful and capable of doing serious damage. Understanding this, you need not rush out and trade in the family dog for a fish tank of guppies, but it's worth remembering that Mother Nature armed the dog with a variety of skills and weapons that can be deadly. A full appreciation of what the dog is capable of makes us all the more astounded by and grateful for how rarely they bring their power to bear. It should also make us aware of the tremendous responsibility we have as dog owners.

16

PUT DOWN THE PANCAKES AND NO ONE GETS HURT

Everyone believes very easily whatever they fear or desire.
JEAN DE LA FONTAINE

IF WE DELVE DEEPLY ENOUGH INTO OUR OWN RESPONSE to what we perceive as aggressive behavior, we may be slightly embarrassed to realize that our trust of dogs in general or even of particular dogs we know extends just so far. It halts precisely at the point where our understanding runs out. The less we know, the less we are likely to trust a dog when he is acting in what we consider to be aggressive ways. If we do not know what our dogs' behavior means, we may respond with aggression of our own—because we are afraid. If we are unable to distinguish a playful growl from a warning, a complaint from a threat, we have learned only a small portion of our dogs' language and will inevitably respond inappropriately and in doing so, run the risk of damaging the relationship.

It's Sunday morning, and I'm preparing breakfast for a guest. As always, the kitchen floor is awash in dogs (our only carpets are live ones done in natural colors, like black and tan). I hand the guest her plate of pancakes, urging her to eat while they're still hot. Carson moves to sit politely watching at her side, hopeful that the guest might be abducted by aliens leaving the pancakes ownerless, or at the very least that the guest might offer a starving dog a bite or two. A dog owner herself, the guest is accustomed to eating under close surveillance and fending off potential plate raids, so I don't bother to tell Carson that staring at people while they eat is considered rude in some countries. Other than assuring Carson that the pancakes are indeed delicious, my guest pays the dog no mind *until* she hears a growl and looks down to see Carson curling her lips back in an unmistakable snarl. Though a dog lover, my guest is somewhat intimidated by our small army of German Shepherds. Suddenly finding herself with a growling dog's head aimed at her lap, she freezes, her forkful of pancakes held in midair.

I've heard the growl and, knowing my dogs, don't even bother to turn around. I have no doubt that it's just part of a dog-to-dog communication; the times they've ever directed a growl at a human being were few and far between, and usually in response to threatening behavior directed at me. But I have forgotten that my guest is not as sure of my dogs, so her tremulous "Why is she doing that?" surprises me. (It's easy to forget that not everyone lives amongst a swarm of dogs and listens all day to the conversations and currents of the pack. Dogs do swarm, you know— ask anyone who's visited us.)

As I turn, I'm already mentally assessing the situation's components: Carson, pancakes (Carson's preferred breakfast food), guest (viewed correctly by my dogs as a gullible pushover who might be conned into giving them her whole plate of food), and one or more of the other dogs present. Sure enough, under the table where she cannot be seen by anyone sitting there, Otter has moved in to cover the guest's other flank. Carson's growl and snarl are not, as my guest fears, aimed at her vulnerable thighs but rather across her legs and directed solely at Otter. Her message might be roughly translated as "If there's any pancakes to be had from this sucker, they're mine."

Quickly, I tell both Otter and Carson to go lie down, and I warn Carson that those pancakes are not hers to defend. She looks at me, and for perhaps the thousandth time, I'm glad she cannot speak. I think she might sound too much like a lawyer for my taste—she's got a defense for everything. "Your Honor, I was simply defending my food from another dog, which, as we all know, is a God-given right and a time-honored dog law." Questioned as to the actual ownership of the pancakes, Carson might develop the interesting argument of defense by proxy and note that she was not only protecting her potential future interests in the pancakes, but that she was also acting nobly in assisting the guest in staving off a possible raid by Otter. As Carson throws herself into an exasperated heap, sighing dramatically to underline how unfair she considers the whole situation, the guest begins to breathe again.

What might have happened if I did not have a deep trust in and understanding of my dogs and a good understanding of dog behavior? Carson was doing nothing wrong—she was communicating to Otter, not threatening a guest. Carson's actions were no different from a mother yelling across a guest at a bratty kid threatening to pour ketchup on her sister's head; the person being yelled across certainly understands that the warning or promises of various punishments are not directed at her. Having warned the kid against trying to turn her sibling into one of the Heinz 57, a mother might turn and resume a conversation or sweetly inquire if the guest needed a refill on her coffee. Smiling at the guest, the mother might then turn a split second later back toward the kid and assume a frowning, threatening expression of warning, and then soften her expression as she turned back to the guest. She's not crazy; she's just a mother.

Dogs make such conversational shifts as effortlessly and frequently as we do—it's part and parcel of life as a social species, which sometimes necessitates holding several conversations at the same time or in very rapid succession. We, on the other hand, speak a very slow, stilted form of Dog, so that the mere concept of shifting effortlessly between conversations is beyond us, and—being a somewhat arrogant species—we assume that if it's beyond us, dogs can't do it either. Unfortunately for dogs, our ability to see these normal shifts is either nonexistent or it halts the moment a growl begins so that from that point on we literally don't see what the dog is really doing second by second. Carson, once done with Otter, might have looked up, pure doggy politeness, and wagged her tail at the guest who from Carson's point of view was not included in her conversation with Otter. The guest, stuck in time back at the growl, would be unable to notice and understand Carson's unmistakably friendly expression toward her and her pancakes.

If all I saw was a growling dog snarling at a guest, if I did not trust Carson, if I feared that my dogs might be dangerous, if lurking in the back of my mind was a fear that maybe German Shepherds do turn on people without warning, I might have leaped to the wrong conclusion. I might have felt justified in "correcting" Carson by grabbing and yelling at her, which understandably would have been perceived by her as an unprovoked attack by me. If she were not Carson (a stable, trusting dog) but an unstable dog who did not deeply trust me, she might justifiably respond to my unprovoked attack by growling or even snapping at me in self-defense. And if I did not see *that* as reaction, an understandable act of self-defense, but instead interpreted that as a further threat to me, things could escalate quickly into a pitched battle, hurt feelings if not actual injuries, and my final assessment of Carson as a dangerous dog who had threatened a guest and attacked me. All because Otter hoped to share in whatever pancakes Carson might be able to con out of a guest. Fear seems especially fond of hanging out in vicious circles.

Dogs find themselves in this situation time and again, their absolutely normal, blameless and nonthreatening-to-human behavior wildly misconstrued by the people around them. It must be very confusing for them.

GIVE A DOG A BAD NAME AND . . .

The majority of dogs presented to me and trainers all over the world as "aggressive" are more often simply out of control, responding to inconsistent or inadequate leadership, undersocialized, afraid, misunderstood, in pain or defending themselves against violent acts against them, some disguised as training. This is not to say that such dogs are harmless—a confused, scared, irritated, angry or disrespectful dog can be quite dangerous; the label "aggressive" is neither descriptive of the scope and potential danger of the behavior nor helpful in resolving the problem behavior. Yet even among professional trainers, there is an appalling lack of understanding of the wide range of behaviors that are broadly categorized as aggression. For some dogs, the lack of understanding can prove fatal. Others get lucky.

The puppy, Chelsea, entered the room pulling so hard she looked like a fugitive from the Iditarod. Towed along behind her, the human on the other end of the leash was serving more as a speed-moderating device than a guidance system. Tail and ears up, the puppy eagerly bounced around, unable to stand still for more than a second or two as she looked and sniffed. All signs were that she was simply very excited—and more than a little out of control. Upon spotting me, her body posture and attitude changed dramatically: The dog backed up rapidly and began to bark, her tail dropped and wagging though held low in a classic anxious attitude.

"I suppose you can see the problem," the woman yelled over the din of the dog's barking. I just smiled and asked her to have a seat about ten feet away from where I sat quietly. I didn't see an aggressive dog, only an excited, out-of-control adolescent dog who was also uncertain. While her barking was loud and impressive, there was no serious threat in it— it was fairly high pitched and quick in its repetitions. It was hard to reconcile this dog with the opinions of the owner's previous instructor: that this dog was very dangerous, would eventually bite, and should be euthanized before she hurt someone.

While we sat and talked for a while, gathering some background information, the puppy explored as far as she could on leash, leaping back with a startled woof when she accidentally moved a chair. She retreated to her owner's side to consider the chair with furrowed brow, but when it didn't move again, she decided it was safe to approach it again. I invited the woman to move closer, intending that the dog would be able to reach me if she wanted to. Cautiously, Chelsea approached and sniffed my shoes and legs. Ready for her approach, I opened my hand and let a small chunk of chicken fall to the floor. This pleasantly surprised the puppy, who eagerly ate the unexpected treat and sniffed around for more. As soon as she glanced my way, I let another treat fall and this time, made sure the dog saw my hand open. She ate it and then stood staring at my hand. I ignored her until she touched my hand with her nose, and then opened my palm to reveal several treats. I gave her one and then quietly asked her to sit, which she did, and I rewarded that with soft praise and the remaining chicken. Surprisingly gentle she cleaned my hand and then looked up at me, her eyes bright and interested. We considered each other, and I noted that direct eye contact, at least in this particular moment, did not bother her. Her gaze was steady, alert and relaxed.

Keeping an eye on her, I shifted slightly in my chair to reach the bag of chicken on a table behind me. As I suspected it might, my movement made her back away a few steps, her expression shifting from relaxed to somewhat worried. For a while, we played the simple game of approaching and doing simple things like sit and down in exchange for food, and soon I was able to pet her, tug gently on her collar and run my hands down her back. A touch near her rump made her dance away, neatly placing her hind end well out of my reach; at the same time, she wagged her tail and bumped my hand with her nose—a combination of gestures that I read as, "Please don't touch me there, though I still want to be close to you." Her owner spoke up, noting that she'd forgotten to tell me that Chelsea did not like to have her hindquarters touched by strangers, a detail that did not surprise me. In my experience, dogs who are fearful or anxious often do not want their hindquarters touched. Some, like Chelsea, just move their bodies out of reach; others protect themselves with growls or more. As bodywork therapists and trainers like Linda Tellington-Jones have known for a long time, emotional patterns are often correlated with physical patterns. We do this ourselves, holding the tension created by our emotional states in various places, such as our jaws, our neck and our shoulders. For fearful dogs and horses, it is quite common to see "goosiness" in the hind end. Like the classic chicken-or-the-egg scenario, it's hard to say whether goosiness in the rear helps create the fear or the fear creates the goosiness, but in working with dogs who are fearful, teaching them to feel comfortable with having their hindquarters (in fact, their whole body) handled is an important part of the treatment program.

Far from the original instructor's assessment of aggression caused by "dominance" (which would more accurately describe a very confident dog using aggressive behavior to get her way), what I saw in this puppy's behavior was a lack of confidence. Each time I asked for a little more or touched her in a new place, there was a flash of concern in her eyes and she drew back, though I did not push her to the point where she felt the need to add barking to further warn me. Her barking retreat was also a classic sign of low confidence. But the tasty tidbits quickly helped to convince her that this wasn't so bad after all. I asked the owner to take off the leash and turn the puppy free in the training room.

Chelsea began to cautiously explore the room, sneaking up stealthily on the box of dog toys in one corner. Her behavior was an interesting blend of curious investigation and an occasional fearful retreat when she encountered something strange, like the pile of jumps in one corner. Waiting till her attention was turned elsewhere, I quietly stood up, being sure to arm myself with more chicken. At first, the dog didn't notice this change as she blissfully snuffled along the carpeting, eyes half closed, no doubt reading fascinating sagas of other dogs who had come before her. She was within six feet of me when she realized something had changed. Despite our previously pleasant encounter with me sitting, I was now standing, and that changed everything. Her eyes grew wide, and she began to bark while she backed away to what she considered a safe distance.

"Oh my God!" the worried owner gasped. I knew she was concerned that the dog might attack me. Smiling, I reassured her that everything was fine. And it was. I didn't doubt that if at this moment I were to back the puppy into a corner or try to forcibly restrain her she might feel the need to snap toward me or perhaps even bite, though I suspected she'd simply try to get away. Chelsea wasn't a little killer honing her deadly skills in preparation for an adult career as a canine terrorist. She was simply uncertain and anxious in certain situations, like those that contained strangers and odd items like a moving chair. And as the owner confirmed when I asked, this was Chelsea's pattern of behavior in such situations: bark and retreat. Given her ever-increasing size and the pure volume of her barking, this behavior had worked rather well—at least from the dog's point of view—to resolve scary situations. Approaching people or dogs quickly retreated in the face of such a fierce-sounding display. Backing away as far as possible left the dog feeling a little safer.

But in the long run, this pattern of bark and retreat had not given the dog any skills for dealing with scary situations. Chelsea was not being a bad dog. She was simply using the best solution she had for coping with what she did not understand. Unfortunately, her solution had earned her the label of "aggressive," and was one that without a caring breeder's insistence on a second opinion might have resulted in her death at an early age. As she matured and grew more confident, bark and retreat might still be all she ever did, and it was possible she might never bite a single soul. But to underestimate the potential for serious problems would be to underestimate what happens when a dog feels he is pushed into a situation that can be handled only by fighting or fleeing.

Any situation that creates anxiety, anger, pain or fear in a dog is a situation where a bite might be triggered. The most dangerous dog behaviors are the aggressive behaviors (especially fearful ones) that are managed, but not dealt with and resolved by providing the dog with new skills for coping with the triggering situations. (Actually, within any relationship, the combination of intense emotion—especially fear or anger—and inadequate coping skills for the situation that provokes such feelings is a minefield of potential.) Closed doors, locked gates, carefully controlled environments and even complete agreement of family members to protect the dog or manage the behavior do nothing to defuse a potential time bomb. Accidents happen, dogs get free, people make mistakes. Here in a comfortably sized training room, Chelsea had the room to retreat to a safe distance and still keep me in sight. At home, in the more crowded spaces where walls and furniture might block escape routes or trap an already anxious dog, there might not be—to Chelsea's mind—any option but to snap or bite. At the moment, she also benefited from my desire to keep her feeling safe. In another situation, a well-meaning but uninformed person who simply wanted to greet her or who stumbled toward her might accidentally pressure Chelsea past her ability to cope, and without meaning to, trigger a snap or an actual bite.

Chelsea was not a dog with deep fear, just a dog with a fair amount of insecurity. If Chelsea's alarming behavior had been correctly interpreted as a lack of confidence and handled in ways meant to build her confidence and not simply punish her fear, she might have sailed through without any real problems. The puppy's strong genetic soundness and her early socialization came shining through as I worked to build her confidence. Within a few minutes, she was able to stand in front of me, happily nudging my hand for more food. Knowing that her owner had faithfully done the obedience training at home, I began to put the puppy through her paces, asking her to do everything she knew: sit, down, stand, stay, heeling and coming to sit in front of me. (Nothing like being asked to do what you know how to do to restore confidence to anyone who's feeling anxious: "I know how to do that!") She knew her stuff and was a delightful partner in our work together. As she realized that I would not hurt or frighten her but instead made things very enjoyable, she threw herself into the spirit of the game. Initially, I moved carefully, making all my gestures and movements slow and deliberate. But as Chelsea's confidence and trust in me grew, I moved faster, made my gestures larger and quicker. In less than ten minutes, we were able to romp around the training room like lunatics, whooping and laughing and dancing around, mixing up commands as fast as I could think of them and she could comply. The out-of-control, fearful, retreating puppy was actually a genius who thoroughly enjoyed working with people.

What alarms me in cases like this is not the dog's behavior, but the sad reality that the dog's behavior was badly misunderstood and misread as "aggressive." In Chelsea's case, the lack of understanding from a professional trainer nearly resulted in her death. Only her breeder's insistence that the owner seek a second opinion from another trainer (in this case, me) saved the puppy's life. Unfortunately, this misunderstanding is not uncommon. And it is the dogs who pay with their lives for our failure to understand what they are often trying to tell us in their behavior— that they are uncertain, afraid, lacking the skills they need to share the complicated and confusing human world.

CAN YOU HEAR ME?

A few years ago, I received a letter from a woman who was seeking help with her dog Baron, a very large breed that at maturity weighed 125 pounds or more. From her description, the dog sounded like a pretty normal dog with good socialization and training. Apparently, Baron had been limping, and when she examined his paw and leg, he had growled at her. Shocked, she immediately yelled at him and pushed him to the ground in a "dominant down" to remind him who was the "top dog" before running him through a series of obedience exercises for ten minutes or so (although he was still limping). When she reached for his paw again, he growled before she even touched the foot. Again she yelled at him and threw him to the ground. The third attempt resulted in a short growl that stopped when she yelled at him. Finding nothing, she took Baron to the vet.

When the vet tried to examine the dog's paw, there was no growl before Baron silently grabbed the man's hand, doing no damage, leaving nothing more than spit. Embarrassed and upset by her dog's behavior, the woman repeated the cycle of yelling, dominant down and obedience work. Eventually, after a struggle, the dog was immobilized and his paw was examined. Nothing serious was found, though the dog continued to limp for many days.

In her letter, she stated her deep concern that this dog was potentially aggressive. Although she had embarked on a course of handling the dog's paws many times a day, punishing all growls or mouthing by the dog, Baron was still growling. In her mind, a growl allowed to exist only opened the door for more aggression, and to her way of thinking, the dog's mouthing of the vet's hand proved that she was right to think so. Having sought help from local trainers, she was horrified by the recommendations she had heard, which included putting an electric shock collar on the dog to teach him not to growl when his paw was touched. Her question to me was this: "How do I teach my dog never to growl or put his mouth on me even if he is in pain?"

Every now and then, I get letters that make me very sad; this was one of them. While the woman was without question well meaning, the philosophy that lay at the heart of this dilemma was beyond what I could address in a brief response. If I took away her voice or ability to write, how might she communicate when she was hurting or afraid? What she was asking for was not only unrealistic but unfair—a dog who never, ever communicated with her except in ways she found acceptable.

Unable to see the dog's growl as a communication, the woman ended up fearfully interpreting the growl as a threat and was quite worried that this "aggression" would get worse. Threats (real or perceived) frighten us; in our fear, we often strike back against a perceived attack. Sadly, many "training" techniques are little more than thinly disguised attacks on dogs who have perhaps threatened us in some way, with such justified attacks meant to teach them "respect," which really means meekly submitting to us no matter what we do to them. This approach reminds me of the scene in *The Maltese Falcon* where, for the second time, Humphrey Bogart has slapped Peter Lorre. When Lorre threateningly complains about this insult, Bogart responds, "When you're slapped, you'll take it and like it."

Most of us, in similar situations, would probably meekly do as this dog did. If you warned someone that you were afraid of having your hand touched, and they disregarded this but grabbed your hand anyway, you might raise your voice: "I said leave me alone!" If in response to this understandable outburst, they attacked you and threw you to the ground and then made you recite multiplication tables, you might find that a very frightening scenario indeed; that is hardly a normal response to your verbal warning. If this scenario were repeated, you'd probably learn that allowing your hand to be examined was the lesser of two evils, but your trust in that person would be damaged. Our lack of trust and understanding must be terribly confusing for dogs, who are communicating to us in the clearest way they know how: fully canine ways.

From the dog's perspective, this is a very different story. If we were able to go back in time and witness the events, keeping our eye on the dog at all times, we'd find another version of what happened. The dog is limping, a clear sign that something is painful. As the woman reaches for his foot, some subtle changes occur in the dog's expression and body. Unseen, his tail droops slightly. He turns his head away from her, perhaps licking his lips, or—depending on his temperament—may hold his head over and near the foot, protecting it from contact much like a dog uses his head to cover a toy he does not want taken away. Like anyone anticipating a touch in a painful area, he holds his breath; his lips might compress slightly, and his ears slide back and down. In each and every one of these signs, he is saying, "Be careful. This is a problem for me." But intent on her examination, she does not notice these things. The dog probably tries to pull the paw out of her hand, but she does not let him. As she examines the foot, the dog—having had all his more subtle signs disregarded—growls. To his relief, the woman apparently understands the growl and lets go of the foot.

What happens next is not at all what the dog expects: The woman roars at him and pins him to the ground. From the dog's point of view, this act of aggression is shocking and without any rationale. She snaps a leash onto his collar and begins to insist that he heel, and sit, and lie down. Anxious to appease her inexplicable wrath, not wanting to trigger another aggressive act by her, he complies. Finally, she appears mollified, but to his dismay, she reaches for his foot again. In addition to the pain in his foot, he now has another concern: his unpredictable owner who may attack him without provocation. Anxious and hurting, upset and confused, he does not wait till she has touched the foot—he growls as soon as she begins to reach for him. When once again she screams and throws him to the ground, he begins to understand that she is responding to his growl. From his canine point of view, this makes no sense. In all his body language, he is clearly indicating a warning, not a challenge to a fight; yet her response is (from a dog's perspective) abnormal, dangerous, clearly aggressive. When he growls the third time, he pays attention to *her* verbal warning and thus avoids her aggression. Though he is still afraid, though his paw still hurts, he decides that allowing her to examine his foot is not as bad as being attacked by her.

When he gets to the veterinarian's office, he again tries to warn all involved using many subtle gestures, but his communications go unheeded. He makes the warning as clear as he can, though he now knows better than to growl—his owner has taught him that growling is not acceptable. What amazes me is that the dog—despite what he might very rightly view as attacks on him physically—still remains cooperative, still inhibits his behavior, does not do what he's well capable of doing: biting. This is a very large dog whose mouth easily encompassed the veterinarian's entire hand, a dog with sufficient jaw pressure to have badly maimed or even bitten off fingers without much effort. But he did not even leave the tiniest bruise—exerting no pressure whatsoever, he simply holds the man's hand, trying to make his point very clear: "Please, don't do that."

In working with dogs, I've more than once caught a flash of surprise and relief in a dog's eyes when he realized that I heard and heeded his subtle communications, that there was no need to growl or bite. Clients are often surprised when I cheerfully assure them that it's a good sign that their dog is growling before he bites (or is simply growling without the bite). While I'd much rather that a happier relationship existed between client and dog so that growling wasn't necessary, it's good to know that the dog is still willing to offer warnings, giving us a chance to change our behavior. He's letting us know just where the tricky spots are, not simply attacking. "Be careful," he tells us, "you are treading on thin ice." Though their method of communicating may sometimes be alarming if we do not understand that growls and snaps are valuable messages, I am grateful that dogs keep trying.

In any relationship, feedback (even unwelcome feedback that indicates great frustration and anger) is an opportunity to examine the underlying problem and work to find a resolution. To ignore what others tell us about their frustration or anger or fear is emotionally cruel and will eventually erode relationships at a very deep level. Dogs who do not warn but bite are difficult on many levels. Be grateful for and *do not punish growls*, but do work to resolve whatever has prompted the growl. Punishing or suppressing a growl does not change the underlying feeling, no more than biting back "Damn!" in the presence of delicate Aunt Tillie changes the feeling that prompted it. Punished into silence, the dog learns to not give you that very important warning signal. Though it may be more surprising to us when he bites "without warning," we forget that we've told him we don't want to hear any warnings!

A growl can simply be a trigger for us to indulge in our own worst fears, or it can be an important signal and an opportunity for greater understanding. We have to be willing to accept that not all of our dog's communications will be happy and pleasant messages; a dog may need to tell us he is afraid or hurting or angry. If we turn a deaf ear to all but what we want to hear, we are going to miss opportunities to help our dogs resolve or learn to handle whatever it is that has frightened, hurt, irritated or angered him. If, as is far too common, we actually punish the dog for these communications, we will seriously undermine the relationship. No relationship can thrive when communication is blocked.

LISTENING

When we seek understanding of a dog's behavior—and particularly what we consider to be aggressive behavior—we cannot lose sight of the fact that behavior is communication, and communication does not occur in a vacuum. It is aimed at someone for some reason, and the full story is unimportant to our understanding and to our ultimate decision of how best to respond.

Understanding that aggression is a form of communication does *not* mean that the behavior is acceptable, no more than a child slugging his brother out of frustration or an adult yelling at the bank clerk because a check was bounced is acceptable behavior. It does mean that we make the effort to look for the message behind the behavior. A dog who growls at a veterinarian trying to examine painfully infected ears is quite different from the dog who growls at someone for making eye contact with him. A dog who attacks and kills a rabbit is in a different category from the dog who attacks and maims a child. A dog who bites a burglar who has broken into our home is quite different from the dog who bites visiting Aunt Tillie when she stands up to totter off to the powder room. A dog who acts aggressively on our behalf, scaring off a would-be attacker or thief is considered a hero; biting the hand that feeds you is the act of a scoundrel.

When we understand the motivation behind the behavior, when we can see what the dog was trying to communicate, when we can see the situation from the dog's perspective, we are better able to intelligently assess and humanely correct the problem.

Whether with another human or with an animal, relationships can reach new levels of understanding and intimacy only when we learn to listen for the real message behind the behavior rather than simply reacting to it ourselves. If your closest friend suddenly began yelling and punching you, how would you respond? I'd be shocked, and would definitely take care to keep myself safe. Depending on my experience with yelling and screaming people and this person in particular, I might wisely choose to leave, fearing that I will be hurt. If I don't have trust in my friend and believe she must have good reason for acting this way, I might take her behavior very personally and react emotionally, yelling back and maybe taking a swing or two myself. My reaction does nothing to resolve the situation—reactions rarely resolve anything but can keep us alive in a threatening moment, which is precisely what they were designed to do. When she installed the fight-or-flight response, Mother Nature did not intend this as a mechanism by which deep, intimate relationships might be developed; she was just making sure that we'd live long enough to enjoy such connections. It's a good basic rule that if you're reacting, you're not connecting.

My reaction does not arise from a compassionate interest in understanding why my friend might be acting this way; it is simply based on the fear or anger her behavior has now generated within me. This creates a vicious circle of reaction: yelling and punching (prompted by a yet-undetermined internal state in my friend), met by my reaction (prompted by my fear, which leads me to yell and punch), which is in turn met by yet another reaction (my friend is now reacting to my yelling and punching as well as the original, underlying cause). This vicious cycle is characteristic of immature human relationships, but sadly typical of animal/human relationships as well. If I am mature enough to understand that not all behavior directed *at* me is *about* me, I am then in an even better place to carefully search for the real message behind the behavior.

This book cannot and does not address specific treatments or resolutions for aggressive behavior. What it intends to do is place aggressive behavior within the context of the dog/human relationship and open the reader's mind (and heart) to the understanding of aggression as communication. I also intend to raise the caution flag in every reader's head—*any aggressive behavior is a warning that needs to be heeded and given careful consideration.* Even in the best of cases where there is no real problem except that we have misinterpreted a dog's innocent behavior as aggressive, this is a sign that the relationship is not built on deep, intimate understanding; we need to know more so that we can accurately understand what our dogs have to say. Aggressive behavior may be a warning that something is terribly wrong in the relationship, a warning that we need to rebalance the relative status between ourselves and our dogs and provide clear, fair leadership. Aggression may also warn us that something is wrong within the dog, that he is experiencing fear or anxiety or pain and that he needs our help. In a loving relationship, we cannot turn away from such warnings; we must respond, hopefully from a deep desire to resolve whatever troubles the waters, and—at the very least—from a recognition that in taking a dog into our lives, we have accepted the responsibility to answer his needs.

Quite understandably, within the context of our relationships with dogs, we tend to take things rather personally. It's one thing to read an academic discussion of aggression; it's something else altogether when *our* dog growls at *us*. We are rarely grateful for this communication.

"Well, my goodness, Jethro. Thank you for that timely comment on my behavior or gestures, which may have threatened you in some way. I shall examine what I may have done to provoke that and study on how best to resolve this matter. I deeply appreciate your growl, which I understand is your attempt to resolve the perceived conflict between you and me." When we learn to value the communication behind a dog's growl or snarl or snap, we move closer to an understanding of that dog and, quite often, an understanding of ourselves.

17

WHAT TIMMY NEVER DID TO LASSIE

Until we have the courage to recognize cruelty for what it is . . . whether its victim is human or animal . . . we cannot expect things to be much better in this world.

RACHEL CARSON

VICKI IS UPSET THAT HER DOG SALTY IS DIGGING HOLES in the yard. Looking at the hole her dog has dug, she has an idea. She grabs a spade and a shovel and makes Salty's hole larger, more perfectly round. When it's just perfect, Vicki dances a jig of delight and, still dancing, uses the garden hose to fill the hole and then holds Salty's head underwater. She's surprised when Salty struggles to free herself, and tells the dog, "But I thought you loved hole digging!" Every day for three weeks, Vicki improves Salty's new holes or redigs the old ones and fills them with water and holds her dog's head underwater.

Vicki exhibits no apparent remorse whatsoever for her actions. In fact, she writes about it in some detail, noting that she "has this crazy, incurable response to the sight of a hole." The only way to stop her from doing this to Salty is, she says, to "keep me away from holes." She notes that Salty is no longer digging holes in the yard and is nervous even when she sees a hole out in the woods, a hole she did not dig.

How do we respond to Vicki and her treatment of animals? If Vicki were a child, we might be urging all involved to get her professional help. While not all children who abuse animals go on to commit violent crimes, such behavior is a red flag of warning that this is a child who needs help, and most children who abuse animals are also victims of abuse themselves. But Vicki is not a child. She is an adult, and a dog trainer who offers to help people discover the "poetry in obedience."

219

She was a very real person, the late Vicki Hearne, dog trainer, author, professor and poet, and the actions described above are taken directly from her own words in her critically acclaimed 1986 book, *Adam's Task: Calling Animals by Name.*

Far from being censured or sent into therapy, Hearne was lauded for her beautifully written philosophical exploration of our relationship with animals. How is it that Hearne's behavior is acceptable? Is it merely because she is not a child? Most readers would be appalled if a child did to a dog what Hearne did to Salty, yet are strangely silent when an adult—and particularly a *trainer*, and *expert*—does the same thing. Evidently, somehow, at some point, children become old enough to practice other ways of dealing with their old pal Fido, ways that are unmistakably not nice. Is this a rite de passage that goes unremarked or uncelebrated but is nonetheless real? Just where is that point where we no longer need to be nice to the doggy? If maturity entitles us to treat animals in such ways, where exactly on our development path do we take the turn that leads to this ugly landscape devoid of a consistent compassion?

Somehow, there is a socially acceptable progression from being horrified by the treatment of Black Beauty to this question: "How hard do you hit the dog? A good general rule is that if you did not get a response, a yelp or other sign, after the first hit, it wasn't hard enough." Who on earth would buy such a book for their children? We would be horrified to discover such advice included in a 4-H manual or as part of a national "Be Kind to Animals Week" program. If any teacher proposed to include such a notion in our children's curriculum, the resulting outrage would probably both curl and gray the school board's collective hair. And yet, many adults have bought the book from which I took the "how hard do you hit the dog?" quote—*How to Be Your Dog's Best Friend* by the Monks of New Skete, first published by Little, Brown in 1978 and still on the shelves of nearly every bookstore in the United States. It is a title that answers the question of how hard to hit the dog, but also talks about the spiritual nature of the dog/human relationship. Strange bedfellows, these two topics—or so it seems to me, though I am well aware of the many justifications and rationales for not "sparing the rod."

In *Spare the Child*, historian Philip Greven offers a startling study of both the roots and consequences of corporal punishment of children in America. Reading Greven's work, I was struck with a tremendous wave of sadness for the violence woven through so many of our most intimate human relationships. Little wonder then that we may, without thinking or with full acceptance, also weave this ugly thread through the fabric of our relationships with animals. But this is an old thread, handed down from generation to generation, and in taking hold of the life cloth we are given as children, we may not realize that among the bright and beautiful threads, there lurks a darker one. We can cut this thread, and remove it from the tapestry of our lives, but first, we must tease it out from where it is woven in and through.

THE EMPEROR'S NEW CAREER

Adam's Task was not lightweight reading, and it's reasonable to assume that reviewers and readers were intelligent people. And yet the jarring image of a woman holding her dog's head in a hole filled with water somehow glided by without leaving an outraged cry of disgust in its wake. Blinded by lofty prose and philosophical contemplation, deft quoting of Nietzche, Vonnegut, Auden, Xenophon and Shakespeare, readers evidently lost sight of the real dog in the real moment when a real person perpetrated a real cruelty. Or perhaps the ugly contradiction was noticed, but no one raised a voice in protest. I hope not; I'd prefer to think that readers simply were moving through page after page in dull, unthinking incomprehension. While unthinking acceptance is dismaying, it can't hold a candle against the ugly darkness of soul involved in observing inhumane behavior and saying nothing.

Forget the glistening, polished phrases. For a moment, narrow your view to see only this: the dog. See the dog standing beside her, even helping her dig. The dog is a bit bewildered by but pleased to join in the dancing jig Hearne does as she digs the hole farther. See the dog's tail wagging, and the questioning but happy look on the dog's face as she trots along behind Vicki as the garden hose is dragged to the hole. See the dog watching with curiosity and interest as the water splashes into the hole, swirling, churning the freshly dug dirt into a minute muddy pond that rises toward the dog and the woman who stands at its edge. See the dog's surprise when the woman grabs her and pushes the dog's head into the hole where the water is still chasing itself around. See the reflexive arching of the dog's body upward, away from the shock of the cold muddy water that has covered her head, splashing into her ears and up into her surprised nostrils before survival instincts take over and stop the intake of breath. When the dog fights free and looks into the woman's eyes, tell me what you see in the dog—trust? joy? the poetry that Hearne tells the reader exists in the dog's soul?

I think we've had our blinders on for a long, long time.

It would be almost a welcome thing to be able to write about Vicki Hearne as some sort of depraved monster, a singularly disturbed individual whose philosophy is so far from that of the average person as to make it nearly impossible for us to fathom the world in which she lives. If Hearne were a bizarre, inexplicable blip in our society, one of the unusual fringe people so far out that they barely even appear on the societal radar, we might more easily rest, able to dismiss her as a kook or perhaps even a sad case more to be pitied than censured. But Vicki Hearne was not in any way an aberration, nor are people like her unusual. She was an articulate, even elegant voice that raised some provocative questions and posed some intriguing notions of how it is we connect with dogs and other animals. Her flights of poetic musings are seductive, if we allow ourselves to be lulled by the beautiful words and forget the living breathing dog who is not a concept to be toyed with, an idea to be played with in the rarefied air of thought. Always, we must remember: *See the dog.*

Hearne was not a monster, simply an easy example, and one of many who, though they may give forth on the joys of a relationship between humans and dogs, nonetheless bring their philosophy to life in hurtful and often inhumane ways.

Though we might prefer to think that such incongruency between pretty thoughts and not-so-pretty deeds would be astoundingly evident, the truth is that this uneasy (though often unremarked) gap between philosophy and practice is all too common. In just a few moments of browsing the selections available at a bookstore, I encountered trainers who assured me that a leash, a collar and a flyswatter were all I really needed to discover the "magic" of dog training; encouraged me to jam my fingers down a puppy's throat until he gagged on them and thus learned not to indulge in normal puppyhood exploratory biting; earnestly told me how to effectively slap my dog under the chin or throw him to the ground in an imitation (staggeringly inaccurate, I must add) of an "alpha" wolf; how to inflict any of a sad, long list of "training techniques." And each of these titles also touched on the wonders of the love and fellowship that were possible with a dog. Man's best friend would do well to mutter, "With friends like these, who needs enemies?"

Incredibly, such incoherence of philosophy and practice is rarely questioned. Those who can weave a cloak of beautiful thoughts about ugly actions may not only be allowed to proceed without fear of protest, but embraced as a shining light of wisdom. Add a catchy phrase and a cute gimmick, and chances are good no one will notice the dog's ears flattening on his head in apprehension during training sessions. Smile and chuckle while snapping the dog's collar harshly, drop some celebrity names and maybe quote a philosopher or two, and it's a safe bet no one will notice the dog's tail wagging anxiously between his thighs. Justify your actions with conviction, and no one will appear to question why the trust and joy we would include in our relationships are sometimes little more than words and intent, not action and deed, and certainly not evident in a dog's eyes. The emperor not only has new clothes, he may also be working on a new career as a dog trainer.

In our minds, we can pity Black Beauty, be moved to tears by the poetry in a dog's soul, and yet still ask the question, "How hard do you hit the dog?" Coherence seems a rare thing, and the human mind is sometimes quite careless about insisting on it. In the long run, however, I think our lack of coherence eats at us, undermines the sureness with which we know our own minds, and thus blocks us from knowing our souls. We may choose to glide unthinking on the surface of our relationships, never asking how it is that we actually practice the art of loving friendship. But always, silently, our dogs remind us that our intellectual honesty and spiritual integrity depend upon our willingness to question and thus defend against the inevitable cruelties small and large that accompany a philosophy at odds with its practice.

BE NICE TO THE DOGGY

Once upon a time, most of us reached with chubby toddler hands for a dog and heard a cautionary, "Be nice to the doggy." At a tender age, we learn to touch animals softly, with respect, and not to pinch, pull, prod, twist, poke, slap, punch or bite them. No healthy, normal adult would encourage a child to hurt an animal. Instead, part of our education as children is a compassionate, gentle approach that emphasizes the development of empathy and respectful caretaking of the creatures around us. In fact, research into the psychology of criminal behavior and interpersonal violence has proven a disturbing connection between animal abuse and violent human behavior: cruelty to or abuse of animals is seen quite rightfully as a warning sign that something is very wrong. Children who abuse or mistreat animals are not considered dog trainers in the making but troubled people in need of therapy and intervention.

But these warnings only seem to apply to children, not to the adults who employ punitive, cruel techniques in the name of training. Without risk of being considered a psychologically disturbed individual, you can "train" a dog using any number of techniques: slap him; slam him; push, pull or pinch him; choke him and drag him and so on. And that's for the good dogs who aren't stupid enough to think about fighting back.

Should a dog actually protest such treatment, he'll encounter a whole new set of horrors, such as the trainer willing to "string a dog up" so that the dog dangles and chokes in midair at the end of the leash until he's reached the appropriate state that trainer Bill Koehler (whose techniques Hearne unabashedly champions throughout *Adam's Task*) describes thus: "physically incapable of expressing his resentment. . . ." Koehler does note that "the sight of a dog lying, thick tongued, on his side, is not pleasant, but do not let it alarm you." Of course not. That the dog is vomiting and staggering (as Koehler indicates he might) after such training is to be expected, right? To be fair, Koehler cautions that such training is not appropriate for all dogs, just the dog who is a "real hood"— the type of dog who has the audacity to "express his resentment by biting."

It would seem fairly obvious that a philosophy that would admit such techniques is not one that is concerned with the relationship, or is at best Machiavellian in its defense that the ends justify the means. What is not so obvious is how humane, caring people nonetheless end up employing such techniques. Uncomfortable though it may be, our growth as human beings requires that we examine the ways in which we justify our sometimes inhumane actions and our very human tendencies to accept an authority beyond our own hearts. Unless we are willing to learn to see cruelty in all its many disguises, we cannot create a philosophy that protects against it.

No Apologies Needed

How do we define cruelty? Cruelty may be a good deal like obscenity—tricky to define, and to some extent, existing largely in the eyes (and heart) of the beholder. One trainer may view certain training techniques as nothing more than what Koehler calls "the necessity of stern measures" while another trainer may view those same techniques as abusive and inhumane. How then to define what is cruel? Frank Ascione, a respected authority on the connection between animal abuse and domestic violence, offers this definition of cruelty: "socially unacceptable behavior that intentionally causes unnecessary pain, suffering, or distress to and/or death of an animal."

At first glance, this seems reasonable. Our eye falls on the words *pain, suffering, distress, death,* and we readily agree anything that might cause such would indeed constitute cruelty. But in this phrase—*socially unacceptable behavior*—and with these two words—*intentionally* and *unnecessary*—Ascione leaves unspoken volumes for us to wrestle with in our individual consciences and in our larger collective conscience as a society. Implied is the notion that there may exist socially acceptable behavior that out of necessity, intentionally causes pain, suffering, distress or even death. And he is right.

It is socially acceptable behavior in our neck of the woods for our local butcher to calmly place a bullet deep in a cow's brain so that the animal does not even blink or take another breath before dying unaware, a last mouthful of grain still held in its jaws, though my guests eagerly reaching for another serving of pot roast do not like to think of this. In most Western countries, it is socially acceptable for a veterinarian to kill an animal in the name of mercy (whether merciful relief from terminal illness or simply being unwanted), or to perform procedures that may cause pain or suffering but with the goal of helping and healing. And though the tide is slowly turning toward gentler techniques, it remains socially acceptable behavior to use even considerable force to train dogs, to employ techniques that without question can and do cause both pain and suffering.

When we take off our blinders and peer closely at this line between acceptable behavior that causes an animal pain or suffering and unacceptable behavior that has the same effect, we see that it is not a clear, hard line. We can see situations in which compulsion might be well justified, and yet still others where the use of force is inhumane. Though we might like to try to fix this line firmly so that we know just what to do or not to do if we wish to stand on the side of fairness and humane treatment of others, the line does not yield to such definition. If we tread in the delicate territory close to the line, as we almost cannot help doing if we try to be responsible dog owners, we must be willing to question every step we take and put a foot down only when we are sure we know on which side of the line we will end up.

At one level, a commonsense rule of thumb may be helpful. A humane approach rarely has to be explained or defended to even the most uniformed passerby. No apologies are needed for treating anyone kindly, compassionately and fairly. Cruelty and approaches that give the appearance of cruelty often need to be defended. But the ground covered between cruel and kind is vast, and it does not yield to tidy delineation of which land belongs to which camp. There are humane actions that may appear to the uninitiated as cruel. On the other hand, it is possible to be so "kind" as to be cruel, ultimately creating the same effect as outright and deliberate abuse. A more comprehensive definition is needed.

In his book *Creating Love*, John Bradshaw offers a definition of violence against another. Though he is discussing people, his words hold a great deal of truth for animals as well: "I consider anything that violates a person's sense of self to be violence. Such actions may not be directly physical . . . though it quite often is. In my definition, violence occurs when a more powerful and knowledgeable person destroys the freedom of a less powerful person for whom he or she is significant."

Bradshaw goes on to describe other, less-obvious forms of violence toward children, many of which are also found in our relationships with both animals and other adults:

> cause them to witness any form of physical violence, not pro-
> tect them from bullies, desert them emotionally . . . refuse to
> set limits, use them to supply your own need to be admired
> and respected, use them to take away your own disappoint-
> ment and sadness by demanding that they perform, achieve,
> be beautiful, be athletic, be smart, etc. . . . use them as a scape-
> goat for your anger and shame, refuse to resolve your own
> unresolved issues from the past.

Bradshaw's list reveals a truth about cruelty and violence—though it may be directed externally, its roots lie within us. To the degree that we are aware of and willing to chart the complex territories of our souls, we will be able to safely navigate a path that leads away from cruelty and violence. But this is not easily done. Violence against others takes on many guises, wrapped in the cloak of justification, hitching a ride on habit. It is easy to talk about being humane and kind; it is tiring work at times to question, always, how and why you will choose to behave regardless of the dog's response, regardless of who tells you what you "ought" to do. And it is easy to be kind and fair and gentle when all is going our way. The test of who we are and where we are in our journey toward humane relationships comes when the weather turns stormy.

When an intimate connection is sought, we open the doors to dis-agreement, conflict. By the very nature of the dog/human relationship, we have created the need to impose our will on the dog if for no other reason than our moral obligation to keep the dog safe from the realities of animal nature bouncing against the confines of the often highly unnat-ural human world. We may be guilty of a very great cruelty (perhaps the ultimate cruelty since it is a perversion and denial of our obligation) if we fail to do what needs to be done to keep our dogs safe. Yet if we use our obligation as moral justification for resolving conflict by doing anything and everything in the guise of "for your own good," we have not excluded possible cruelty but practically assured its inclusion.

We have two basic choices when trying to resolve any conflict within a relationship: persuasion or coercion. Persuasion is possible only where freedom exists. If I am willing to accept *whatever* choice you may make, I am able to use persuasion and nothing more in my attempt to get you to do what I'd like you to do. Persuasion contains no elements of cruelty—by its very nature, persuasion contains the freedoms of both involved, and within that freedom lies profound respect even if disagreement exists. If the dog is truly free to say "No, thanks" and we are truly willing to accept that answer, then we are engaged in persuasion. Often while out walking, I'll tell Bee, "Gimme that!" Whatever her response—giving me the toy so I can throw it or keeping it herself—is fine with me; she is truly free to do as she likes in that situation. "Gimme that" is not a command but a suggestion, an attempt to persuade her to let me have the toy. I have to be very clear in my own mind what is a suggestion and what is a command and maintain absolute consistence on the distinction.

But persuasion has limits, and especially within the context of our role as guardians and caretakers, persuasion may fail. In some situations, compulsion or coercion may be justified, especially if the consequences of a failure to respond or act in a certain way can be dangerous or even deadly. Few of us would choose persuasion to deal with a child about to stick a fork into an electrical outlet or walk into traffic; most of us would simply forcefully compel the child to stop.

The moment we begin to limit the dog's options, when "no" is not an acceptable response, we are no longer persuading but coercing. *Webster's New Collegiate Dictionary* defines *coerce* as

1.   To restrain or dominate by nullifying individual will
2.   To compel to an act or choice
3.   To enforce or bring about by force or threat

Coercion covers the full gamut from mild restraint (physical or psychological) to outright physical assault, but it always involves denying another complete freedom in some way. Though coercion contains the possibility of cruelty, it is not synonymous with it. It might be helpful to keep in mind that dogs use coercion (both physical and psychological) among themselves.

No matter how loving we may be, no matter how humane we are in our treatment of our dogs, at some time we will find ourselves with no option but coercion. We cannot humanely offer dogs complete freedom to do only as they please, no more than a loving parent allows children to do only what they want to do. At some point, in some way, we give the dog no option but to do what we need or want him to do. In some way, we will make it happen, whether by gently restraining the dog for a veterinary procedure or by simply using a leash and collar to hold him back from chasing a squirrel or even by withdrawing our attention from him in order to make our point that his behavior was unacceptable. However gently we apply the force, regardless of how much love and good intent accompanies our limiting of another being's freedom, our actions remain coercive.

There are times when the simple obligations of being a dog's keeper and guardian brings us into conflict with the dog's impulses, needs, desires and even his instincts. *How* we will handle the inevitable conflict between us and the dog, how we will use coercion, is the question. And this is where we tread on treacherous ground. Cruelty does not rear its ugly head in moments of agreement; only where conflict exists can cruelty germinate. A friend of mine once noted that anger was not possible without a goal. No goal, no possibility of anger. I thought about this a long time and realized that no matter how modest or unimportant the goal, the moment I have something I want, an outcome I desire more than other possible outcomes, there arises the possibility for anger, and further along that spectrum, the possibility of cruelty if I am willing to pursue my goal at any cost, even at the expense of another living being. We may not take the achievement of a goal to Machiavellian extremes. But simply shaping a goal and focusing on it has the additional effect of narrowing our perspective; aimed at our goal, we may forget the dog beside us.

ESSENTIAL AND NONESSENTIAL

Despite an unpleasantly substantial knowledge of how animals are abused in the name of training, I remain fascinated with what is possible between a human and an animal. I know what it is to set off in pursuit of a goal with an animal as my partner, and I know how easy it is to gaze in desirous unblinking thrall at the goal and lose sight of the very real animal at my side. And yet, the pursuit of excellence is a good and noble cause, one that asks, What might be? What is possible? How far can we go?

When we ask these questions of ourselves, we are bound only by the effects of our actions on those around us and are relatively free to push ourselves quite hard in pursuit of a goal. But a far more problematic question arises when we select an animal as our partner. How far can we ask animals to go with us without crossing the line into inhumane? After all, what is it that allows an animal to shine, bringing his utmost to a task, displaying his talents with confidence and joy? In the best of all possible worlds it is simply this: the relationship between the animal and a human. If within a healthy and mutually joyful relationship, the dog/human team strives for the highest performance of which they as a team are capable, then that is gilding on an already lovely gem.

To the best of my knowledge , no dog has ever leapt on to his owner's bed with a dog magazine in his teeth and announced, "You've got to read this! They're now offering a new title! If I can just learn to do x, y and z, and do it in less than fifty-three seconds without any mistakes, then I could be Champion Oh My Goodness Gracious!" And this is the little notion that somehow is overlooked at one time or another by even the best, most loving dog owners: The dogs aren't volunteers. They are drafted. I have no problems with "drafting" a dog to learn new skills and hone his God-given talents. To a large extent, dogs and other animals who are highly trained often lead interesting lives with a degree of stimulation simply not found in the backyard or pasture. I've seen the eagerness in the eyes of a dog who is asked to work at that which he loves best, whether it is herding sheep or hunting birds or prancing at heel in precise harmony with his handler or providing gentle, loving company as a therapy dog. Deprived of the natural stimulation of life in a pack, dogs are highly intelligent beings who welcome the opportunity to use their minds in new ways. So, in theory, educating an animal is a good thing. In practice, however, something else often happens.

There are many approaches to training, all promising to help you turn your dog into a well-mannered canine citizen, a goal that at first blush seems laudable indeed. Though the end result may be a good thing, not all ways of getting to that end are; not all of them are fair and humane. Though the goal of a well-mannered canine citizen is a good one, we must be careful about what we are willing to do in order to achieve that goal. We need to make the distinction between essential life skills and nonessential life skills. Such a distinction helps us to clearly define the relative importance of what is being taught. Without such a distinction, how do we choose what might be most appropriate for our dogs, our lifestyles, the kind of relationships we hope to have?

The emphasis we place on the importance of teaching a dog x, y or z says a great deal about us, and about the relationship between us and our dogs. Care should be taken that we are clear in our own minds about what we consider important enough to achieve at almost any cost and what we will not do. It's far too easy to get caught up in niceties that have nothing to do with cooperation and good manners from the dog. Common sense would tell us that when essential life skills are involved, there may be some convincing rationale for working persistently to make sure the skills are mastered, regardless of whether a dog or person actually enjoys the process, though I think we have an ethical obligation to do our level best to make learning as pleasant as possible.

Humane training is possible when we are very clear about what we are trying to teach, and how we are going to teach it, and also *why* we are convinced that it is important that our dog know a particular something. The importance we assign any particular goal will dictate our willingness to accept even distasteful ways of achieving that goal. Whenever we forget that we are dealing with draftees and not volunteers, when we mistake willingness and enthusiasm for informed consent, we begin a dangerous movement away from the dog as our friend, our partner and toward the dog as an object to be shaped—however necessary—to suit our needs and expectations.

Essential life skills are the skills and behaviors that a dog needs to learn so that he has maximum freedom and minimal risk and stress *in his world*. For each dog, this means something different. There is no book that will outline behaviors and neatly assign them a category: essential or nonessential. It's not even possible to pick a single behavior and say it is essential for all dogs. The set of life skills that each dog needs to have varies tremendously from dog to dog and is uniquely shaped by his life.

For example, I could ask my dogs to heel precisely on the way to the barn, but I don't need them to do that. Since we live far from any road, there is a lot of flexibility in how we and our dogs move together through the farm. In their life, precise heeling does not constitute an essential life skill. What I do consider an essential life skill is a willingness to lie down quickly when asked, and to stay where dropped until released. Such action may save their lives or keep them from harm's way, and so I do insist on a fairly high degree of precision on this score. Because I consider this an essential life skill for my dogs, I am willing to use some degree of force to assure their compliance.

But I have to be critically honest about my expectations and a dog's understanding. To the extent that I bring my time, attention and investment of myself to the practice of this essential skill, they comply largely without need for anything but the mildest compulsion—a mildly scolding "eh!" or a light hand of reminder on a neck. When I let quick drops and steady stays slip, *they* let it slip as well not because they are lazy or resistant dogs but *because it does not matter to them*. It only matters to me, and thus it is my responsibility to maintain a high level of awareness about this, and my obligation to remain invested in maintenance of the behavior. If I am unaware of my responsibility and blame the dogs, who do not understand the importance of the behavior as one way to keep them safe in their world, then I might slip over the edge and justify using force, placing the blame on the dogs and not on myself where it belongs.

WHEN THE ANSWER IS NO

It would be nice if a checklist existed that neatly pointed us to what was naughty and what was nice in terms of our response to a particular situation or behavior. But nothing is as clear-cut as we might like, and within the context of a relationship, we have to do the work of making choices for our own behavior in every situation. In a situation where I am going to compel, not persuade, I do my level best to use the absolute minimum of compulsion that will be effective. This is an ongoing challenge, because there is no set limit of what is or is not effective with any particular dog at any particular moment. The situation, the respective moods of the dog and myself, the weather, what happened a moment before or a week before, what we had for breakfast or lunch—because all this combines to create a unique moment, there's not a way to predict or recommend the level of compulsion that constitutes an effective communication in that moment. Fine points must be considered and taken into account.

If, for example, I say that a dog refused to lie down on command, that is insufficient information on which any humane trainer could make a recommendation as to how this should be handled. "My dog will not lie down on command" is nothing more than the first line in a possible lengthy discussion and examination of why this might be so and therefore what is to be done. To the extent that we are willing to thoroughly engage ourselves in this discussion, sincerely interested in the possibly answer, we are working in a humane and loving way. When we are no longer curious, when we no longer care what the explanation might be, we have opened the door to cruelty. There is nothing humane or fair in a refusal to acknowledge another being's legitimate reason for doing something other than what we wanted or expected.

Why didn't the dog lie down? The simplest answer—the one we allow for in our human relationships but rarely in our relationships with animals—is that the answer is no for whatever reason. Far too often when communicating with dogs, we are not really interested in communication or a dialogue; we are interested in finding ways to tell the dog what we want him to do (or not do). And this is where communication ceases to exist, and dictatorship, no matter how benevolent, begins.

If someone we loved or at least deeply respected said no to us, a healthy and respectful response would be "why not?"—asked with the sincere intention to understand the other's point of view. If we can get past the flare of annoyance or even anger at their refusal, if we are sincerely interested and open ourselves to listening, we can learn perhaps that while they might like to respond to us, they can't for any variety of reasons. Before we can choose a humane and fair response, we need to hear the full message that the dog is sending. Is the dog saying "No, I don't understand how to do that" or "No, I'm confused" or something else? Perhaps they are physically unable, or they find the act frightening (never ask my mother to hold a horse, even briefly!) or they have something else they'd rather do. They may be bored or uninterested. We may have hurt them or confused them, making them reluctant to work with us again. They may have other priorities. They may have no respect for us—this is a possibility that should be carefully examined when we have gone past the point of friendly conversation and request and are now in the demand/command stage of insisting. If we love them, if the relationship is important to us, we will listen for the rationale behind the refusal or resistance, and our hearts will be guided by the trust that even if it cannot be fully understood or articulated, they have a good reason for saying no.

This does not mean when a dog or anyone says no we simply give up and wander off in search of someone more compliant. It is possible to honor the reason behind a dog's refusal and still decide how you will insist on compliance. My experience is that very often, an animal needs an acknowledgment of the motivation behind his resistance more than he needs us to simply withdraw our request. Though it sounds terribly simple, I am endlessly amazed by what happens when I assure an animal that I do understand why he finds something unpleasant or scary, and I believe that like all people I know, animals also need to be heard. It may be only that the animals are responding to the shift in me when I work with them in such moments, offering my sympathy, which in turn shapes and informs my very actions. But this limited explanation does not explain the look I have seen in the eyes of creatures too many and too varied to list—a look of gratitude for having been acknowledged. Whatever the truth behind this phenomenon may be, I don't care; it is enough for me to know what can happen when I respectfully acknowledge another being's resistance as something as fully justified and real as my insistence on another path.

If you understand what lies behind *no*, if you understand why you have placed a particular value on compliance, if you know your own heart, then you are clear to make a choice to compel and to do so as fairly as your knowledge and skill allow. If you understand what lies behind the refusal, you are also given the gift of understanding that perhaps changing course is necessary, or that in the future, when you come again to a crossroads, you'll do better to choose another route.

While we may be uncomfortable thinking about coercion as part of a relationship, it is something we need to consider in our pursuit of humane, loving treatment of a creature in our care. At times, we may have no option but to coerce the dog's compliance. But even in those moments where we cannot fully honor another being's complete freedom, we do need to honor his refusal as a valuable communication that will be taken into consideration and may influence our own actions. If we are going to use coercion—however gently—then let us do so with awareness, lest it become both justified and comfortable for us, perhaps leading to a complacency we ought not to feel. Complacent, we may stop seeking—always, relentlessly, in the name of love—for ways to engage a dog's voluntary cooperation without the need for force; such ways often do exist, though they may require a far greater investment of ourselves. If we are unwilling to invest ourselves to achieve a more humane end, we need to be honest with ourselves about this, not rationalize our behavior as necessary. Coercion is a slippery slope, and in whatever varying degrees we bring it to bear, it permits (though does not guarantee) the existence of cruelty. So we need to tread very carefully and be very clear about which side of the fence we are on: Are we persuading or coercing? Coercion may be inevitable and a part of life, but it need not equal cruelty, especially if we are willing to keep our eyes clear so that we can truly see the dog.

What happens if we mistake a nonessential for an essential? One would hope that there's nothing more at stake than some wasted time, and a dog's mind that now contains a bit of interesting but relatively unimportant trivia. Of course, if that is the case, we may have proven James Thurber's point: "While man has sometimes succeeded in dragging the dog down to his level, the dog has only occasionally succeeded in raising man to his level of sagacity."

Unfortunately, if we mistake nonessential for essential, we may do more than simply waste our time and the dog's. We may be willing to justify the use of force in foolish, frivolous and quite possibly unfair ways. Because a living being will pay for our mistakes, we need to think long and hard about what we consider important. Assignment of relative value in our lives can easily go askew. We may assign great importance to things that help us gloss over sad or empty places in ourselves, and clutch these things (ideas, possessions, religion, people, animals, work and more) to us with fierceness, holding on at almost any cost. The risk of cruelty runs high any time we shield the bare, naked ladies of our soul with another living being, be that a man, woman, child or dog. Perhaps saddest and most ironic is this: Of all whom we might hurt as we use them in some way to shield or soothe ourselves, the dog is the only one who would stand unflinching before our darkest secrets and most painful wounds and love us still, forgiving us again and again for being human.

18

IN SEARCH OF SOULFUL COHERENCE

Shall we make a new rule of life from tonight: always to try to be
a little kinder than is necessary?

J. M. BARRIE

IT IS SAD THAT WE ARE WILLING TO ASK "How hard should I hit the dog?"
It is sad that incoherent philosophies go unchallenged, but until we can
clarify for ourselves what it is that we think and feel and therefore how
we shall act, we cannot raise much protest. How then do we begin? As
Philip Greven writes in *Spare the Child*: "We need to create for ourselves
charts and maps, however flawed or inadequate they might initially be,
so that we can find our way through this maze of punishments that
stretch back in time as far as we can see." We have to demand coherence from ourselves, congruence in our actions, words and deeds. We
have to be, if we claim to be our dogs' best friends, the kind of friend we
would like for ourselves.

However sincere and honorable in our intentions, mistakes are
inevitable. Though we can try to live a life that is unfailingly in agreement with our deepest desire to be fair and humane, we are only human.
Set against the broad background of love and respect, our mistakes may
sting, but they also offer a chance to correct our course, to learn more,
to accept the grace of forgiveness. Though always miserable with my
mistakes, I have learned not to throw them away like something foul to
be discarded as quickly as possible. Instead, I embrace them, sifting
through the unpleasant layers until at last I find what lies at the heart
of all my errors: a small gem of self-knowledge.

While working on this book, we were blessed by the arrival of Badger, an adolescent Labrador/Chow cross that many might label a problem dog. His owner had grown afraid of him, and it was easy to see why. Pushed to do something he did not want to do, Badger would physically resist, using his nearly eighty pounds to good effect as he pulled away, leaped up or pushed with stiff legs at an insistent person. If the person persisted—trying, for example, to get the dog outside and hooked on his tether—Badger would grow still, his lip twitching in the beginnings of a snarl. Pushed a bit further, he'd reveal more teeth, offering a startling display of white against his dark muzzle. And pushed further still, he'd make an openmouthed gesture toward the offending hand. If he deemed it necessary, he would firmly grab a hand or arm, never breaking skin, never even leaving a vague welt, but with the pressure of his jaws and a steady look in his eyes, he'd give the clear impression that if forced to really bite you, he just might. He had never yet hurt anyone, but at some point, it was possible that he might feel that he needed to bite in order to make his point.

Though it would have been easy to do as others already had and label Badger as "aggressive," the truth of who Badger is as a dog was much more complicated than that. But our descriptions of dogs do not usually encompass the fullness of both the light and the dark. Labels tend to exclude all but the quality or set of qualities they are attempting to describe. I am endlessly bemused by how quickly we leap to label others (something I am as guilty of as anyone else), and yet what we long for from others is an acceptance and recognition of all that we are, not merely that which fits within a label. We resent being pigeonholed in neat ways that exclude the fullness of who we are, even the seemingly contradictory facets of ourselves that reside merrily side by side in the same mind: the brusque football player who serenely knits, the cynical parole officer who breeds canaries and finches, the avid deer hunter who steadfastly refuses to shoot rabbits even when they destroy his garden. Badger was a dog with some unpleasant habitual responses to certain situations, but he was also much more than that. If we would know another being on an intimate level, we need to allow for and even deliberately create room in our own minds and hearts for the contradictions and juxtapositions that make each of us unique though perhaps also maddening or puzzling. If we see nothing more than can be neatly contained with a label, the fullness of any individual light will never be able to shine, at least not on us.

Badger was much more than a dog who had learned that the threat of biting was an effective way of communicating his confusion, frustration and resentment. He was also loving, funny, forgiving, tolerant of other animals, deeply intelligent and most of all, a dog who wanted nothing quite so much as the opportunity to be with or near us whatever we were doing. This was not a dog who would simply become aggressive for no reason—in face, unless triggered in very specific ways, he was remarkable for just how easygoing and pleasant he was. And there was no joy in his dental displays, just an exasperated reluctance to have to make his point clear. I was sure that some attention, exercise and clear, consistent rules were going to eliminate Badger's need to threaten. I was also sure that conflict was inevitable as we learned about each other.

Our first conflict with Badger arose on the very first night. Having had him for less than six hours, it seemed prudent to have him spend the night in a crate next to our bed, an arrangement that made it clear he was part of the family and also kept him safe and unable to make any mistakes while we slept. Though nearly eighty pounds, Badger was—as we kept reminding ourselves—just a big puppy in terms of what he knew, and we needed to treat him as we would any untrained pup and not provide more freedom or privileges than he had earned.

To us, putting Badger in a comfortably bedded crate just an arm's length from my pillow seemed quite fair. He was, after all, well accustomed to a crate. But that was also the underlying problem. Our perspective was that a crate was a necessary safety, and we had the additional knowledge that Badger would be crated as little as possible; given our at-home, on-the-farm lifestyle, that meant very little indeed. Badger's experience was that stepping into a crate was just the beginning of a very long and lonely day—his owner had worked a full-time job. Little surprise then that having enjoyed more freedom and excitement in his first night with us than he had ever known in his entire life, Badger was unwilling to give it up, bracing himself as if we were trying to push him over a cliff instead of simply guiding him into a crate. Fortunately, he was rather taken with the tasty treats we offered, and without thinking it through, he followed the handful of treats we tossed into the crate.

Swallowing the goodies, he turned to face me and pushed his nose against the crate door, dismay crossing his face when he realized he was locked in. He stood for a long moment and then lay down with a deep sigh, his eyes still on my face. In that thoughtful, considering gaze, I could see an intelligence that would not as readily sell out for a mess of pottage again.

Sure enough, Badger proved to be the kind of dog who was an acute observer with a prodigious memory and the ability to sit back and consider a situation before acting. Aware of the potential conflicts and committed to doing what was best for our long-term relationship, both John and I were ready, armed with patience, the necessary time, delicious treats and a soft hand in the collar to ask and guide. Though it might take a few extra minutes, though there were inevitable moments where our requests outstripped his agreement and he would begin to mouth our hands or arm in warning (gently, always) Badger eventually ended up where we needed him to be, and we heaped praise on his head.

ALWAYS DARKEST BEFORE DAWN

What do they say about patience? That you become aware of needing it only when you run out of it? I ran out of patience for Badger about two weeks after his arrival, on an icy morning when, with less than two hours of sleep under my belt, the dogs let me know that they needed to go out. Tired, cold and wishing I lived with African violets and not dogs, I stumbled downstairs to make sure that Badger and puppy Bird actually made it all the way outside. Bleary eyed, I offered praise for well-placed puddles (it's hard to sound genuinely pleased when your teeth are chattering wildly) and headed back to bed, a swirl of happily empty dogs around me as I climbed the stairs. I noticed Badger in the crowd of dogs and smiled to myself as he rounded the corner toward the bedroom with wagging tail. "He feels right at home," I told myself, little suspecting how right I was. By the time I reached the bedroom, I could see an unwelcome sight in the faint predawn light: Badger was sprawled across the bed.

With a sigh, I grabbed the dog biscuits, and with an enthusiasm I did not feel, I began asking all seven dogs to sit and lie down for their biscuits, a ploy meant to lure Badger off the bed. He was willing to leave the bed in order to get his biscuit, but when I reached for his collar and tried to guide him toward the crate, he twisted out of my hand and leaped back into bed. Annoyed, I reached for him again, and this time he flipped over on his back, all four legs wildly punching the air and pushing me away. Long accustomed to dealing with such shenanigans from dogs, I expertly reached past his legs toward the collar—and was met with a display of teeth that gleamed in the predawn dark. Unafraid but increasingly annoyed, I tugged on his collar and struggled to get him on his feet. "Dammit all, Badger, just get in the crate!"

His response was to grab my arm, and anger flared up in me. My anger wasn't from pain; his jaws on my arm didn't hurt in the least. Though there was pressure that was not to be ignored, Badger was always precise and well aware of what he was doing, and I trusted this (though I might not have with another dog). I was angry because something as simple as getting a dog into a crate involved such a bloody waste of time when I was exhausted and cold and all I wanted was for him to be safe while I slept. This did not seem to be an impossible request, especially for a dog who knew perfectly well how to get into a crate. At that precise moment, focused only on what I wanted and how I felt and how pissed off I was by the whole damn thing, I fell a long, long way. Out of patience and not even a little curious about Badger's feelings or his point of view, I was a long way from empathy or fairness and much closer to the edge of cruelty than I'd been in a long time.

When we experience the death of curiosity or patience, empathy is shut down. To be empathetic, a few conditions are necessary: We are interested, curious, intrigued by the other's point of view. We extend the time and patience to explore what may be possible. We are both willing and able to set aside our own fears, feelings, and even needs, making room for the other's needs and feelings to be laid out for examination and study. When we do this, when we engage our curiosity in a patient way and empty ourselves of ourselves in order to fill ourselves with another's perspective, then we are acting in a soulful way. The connection thus achieved is not only powerful, it can be profound in its ability to change us. The most difficult work of empathy may be just this: truly clearing the table of our own stuff, at least for the moment, and not begrudging the space required for another's stuff.

But there was nothing soulful about what I was doing, and the only thing on the table at that moment was my stuff. With gritted teeth and a fire of righteousness burning in me, I unceremoniously hauled Badger to his feet by his collar and snarled at him to get in the crate. By way of response, Badger proved to have far more control of his emotions than I did of mine: He did not bite me. He grabbed me harder, though still without really hurting me, and twisted upside down again, my arm still in his mouth, my fingers painfully trapped in his collar (which hurt like hell). For a long moment, we struggled, and all the while I was angrily wondering why on earth I had ever agreed to take on this brat of a dog, this spoiled, foolish, idiotic animal, this stupid beast. Finally freeing my fingers from his collar, I slapped him on the muzzle. No longer thinking, hurting, out of patience and past the point of caring, I slapped him. Once. Hard.

With a snarl of surprise, Badger let go of my arm and reared back, showing me all his teeth, watching me with wary eyes. For a long heartbeat, I found myself staring into the eyes of a very angry dog and felt the heat of my own anger—I was no longer cold as I had been only moments before when I stood watching dogs pee in the frost-glazed yard. Suddenly aware of how off balance I was at the bed's edge, I adjusted my stance, and as I did, I saw Badger's eyes go wide. Anticipating that I might again reach for him, he pulled back slightly. Never taking his eyes from mine, he snapped at the air and barked, a rising shrill bark of clear frustration.

And then, called to myself by the *clack-clack-clack* of his deliberately impotent jaws in the void between us, I could see again. My anger melted in a rush of empathy, and I could see Badger again. And what I saw was a dog whose only crime was that he wanted to sleep beside me in a warm, soft bed; a dog whose experience had taught him that crates meant loneliness; a dog who believed that people would yield to a show of teeth. I saw a dog who found himself confused by my response and frightened by my sudden anger, especially when he had met nothing but patience from me up to that moment. This was not a bad dog or a defiant dog. This was an untrained dog pushing for what he wanted, a dog testing—as all adolescents do—and trying to find out what the rules were. Most of all, this was a dog defending himself, with dignity and restraint, against what I knew was a sad moment. Though I pride myself on how far I've come from the harsh past, my grasp on what it is to be humane and fair proved too tenuous to allow me to swing safely past that dark moment when a dog's teeth gnashed in the predawn silence.

All the fight drained out of me. I apologized to Badger, who heard my apology with wary watchfulness, and then I headed downstairs to regroup in the kitchen, where I asked each dog to sit and rewarded them with a small treat. I quietly snapped a leash onto Badger's collar before handing him his treat, relieved to see that he did not flinch or draw back from my hand but wagged his tail and looked trustingly into my face as I smiled down at him. And then we made our way back upstairs. With a bit of beef jerky, a little careful but nonthreatening maneuvering and judicious use of the leash I was able to get Badger to enter the crate without much fuss. (I think that much like me, Badger was shocked and surprised by our nasty encounter. Given an opportunity to avoid another confrontation with someone who had proven herself possibly quite aggressive, he was all too glad to get into his crate.) I lay down with a heavy heart and turned to face Badger in his crate as other dogs settled themselves beside me in their accustomed ways. In the faint light that held the promise of the coming day, Badger's eyes gleamed steadily, watching me.

In the dark, I lay watching him. Thinking about our predawn fiasco, I realized that if he had not been wearing a collar I would have had no option but to bring my full attention, creativity and respect to asking Badger to kennel up. There would have been nothing unusual about this. John and I routinely move the cattle on the farm not by force or even halters, but by creating an invitation, by opening a place where willing partnership can exist. Badger's collar had been left on ostensibly as an aid in guiding him through the complexities of the new rules he needed to learn, a strange justification when we regularly handle animals that weigh half a ton or more without such aids. Instead, the collar proved to be a crutch. Hand in collar, I had been tempted to force Badger instead of seeking his cooperation. Hand in his collar, the sleep-deprived, irritable, cold and selfish me could justify using more compulsion when Badger did precisely what I knew he would do in response to being forced—fight back, threaten. How foolish and unfair of me to approach him in a way that I knew he would resist, and then feel justified in punishing him for that resistance.

When I woke up a few hours later, I took his collar off. This was both a profoundly symbolic gesture and a heartfelt promise. None of my dogs wear a collar at home since the setup of the house and farm makes collar and leash unnecessary except for walks in town or while traveling. In our home, dogs wearing collars are easily identified as guests or temporary members of the group. In the simple act of removing his collar, I made Badger a family member, not a conditional guest. I also made a promise to Badger and myself to honor our relationship and to build it one moment at a time.

I am deeply grateful for Badger's forgiveness, though I know that in our relationship, he has good cause to be glad of my forgiveness as well. Badger is not a perfect dog, which is a good thing, because I am not a perfect person. Each of us forgets at times to listen to the other. Each of us gets lost in our own view of the world; each insists and resists in silly, prideful ways. But we don't go very far down the path in those dark woods before we turn back. He keeps me honest. Arriving with his own baggage and knee-jerk responses, he helps me sort through my own. Not as fortunate as the dogs who were born here and thus grew up never knowing the need to threaten in order to be heard, Badger reminds me of the power of simply listening and really hearing another being. In his expanding trust and joy, he offers a poignant reminder of how much relief can be offered when we hear the faintest trace of confusion or anxiety in a loved one's communication. The traces of where a collar once sat on his neck can no longer be seen in his fur. He wears a collar happily now, for it means rides in the car or a trip to training class or an adventure, not a way to bind him against his will or bind him to mine. What binds us, this beautiful dark dog and I, cannot be seen. This bond we have forged is what the Little Prince spoke of: "What is essential is invisible to the eye and can only be seen rightly with the heart."

DANGEROUS OBEDIENCE

While cooking dinner one night, John and I were discussing the many positive changes in Badger's behavior, especially a noticeable reduction in Badger's tendency to use his teeth to communicate. We talked about the likelihood that in another home, this behavior might not have been understood as just that—a communication—and the unhappy and unnecessary end Badger might have faced as an "aggressive" dog. I mentioned how much restraint Badger had shown even when I slapped him, and I wondered with admiration for his considerable control how far he'd have to be pushed before he really did bite. I also said how guilty I felt for having lost my temper. John's response rocked me back on my heels. "Well, he didn't leave you much choice, did he?"

Oh, how easy it would have been to step into the offered sympathy and soothe my conscience with the notion that Badger had somehow been the one to force me to get angry. But I knew that Badger didn't start the battle of the bedroom. Badger wasn't interested in fighting with me. He just wanted to do what felt good—sprawl out in bed—and avoid what he did not like, which was being confined in a crate. Had I crawled into bed beside him, he would have been thrilled, snuggled up next to me and drifted off to happy dreams, just as he often does these days with his handsome head draped over my shoulder. I was the one who let slip the dogs of war with my response to Badger's understandable desire to be in bed. Though it was a good idea and a reasonable request to have him nap safely in a crate, how I set about making that happen was anything but a good idea. Although Badger told me again and again and then again how unfair I was being, I refused to hear him. I was the one who didn't leave him much choice. The blame was mine alone. Badger was just being a dog with limited options in the face of conflict.

Instead of maintaining a loving awareness of Badger's limited response to conflict (chomp!) and doing what was necessary to help him work this through calmly and as gently as possible, I stubbornly focused on how cold and tired I was. I didn't think of how painlessly I could solve the whole problem with a leash and a few treats—I only thought of how much I did not want to bother going downstairs again. And my selfish, emotional motivation for slapping my dog made this a more terrible cruelty than a calm, unemotional "correction" delivered by a trainer who believed with all her heart that she was acting appropriately and fairly. As willful cruelty does, this brief moment did more damage to my soul than all the countless moments where I acted far more forcefully but without any misunderstanding of how wrong my actions were. When I raised my hand in anger to Badger, I knew better, and I did it anyway.

Right there, chopping the onions, talking with someone who understood how maddening it can be to make the time to work through another being's issues and problems, I could have easily reconstructed the situation in my head and justified all of my actions as reasonable, characterized Badger as the stubborn dog and even excused slapping him as an unfortunate inevitability. It scared me, how easily cruelty could creep in uninvited and end up wearing the Great Seal of Justification. It horrified me that even my own husband would not question me, the professional trainer, if I announced that I had no choice but to slap a dog. The only safegaurd against the cruelty I am capable of is my willingness to constantly question my own motivations and actions. But I have known this for a long, long time. The responsibility for being humane lies strictly within our own hearts; we cannot and should not depend on external authorities to guide us.

Like some readers, I have another responsibility far beyond my personal relationships with my animals. As a professional to whom others turn for advice and guidance, I need to recognize the power that I am granted in my role as "the trainer" (often spoken in quasi-reverent tones by those who are having trouble reconciling the bouncing Buck at their feet with the well-behaved dog who resides, at least for the moment, solely in their imagination). I need merely say, "I am a dog trainer," and with that statement, I claim for myself whatever degree of expertise a dog owner might attribute to that title. If I want to drape myself in more authority, I might call myself a "behavior consultant" or "dog psychologist" or "behaviorist." (It should be noted that there are no licensing or certification regulations for dog trainers in any state as of this writing. In sharp contrast, I could not cut someone's hair or do their nails without a license, at least in my state. Caveat emptor indeed when obtaining the services of a trainer, behavior consultant or behaviorist.) Whatever I choose to call myself, the moment I step forward to offer advice— whether or not it is good advice, whether or not I am paid for giving it—I have wrapped myself in the cloak of authority. Sought and claimed or not, that authority is powerful and needs to be handled with care.

Because I Said So

There are quite a few old jokes that include someone—a child, a husband, whoever—asking semidefiantly "Why should I?" in response to some direction from an authority figure or evidently more powerful person. And the punch line, inevitably, is this: "Because I said so, that's why." And we all laugh, knowing that the would-be defiance evaporates and the instructed meekly goes ahead and does as told. In such jokes, we evidence an understanding of how deeply obedience to authority is ingrained in us. Defying authority is not something that we do easily. After all, the very coherence of society actually depends on the individual's obedience to authority, whether that's the red light at the corner or a federal regulation. But there is also a dark and disturbing side to how far this obedience can be taken.

Psychologist Stanley Milgram devised an experiment to test "how far a person will proceed in a concrete and measurable situation in which he is ordered to inflict increasing pain on a protesting victim." The experiment consisted of a "teacher" (the actual subject of the experiment) and a "learner" (actually an actor), and a simple memory test of word pairings; an "experimental scientist" supervised. The teacher believed that the experiment was an exploration of the effects of punishment on memory and learning, and also believed that the learner was a genuine participant in the experiment as he was. During the test, the teachers believed that they would be delivering electric shocks of ever-increasing intensity for any wrong answers by the learners. In fact, no shocks were delivered, though the actors participating as the learners offered convincing performances of discomfort, fear and pain.

Before conducting the experiment, Milgram asked a wide range of people for their predictions regarding the results; all predicted that nearly every subject (except a tiny lunatic fringe of disturbed individuals) would be unwilling to obey instructions to inflict pain. The actual results were nothing short of chilling. When an authority figure (an experimental scientist) insisted that the experiment continue despite protests and pleas and even screams from the learner, apparently normal people from all walks of life were willing to obey. Of the Yale students participating in the first study, more than 60 percent of the subjects were "fully obedient," which is to say that they obeyed to the point of delivering the most potent, extremely painful shock available— 450 volts. These experiments were repeated with subjects drawn from all walks of life in New Haven, and the results were the same. Repeated further at Princeton, and in Italy, South Africa and Austria, the results were more disturbing, with a *higher* level of fully obedient subjects, as high as 85 percent in a Munich study.

These subjects were not sadists who enjoyed inflicting pain. Some did protest; some wept or grew increasingly anxious as they delivered greater-intensity shocks. Others were concerned but when assured that they would not be held responsible for what happened to the learner, continued on. Some, Milgram noted, displayed only minimal tension from start to finish; the responsibility for the learner lay with the scientist, not with them—they were only doing as they were told. And some refused to obey. (This "defiant" group fascinated me—what inner qualities or resources did they possess that enabled them to refuse? What could they teach us? Were there common elements in their individual philosophies that served to anchor them firmly in their sense of what was right and humane so that even the pull of authority could not break them loose from their moorings?)

In considering the ramifications of Milgram's work, we need to keep in mind a key fact: The authority figure in the experiment had no particular psychological leverage over the test subjects. Refusal to cooperate with the experimental scientist would not result in lower grades, failure, financial loss, physical pain, harm to a loved one—no tangible consequences, in fact, attended a defiance of authority. And yet, the subjects were unwilling to perform poorly, disappoint or, as Milgram notes, "hurt the feelings" of the scientist in charge of the experiment (this despite the fact that they could hear the protests and screams of the learner whose feelings apparently carried less weight in their mental equations!) In order to stop the experiment and answer the uncomfortable proddings of conscience, the subject had to make a break with authority. And they were by and large unable to do this, even in the presence of another human being's suffering, even when no real consequences attended a refusal.

In his *Harper's* article "The Perils of Obedience," Milgram concluded,

"This is, perhaps, the most fundamental lesson of our study: ordinary people . . . can become agents in a terribly destructive process." Not because they are inherently evil or aggressive or pathologically disturbed, but largely because they were unable to defy authority. As Milgram stated, "Relatively few people have the resources needed to resist authority."

Aside from offering an unpleasant look at the human psyche, how does this apply to our relationships with our dogs? Seeking guidance from dog trainers, behaviorists and obedience instructors, we may find ourselves in a real-life experiment when these "experts" tell us what we must do to our dogs in order to train, correct or punish them. Even when our senses tell us that we have stepped past the bounds of what is right and humane, we may find ourselves more concerned with what the teacher or trainer or expert thinks of us than we are with what is happening to our dog. If we are not aware of our very human tendency to obey what an authority tells us to do, even when we are uncomfortable or even horrified by what that may be and the effects it has on our dogs, we may end up far from where we hope to be.

With unhappy regularity, I meet dog owners who deeply regret following the advice of someone who was "an expert," an authority figure who instructed them in how best to train or "correct" their dog. Believing that what they understood about dogs and training was nothing compared to what the "expert" must know (define *expert* as you will, but it's rarely warranted in any field by but a tiny handful), these folks ignored the protests that rose up inside them, bit back the questions that they wanted to ask and, in misplaced faith, treated a dog in a way that made their hearts grow a little harder. And always, the question these folks ask is this: "Why did I listen to them?" And when they ask, they are not asking me. Their gaze is turned inward, and they review the past as if watching a distasteful movie sequence, and sadly shake their heads before adding yet another straw to their burden of guilt: "I should have known better."

It is always an immense relief to such people to know that they are not a minority group of careless, thoughtless or callous folk, but that their response to an authoritative direction is quite typical. This does not excuse our behavior, but it does help explain it and offer us an opportunity to embrace this gift of understanding of how easily we are led down in ways that shrink our souls and leave us regretful. If we understand that being human includes weaknesses and tendencies that pull us toward the dark, unlighted corners, we then can choose deliberately to move toward the light, and thus continue to grow. Our power remains authentic when we refuse to give it away by surrendering to the illusion that others know more than what our hearts tell us; we endanger the relationship, and due to the potential for cruelty that exists in the animal/human relationship, we may actually endanger the dog.

At the moment we set our intention to walk the paths that we believe will lead us to the deeper connections and more profound relationships we need and long for, we have begun to shift our world. Embracing the dog as more than mere object to be shaped to suit our needs, more than mere subject who must heed our every command, more than just a helpless creature in our caretaking, we open ourselves to a new awareness. We can no longer discard as unimportant or meaningless the subtleties of tail and ear and eye, but as we do with any beloved, we thirst for a greater understanding, and so we enter each moment with our dogs in a new state of awareness. If we are diligent in doing the work of relationship, bringing our curiosity and empathy and joy to the journey with another, our awareness blossoms into knowledge. And with knowledge comes responsibility. Finding the authentic power in ourselves and in a relationship means accepting responsibility for our own actions and its effects on others.

Some of Milgram's further experiments offered additional food for thought. In one variation of the experiment, it was left strictly up to the teacher as to how much of a shock they would deliver for wrong answers. Under these conditions, the overwhelming majority chose a level well under the minimal level where the learner showed any discomfort at all. This gave credence to a fairly often heard comment in the original studies, "If it had been up to me. . . ." Real-life message? Remember this: It *is* up to you. See the dog.

If we are aware that the responsibility is ours for being fair, humane and quite unlike the majority of subjects in Milgram's study, then we can no longer lay the blame for what we choose to do at another's feet by saying, "I was just doing what I was told to do." We have to learn to listen to what our hearts have to say. Our own degree of comfort and joy, sureness and confidence comes from within, when we are acting in deep accordance with our true selves.

The relief of knowing that we have acted in all-too-human ways is compounded by the sensation of authentic power and freedom when we accept that the future need not mirror the past. If we are willing to make conscious choices, we can create new possibilities and reach new levels in our relationships. But then, following close on the heels of such relief and freedom is a snapping, snarling mess of guilt. Even as we project ourselves forward into what we imagine for the future, the tangle of our past pulls us back and begins the retroactive replay. It is a peculiar human tendency to flail ourselves with how it might have been if we knew then what we know now. And the moment we begin to look at our past using a light we acquired only recently, things get distorted. We can only accept the responsibility for what we know; it is unfair to look back and assign our then-unknowing selves responsibility for what we did not understand. To do so is as foolish as looking back on our childhood and thinking that if only we'd been able to read at age three, we might not have drawn on our mother's quilt using a marker clearly labeled as "permanent." Even if we destroyed a family heirloom, we cannot hold ourselves accountable for such unknowing actions.

It is both understandable and common to feel regret for the mistakes made when we saw things differently, when we did not understand or know what we do now—even if our understanding or knowledge is but moments old. And generally speaking, we are most horrified by the distances we were capable of moving from the true north of our soul's compass. If the worst thing I had ever done in my lifetime was slap one dog on one cold morning for no good reason and many selfish ones, it might be fair to say that my soul's course hadn't deviated too terribly. It was a brief derailment, an error examined until as much possible wisdom and grace had been wrung from it and a mistake that has served to heighten my awareness since that dark moment. But my experience is long and my memory is good, and I know that countless times, I have stood in a place diametrically opposed to the path my soul would have me take. And for this, I have had to find a way to forgive myself. The only way I was able to do this was to make a list of all the animals I could remember who had been on the receiving end of my mistakes, and to ask their forgiveness and thank them for what they helped me learn. While unable to change the past, I could—and did—make a vow to change the future, so that all dogs and animals who touched my life would (hopefully) benefit from what I had learned sometimes at the expense of the dogs who had come long before them.

We cannot be held responsible for what we did not know. But we are deeply accountable for what we do know—knowledge entails responsibility. And this is where I've found the greatest difficulty in forgiving myself. It's easy to review my life and understand that given what I knew at the time, given the examples set all around me, my choices were the best I could make. For these moments, forgiveness for my younger, more foolish self is easy. But as with all soulful work, I have found that the line between knowing and not knowing looks sharp and crisp only from a distance. Up close, there is a blurring that occurs as we near that line, a knowing that is not yet a knowing but more a prickling in the soul that says something is wrong. The first inklings of awareness come with a sense of discomfort, unease, a protest that dies unspoken on your lips. Seek these pricklings, hunt for them, coax them out of hiding and ask, "What is wrong?" Do not fear these, but honor them. Ruth Renkel wrote, "Never fear shadows. They simply mean there's a light shining somewhere nearby." These uneasy pricklings, these shadows that darken our inner landscape, are the soul's guardians and warn us when we have gone astray. When we turn away from a willingness to be aware of these warnings, then we are guilty with cause—we knew, but we chose to act as if we did not.

In the end, our personal philosophy is also our best protection against cruelty. When we know what we believe and who we are, we stand strong and sure about what we will and will not allow. For those in our caretaking, such soulful coherence offers them a powerful shield against cruelties large and small.

19

MATTERS OF THE HEART

To love is to give hostages to fate.
Jo Coudert

I HAVE CLOSED THE KITCHEN DOOR to keep the other dogs out, so that I can serve Vali a special meal of pressure-cooked chicken without the need to guard against an impertinent youngster hoping for a morsel from her bowl. I have said nothing to her, and yet she stands motionless as the other dogs sweep from the room at my request. We have understood each other for a long, long time. Closing the door, I turn to her, and she looks at me with unwavering, full eyes, her tail wagging a little as I step toward the dog refrigerator and take out the food I have made just for her, my dear old friend.

This is her favorite, and it is the best I can offer her—chickens raised here on our farm, cared for with love, grown with respect. In this now anonymous blend of bones and flesh I hope that everything good and true that helped these chickens grow to their inevitable end here in my pot is also still, somehow, magically present in this food that I serve my old friend. Watching her eat, gratefully noting that she does so with gusto, eager to nourish her old body, I see chickens sprawled in summer sunshine, white-feathered wings akimbo like sunbathing angels pausing for a moment to rest on the greenest of green grass. I see the brightness in their eyes as they catch sight of John bringing fresh food or a special treat of overripe tomatoes. I watch Vali eat, and I hope that the sunshine still lurks in that flesh. I wish those chickens were indeed angels, and that with soft tender hands, they would carry her to a place where the moment is always right to pause, sprawled in the summer sun on cool green grass.

It's been only four days since I picked up the phone, the veterinarian's cool, professional voice unexpectedly filling my ear. Even as I return his greetings, I am looking at the clock and thinking, But I haven't even begun to worry yet. In my mind, Vali is perhaps sedated and being prepped for her surgery. I have thus far kept at bay the image of her ignobly restrained on her back, legs tied with much-used cord that is held by a simple half hitch to each corner of the operating table. I have not allowed myself to imagine the first cut or the red trail that springs up in the scalpel's path, and yet here is the veterinarian telling me that already the surgery is nearly complete, that Vali's spleen is gone. Dumb in my surprise, I ask, "It is? Well, that's good."

There's a pause, and from years of conversations with veterinarians, I know that the absence of assurances to fill the moment means that he is trying to prepare me for what he must say next. Though the actual time is probably just a few heartbeats, I have more than enough time to imagine Vali dead, bled out, dying or beyond all repair before he continues. "It's not good. The spleen was totally engulfed in tumors. It's already spread to the liver, and there are many nodules of cancer scattered throughout the abdomen. We're going to close her up."

So there it is. That ticking I heard all weekend as I looked into her eyes was indeed the final countdown, begun as surely as if some cosmic hand had slapped the button on the clock in a game of speed chess. All weekend, I had watched her, knowing something was wrong, unsure just what it might be. I hoped I was just imagining the discomfort I saw on her face as she shifted positions on her bed, but I thought I also heard that unmistakable sound that I knew all too well. Watching her, I had felt quite urgently that the clock of her life was speeding up, that the final bang (or whimper) was approaching at a speed I did not know or want to recognize.

For a brief moment, I think that it might be easier if the vet had told me that Vali was dead. Such news would transport me to a sad but familiar place. But I've been handed a ticket to the land of grief, and yet no one can tell me just when that flight for the long trip home departs the gate. Staring blankly out the window, I listen to the vet tell me that it's hard to say what will happen with my dog, my old friend. It seems that perhaps I should at least cry, begin grieving now with this confirmation of the final countdown. It suddenly occurs to me how ludicrous it is to have someone tell you that something is fatal. From the moment of our arrival we are moving inexorably toward our departure. Life is fatal for us all. The note regarding the fatality of Vali's condition is really a hidden message that just puts me on notice that Death is not abroad in some distant land but present, here, in my neighborhood.

But I don't cry. Instead, I feel only calm relief. We have come to this point several times, this dog and I. As a puppy, she lay nearly dead in my lap, a victim of parvo, a vicious virus that had killed thousands of dogs across the country. I had whispered to her as I tended to her, "Hang in there, little one. Today is not your day. Not yet. Hang on." With luminous eyes that seemed almost impossibly large for her face, she had stared up at me, the utter seriousness of life in her expression. And she did hang on, and that was not her day to die, just as it was not her day to die a few years later, when eight pounds of cat food stolen in a moment of canine gluttony expanded to fill her stomach nearly to bursting. "Hang on," I had whispered again, and again she had turned that face toward me, serious, hurting and yet clearly working on holding on fiercely to her earthly connections. That was not her day, and it wasn't her day years later when she ate an entire possum, filling her stomach so full that her heart began to labor. Despite the cautious warnings from the university vets who were unable to guarantee her survival, once again, it wasn't her day.

I know that there is a day not too distant when Vali will die, just as there is a day when I will die. In passing, I feel a pang of curiosity about my own death that becomes a singsong litany from high school journalism class—who? what? where? why? when? how? I realize the question of who has been answered, and doubt that the others can be, or at least not in advance. But to the best of my knowledge, for both Vali and me, today is not that day.

As she finishes the chicken (sun-drenched angel food?), thunder rumbles and the lights over the kitchen sink flicker. Though once she might have turned an anxious ear to the storm that is breaking violently, old age has its benefits, and my beautiful old friend's deafness is at least for the moment a blessing. She eats in peace while I anxiously consider the sheets of rain that have hidden the barn, the trees—in fact, the whole world outside. This old farmhouse has seen a lot of storms in its hundred-plus years, and evidently borne them all fairly well, so I relax into the security (though undoubtedly false) that we're safe within while the storm rages without.

Vali's shaved belly is nearly hidden at this angle, and with a habitual eye, I consider her weight and coat and body. She needs to gain weight—the cancer has consumed calories like some evil boarder who has raided the refrigerator unseen—but her coat is soft, shiny, good to the touch. I admire the cleanness of her limbs and cannot help noting that though some arthritis is evident in the stiffness of her back, she is still a sound dog with four good legs, well built with a body that could easily carry her many more years. But I know that within that beautiful body there rages another storm that will destroy her from the inside out. Just as this old house keeps me safe within from the storm without, no beauty of Vali's earthly house can protect her from the cancer within.

Lightning flashes nearby, and the thunder that follows a startled heartbeat later is a rifle crack that makes me catch my breath. Too close for comfort, I think, and step to look out the window. The barn is fine, and cattle graze without any apparent alarm. Noticing my concern, Vali turns to me with a slight question in her eyes. I smile at her and run my hand across her head and down her back. She never breaks eye contact with me, and for a long moment, we look at each other without blinking. Her eyes seem terribly full, reminding me of the look I've seen in people unable to speak but still needing to communicate. "I'm glad you're still here," I tell her. She gazes back at me as if to say, "Yes, I am here." But I get the distinct sensation that there is much more she still needs to tell me, much more that I need to hear.

Today, this old house will not fall down. Someday it will. Today, my old dog still trots beside me as we head to the barn to bring John his raincoat and check on the pig who has hurt her leg. Someday soon, I think, Vali will walk beside me only in spirit. Today is not the day, and I am grateful that today is all I ever have. Funny, I think, walking along next to my old dog. It was a puppy who taught me that.

APPOINTMENT IN SAMARA

Six weeks old, the puppies were sassy, chubby miniatures of the adult German Shepherds they would become. In honor of their Alaskan father, they carried Alaskan names—Sitka, Juneau, Willow, Aleyeska, Dalton, Kiska, McKinley. To them, the veterinarian's office was an exciting frontier ripe for exploration. I prided myself on breeding good dogs, healthy dogs, beautiful companions that lived long, happy lives. One after another I set them on the examining table, confident in their glowing health and fine character. One by one, they squirmed, kissed the vet and showed no signs of any problems. Then my veterinarian looked up from listening to McKinley's heart, his eyes troubled. "He's got a murmur."

This was not an innocent murmur that would be outgrown. Ultrasound examination revealed a fatal flaw in the formation of the heart, a flaw that could not be corrected and that in all likelihood would result in sudden, unpredictable death sometime before the puppy's second birthday; chances were good he would not live to see his first. Euthanasia was an option. Faced with a grim prognosis, I considered how much future grief I would be spared by putting the puppy down now, before he blossomed into who he would be. But I knew that in sparing myself the grief of losing a young dog, I would also be trading away something unknown but also immeasurable. I was not willing to make that trade.

In any relationship, there is one inescapable reality: To love anything is to risk loss. And a relationship with an animal carries a double-edged sword. While we enjoy the unconditional love of our animals, we know that odds are better than good that even if they enjoy a long and healthy life, we will outlive them. We accept this reality and the eventual tide of grief that accompanies it because in the moments between our first reaching out to an animal and when we finally let go, what we receive are riches beyond measure. Yet, as we do for our own lives, we hinge our daily sanity on the fragile belief that our animals will be granted full, long lives, that the inevitable is years away. Marcel Proust wrote, "We say that the hour of death cannot be forecast, but when we say this we imagine that hour as placed in an obscure and distant future. It never occurs to us that it has any connection with the day already begun or that death could arrive this same afternoon, this afternoon which is so certain and which has every hour filled in advance." Years are measured out to us in seconds, and thus it seems when looking forward that the end is a long way away. Looking back, we know it was a very brief time indeed.

Though we may not be comfortable with thinking about it, we are all aware at some level that for every living being, a life clock is ticking. Watching a talk show, I saw an actual clock that could be set to a specific time; second by second it would count down to that final appointment. The creators of this clock showed how a person's birth date, current age and some information from actuarial tables could be used to estimate how much time was left in that life. A fifty-five-year-old man might, according to statistics, have only seventeen years remaining to him, barring unforeseen illness or accidents. This clock would begin the count, relentless second after second. Most members of the audience found this an extremely disturbing idea. The creators were quick to point out that the intention behind this clock was not to underline death's ever quickening approach, but rather to provide an opportunity for living with a fullness of choice and awareness. With such a vivid reminder, people could discard the meaningless in their lives and trade the valuable seconds for what mattered intensely to them.

Depending on our age, experience, religious or spiritual beliefs, each of us keeps the concept of death a certain distance from our daily awareness. For each of us, experiences ranging from the "near misses" of serious illness or minor traffic accidents to actual losses bring the concept a little closer, at least for a while. Each of these experiences offer us an opportunity to examine our feelings and to learn something valuable. We may turn away from the lesson at hand or we may choose to learn; neither approach forestalls the inevitable.

There is an old Sufi tale of a merchant in Baghdad whose servant returns from the marketplace trembling and pale. The servant had been jostled in the marketplace, and when he turned to see who had bumped him, he saw Death, who looked at him and made a threatening gesture. The servant begs the merchant to loan him a horse so that he might go to the distant city of Samara, where Death will not be able to find him. The merchant agrees, and the servant gallops away.

Later that day, the merchant also sees Death in the market, and asks him, "Why did you make a threatening gesture to my servant when you saw him this morning?"

"I did not threaten him," Death said. "That gesture was only my start of surprise. I was astonished to see him here in Baghdad, because I have an appointment with him tonight in Samara."

It seems a sad but straightforward tale: Caring breeder discovers fatal flaw, keeps puppy, life goes on. In reality, it was more complicated than that. I had planned to keep McKinley's sister Sitka. Could I raise two puppies and do them both justice? Would Sitka or McKinley suffer from more attention paid to the other? What-ifs raced through my head, and I sought advice from a close friend. Of all that she said to me, nothing struck me as forcibly as this: "McKinley's lessons to you will be matters of the heart, on many levels." It began with my listening to what my heart told me was right. A few days later, Sitka was on her way to her new home, and I began my journey with McKinley, aware that we were moving toward an appointment in Samara.

WITH DEATH ON MY SHOULDER

As I thought, and told those who cared to listen, keeping this puppy was the responsible thing to do. I would, I bravely announced, love him till he died, and until that day, offer him a full life. On the surface, I was matter-of-fact, pragmatic. After all, as I said repeatedly, the truth is no one knows when the final moment will arrive. Yet in my heart, these brave words fell empty and hollow, floating on a sea of fears. McKinley would nap, and I would find myself anxiously watching his rib cage for movement. If I heard him whimper in another room, my heart would race, slowing only when I could assure myself that he was fine. On the mornings I awoke before he did, I sat up to see his body stretched out in the corner of the bedroom. Was he alive? Had he died in his sleep? Though I did not make a sound, McKinley would raise his head as if woken by my fears and look at me with sleepy eyes: "I am still here."

"It's so hard to allow myself to fully love you, knowing you will die so soon," I told him one afternoon as he raced across the yard to me, full of a puppy's seemingly eternal energy and joy. He sat, staring at me, and in my head, I clearly heard his reply. "But we all die."

"Yes," I agreed, watching the dogs playing around me, "but these other dogs won't die soon."

His answer came quickly, an arrow to my heart: "You don't know that." With that, he turned away and went on with the business of life.

In *The Road Less Traveled*, Scott Peck wrote, "If we are unwilling to fully face the fearsome presence of death on our left shoulder, we deprive ourselves of its counsel and cannot possibly live or love with clarity. When we shy away from death, the ever changing nature of things, we inevitably shy away from life."

One of my students had a wonderful young dog named Clancy who developed a malignant mass (oddly, on her left shoulder). Though chemotherapy offered some slim hope, the veterinarian warned my student that Clancy had perhaps only six months left to live. He recommended avoiding stress (which included, he felt, obedience school), and suggested that Clancy be made as comfortable as possible. Distraught, Anne told me she would not be coming back to class; she planned to spend as much time as possible at home with Clancy until she died. About a month later, she called again. Clancy was increasingly bored, and was depressed when Monday night rolled around and no one got ready to take her to training class. What should she do?

I asked what Clancy's physical condition was. Her answer neatly summed up canine reality: "Obviously, no one told Clancy that she has cancer and is going to die. She gets up every day wagging her tail and does the best she can." And so Clancy returned to class. Some nights, she lay on the sidelines, unable to fully participate but watching the class with great interest, her characteristic grin letting us all know she was having a wonderful time. On those nights, we included her in the down stays—it was all she could do, but she did it well. We would fuss over her, telling her she had the finest down stay of any dog in class, and she responded with a proud, thumping tail. Other nights, Clancy was her old self and performed with precision and style. Always, she entered the room with joyful anticipation, willing to bring her best efforts to the moment.

Whatever we may have managed to teach Clancy paled in comparison to what she taught all who knew her: Life is to be lived, one moment at a time. Guided by death on her left shoulder and the wisdom of a dog who was busy living, not dying, Clancy's owner learned to treasure each day as it unfolded. Though she worked to protect Clancy from unnecessary stress, she no longer tried to protect Clancy from all that made her life worth living.

THE FENCE THAT FEAR BUILT

It is natural to protect what you love. To a certain degree, this natural protectiveness functions to limit or minimize risk and is part of our responsibility as dog owners, part of any loving relationship. All of us would look askance at someone who proclaimed that they loved their dog yet let him run freely in traffic or failed to provide veterinary care so disease and infection did not take hold. To the extent that the protection we offer is founded on caring for the well-being of our canine charges, our protection is a good and healthy thing. But at what point does protection become hurtful in itself?

McKinley was about nine weeks old when I took him to the barn along with the other dogs for a final night check on the horses. Curious about the new puppy, one of the horses leaned over his stall door to investigate. As I have done with every puppy, I picked up McKinley to meet the horse. Alarmed by the giant head breathing down on him, the puppy's heart began to race, every beat registering in my suddenly unsure hands. Why had I done that? What if that was the momentary stress that killed him? My fears about losing him surfaced in a huge swell of doubt and confusion. Although the puppy calmed down quickly, I did not. Watching him gallop away to join the other dogs, I had to face a difficult question. What constituted the "full life" I had promised this dog?

It would have been much easier if his was a "manageable" disease or defect, if by modifying his diet or limiting his exercise or avoiding certain situations I could limit the risks, prolong his life. But McKinley was a question mark, with no more certainty of when and where the bell would toll for him than for me. While I wanted to protect him (and myself from the pain of losing him), there was a fine line between the reasonable precautions I would take with any puppy and overprotecting McKinley. Knowing just where that fine line lay was possible only if I was willing to examine my own feelings and fears.

When I was nine or ten, my mother sometimes washed my hair in the kitchen sink. Lying with my head safely held in her hands, I could gaze up at my mother's beautiful face. One day, looking very closely at her nostrils, I began thinking that I would recognize her face from any angle, anywhere, no matter how old or wrinkled she got. Suddenly, it hit me that the day would come when she would no longer wash my hair, when I would no longer live with her, and then—building to a horrifying realization—there would be a time when she no longer shared the planet with me. What if she died when I was not there? What if I never got a chance to say good-bye? I could think of nothing more awful than seeing her for the last time without knowing it was, indeed, the last time. The fear those thoughts created was palpable: My chest tightened; my throat closed. To my mother's utter surprise, I began sobbing uncontrollably.

Her first thought was that somehow she had burned me with too hot water or gotten shampoo in my eyes. While I could shake my head in answer to her queries about water temperature or shampoo, I was unable to answer her question, "Then why are you crying?" My young vocabulary could not possibly begin to explain the fear that gripped me. It was nearly twenty years before I could explain that moment to her.

To a certain degree, it used to be possible for me to gauge the depth of my love for someone by the intensity of the fear created in my contemplation of their death. While this is not as true as it used to be, thanks to lessons on living and dying that I've been offered by many animals, the fear is still there. No one wants to hurt; no one wants to experience loss. But I also know that to cling sobbing as I did to my bewildered mother is a waste of valuable time. I am well acquainted with my fear of loss, and with the specific physical feelings that it arouses in me. Finding that fine line between reasonable caution and anxiously clutching McKinley was not really difficult—I had only to recognize fear.

For McKinley to have a full life meant that I had to allow him to live. Any actions I took to protect him had to spring from normal, reasonable caution, not from my fear. With each choice I made for him, I first checked carefully for any hint of the wide-eyed monster. My fear would have dictated never leaving him unhappily barking in his crate, never disciplining his actions, never raising my voice to him, never forcing him to do anything he didn't want to do, never letting him run after the big dogs or swim in the pool or face scary situations or anything, anything at all that might trigger the final moment. But in the end, I would not have held off death. I would only have held back life.

When I was a child, my mother appeared fearless. Now a mother myself and much older, I understand that she was often afraid, but to the best of her ability, she privately wrestled with her fears for us, and only rarely did we wonder at her urgent cautions or worried glances. She taught her children reasonable caution, but did not limit our lives because of her own fears. She understood, and taught by daily example, that a full life is not one described by fear, but one of well-considered risks taken with full enthusiasm and no regrets.

She found horses frightening and did not understand what drove me to spend countless hours in their company. At the first and last horse show of mine that she ever attended, she was greatly alarmed when my borrowed mount tried to deposit me (unsuccessfully) on the ground. But she did not limit my horse activities. She knew that this passion was part of what made me who I was; that mattered far more to her than her own fears. The fine balance she struck as a parent is the same one we must find with our dogs—protecting them without preventing them from being who they are, without limiting the fullness of their lives. This is a difficult balance to find.

Years ago, my good friend Judy had a dog who was dying of kidney failure. All tests showed that nothing more could be done for this dog; it was time to put her to sleep before the kidney failure caused her a tremendously painful death. Knowing there were only a few hours left before the situation became uncomfortable and then miserable for the dog, Judy decided that if Dawn must die, she would not do so in a hospital cage. Instead, she would bring her to my farm, a place they both loved, and a veterinarian friend of mine would put her to sleep there.

At the animal hospital, the attending veterinarian gave Judy a stern warning that while Dawn looked fine at the moment, taking the dog out of the hospital would worsen her condition in a few hours. To Judy, this seemed almost laughable. Why should Dawn's life end after nothing but a few more hours of sitting in a hospital when it might also be called to a halt after a last chance to walk in the sunshine? How long, she demanded to know, would it be before Dawn began to suffer in any way? The vet shrugged. "Perhaps three to four hours at most. She'll get weak and begin vomiting at first. Then it will go much more quickly."

Facing death square-on, it seemed clear to Judy that Dawn should be granted the complete fullness of what remained of her life. "Give me my dog," she said.

At the farm, Dawn and Judy wandered happily in the sunshine, played a little ball, waded in the stream. For the first time in the weeks since Dawn had become ill, they both truly enjoyed life together in the way they always had. It was a well-considered risk, this final gift of a few more moments of joy. Dawn never did grow weak as the vet had warned would happen. Perhaps the pure pleasure of those hours sustained her in ways medicine never could. Perhaps Judy's timing was simply the impeccable timing of love. Still comfortable in her body, Dawn was eased with a gentle hand to her death in Judy's arms, a tennis ball still soggy from play at her side.

In a Heartbeat

When it came to McKinley, I wished I had as clear a timetable as Judy had with Dawn. A part of me wanted for the world to pause until we had marked his last day, so that I might not miss even a moment of his life. Above all else, I wanted to accomplish this: to be able to look into his eyes when the end came and know that I had not limited his life or taken his time with me for granted. But trying to live each of an animal's days in a heightened intensity of awareness, in a sort of death watch, is neither possible nor balanced. In waiting for the dreaded moment, I would exhaust myself, deprive others I love of attention and time, and most of all, miss what that animal's life was really about. So I tried to live as McKinley did—in the moment, one heartbeat at a time.

But it was precisely a heartbeat that reminded me constantly of what was to come. Whether curled beside me on the couch, leaping up to deliver one of his special hugs or draped across me in bed, I could not miss the abnormal rhythm of McKinley's heart beneath my hands or held close against my cheek. His heartbeat was like an enchanted seashell that, when put to my ear, whispered of both death and life. Even without a defective heart that beats telltale under our hands, there are other rhythms that also whisper to us, try though we might to ignore them. They are to be found in the gradual slowing of an old dog's trot, in the dimming, blued eyes of a friend somehow grown ancient without our agreement or awareness. Like photos superimposed, it is hard to distinguish between the old dog before us and the young dog he once was.

In the year between his fourteenth birthday and his death just five weeks shy of his fifteenth year, McKinley's grandfather Bear became increasingly feeble. Watching his legs begin to fail him was difficult; his mind and spirit were still strong. Though no longer able to outrun the younger dogs, he could still exert sufficient authority to force any dog near him to relinquish the ball. I was unwilling to have him jostled by healthier, younger dogs or watch his frustration when they kept themselves and the ball outside his range of influence. So playing ball, a game he loved above all else, became a private matter between us, Bear and me. I would toss the ball a short distance on level ground, and with determination, he would shuffle after it. Even at his advanced age, his delight in having captured the ball was tremendous. Grayed muzzle gripping the prize, he would wobble back to me, eyes aglitter in anticipation of the next throw. In those moments, the sadly real image of an old dog playing a favorite game faded, giving way to the more familiar, remembered image of a younger Bear, a dog who could fly through the air to snatch balls in midflight.

It may have been just a mistake or the habit of years that prompted me one day to toss the ball, as I so often had, high into the air. And it may have also been only habit that triggered Bear's gallant effort to leap for the ball, a canine Nureyev against the sky. I can still see his eyes brightly fixed on the ball's trajectory, his mouth opening in preparation, his entire being projected up and away from gravity's pull. For a split second, he was airborne and young again. Then he crumpled in the grass, shocked and embarrassed that his hind legs had failed him. Although I could apologize to him for my mistake, I had no suitable apology for what time's passing had done to his body.

I had often wondered if, like myself, animals felt little of the aging process, so gradually sinister, so insidious yet ruthless in its quiet work. Marking yet another year's passage, did they too feel no different, no older? Did they bear the knowledge, experience and wisdom of their years as I bore mine—a strange overlay on the child within me, the child who never truly disappeared? Were their images of themselves blended as mine were for me, a blur of young and old, past and present, and running through it all, a constancy that I think must be the eternity of spirit? Watching Bear send his mind soaring after that tennis ball, I knew that for him as well as for me, some part of him was forever young, capable of anything. As he struggled to right himself in the grass, I saw the surprise in his eyes, as if he too had been unable—or unwilling—to see himself as an old dog who would fly through the sky no more. I never again threw his ball high against the clouds; he never again leaped to meet it. Looking through my tears, I sadly brought into focus the reality of Bear, my old dog.

One of the most difficult aspects of caring for a very sick or old dog is keeping clear the images our hearts would prefer to blur. My friend Ginny's dog Annie was a proud German Shepherd who had always disdained coddling or assistance. Now ancient, the end was written in Annie's eyes, which had begun to glow with the oddly youthful look animals sometimes have as they begin the process of disconnecting from this life, this physical body. Annie was preparing Ginny for the departure that was not too far away, and Ginny knew it. Still, one night, Ginny and I knelt next to the old dog, hoping to offer some beneficent touch, some assistance for the wasted body. Annie's paws were cold; her circulation had begun to limit its rounds, saving its precious energy for her vital organs.

"Give her a blanket," I suggested. Ginny protested, saying Annie would never accept such coddling, had always rejected such luxury no matter how wet her coat or cold the night. Still, she gathered a blanket and we draped it around Annie's frail form, leaving only her beautiful head exposed. With a brief, apologetic glance at us, the dog who had spent a lifetime needing no assistance snuggled into the blanket, accepting the warmth her old body needed. Ginny, who spends countless hours helping other people with their dogs, was devastated.

"How could I have missed that? Why didn't I think to give her a blanket? How could I be so stupid about my own dog?" Ginny had not been careless or uncaring. In every moment of her life, Annie had created a powerful image of who she was. It was hard to shift a lifetime's focus and clearly see the newer, less-welcome image of Annie as a rapidly aging dog who needed help. Ginny's heart, and Annie herself, clung stubbornly to the more familiar view of Annie as strong, capable, independent.

Two Dogs and a Funeral

In our house, it is a rare year that does not include death. With so many animals of varying life span and age, it is almost inevitable that by each year's end, we have had to say good-bye to one or more friends. Looking forward as we do to Christmas, our favorite of all holidays, we wonder silently and aloud who will be there with us for the celebration. Because death is such a constant in my life, it was not a surprise when a friend called to tearfully inform me that she had just put Blaze to sleep. This thirteen-year-old Golden Retriever had been her first dog, and she did not know what to do, nor how to handle the situation with her other Golden, Kelly. After talking for a bit, she decided she wanted to bury Blaze in the backyard. Knowing that she was recovering from giving birth just a few weeks earlier and that her husband was away on a business trip, I agreed to dig the grave.

If there was ever a suitable outlet for grief, it is this: the backbreaking, mind-numbing work of digging a large dog's grave, especially in the rocky ledges of western New Jersey where I then lived. At first, you begin with somber purpose, mindful of little but the sadness of your task. Tears spill readily as you work. The digging is easy at first, and as you shovel, you cry and talk and remember, and you even laugh a little. Then the dirt becomes rock, and cursing quietly under your breath, you pound away at the stone that eventually shatters under your determination. You begin to feel the effort now in your back and shoulders, and it gets harder to talk. You no longer speak in whole sentences; instead, you merely grunt in sympathetic agreement as the person who is not digging continues to reminisce and weep. (There is an unspoken rule that the dog's owner need not dig unless they choose to; it is understood that their grief is sufficient work for the moment.) What had been moderate-sized stones grow into boulders the size of small foreign cars. Yet when you wrestle these lost pieces of Stonehenge loose from the earth's grasp, you are shocked to see that the hole you have dug is barely as deep as your shin; you need a hole that will reach to your hips. Surely, your aching body protests, surely we are halfway to China by now. As you stand resting on the shovel to catch your breath, you realize also that the carefully sized grave has somehow changed shape, narrowing as it deepens so that perhaps only a Chihuahua could be laid to rest in the space you've cleared. With a groan, you begin to enlarge the hole on all sides (thinking for only a fleeting moment of how tightly you might curl a dead dog to save some space; practicality is breaking through the heavy clouds of sadness and punching a few holes in this responsibility to treat a lifeless body kindly). And it goes on like this for quite some time. By the time you are done, you are numb, a state of being that is oddly welcome in this sad moment.

Eventually, the grave was ready. Not far away, in quiet repose under a blanket, Blaze's body lay in the back of my friend's car. It is time for the next step. "What do you do when one of your dogs dies?" my friend asked. I explained how we bring the other dogs to the body, how they respectfully gather around and how they sit watching as we bury our friend, attentive until the last shovel of dirt has been lovingly, tearfully tamped into place. She thought this over for a few moments and decided that this was a good way to handle this—after all, Blaze had raised Kelly from a young pup. She headed off to get Kelly for the funeral.

In the wild scrabble of Kelly's feet on the garage floor, I had my first inkling that there might be many ways for dogs to act in the presence of death. Foolishly, I assigned Kelly's enthusiastic gallop toward the car to her joy at seeing me. After all, I told myself, the poor dear had no way of knowing that her friend Blaze was dead since when she last saw her a few hours ago, Blaze was ill but alive. Kelly greeted me with enthusiasm, and I tried to calm her a bit as I returned her hello. My friend asked, "Do we show her Blaze's body now?" Nodding, I opened the back of the car and invited Kelly to put her feet up on the tailgate so she could sniff and understand what had happened. Never a dog to do things halfway, Kelly responded by leaping into the back of the car, merrily bouncing on her dead friend as if this were a new but oddly uncomfortable cushion under the tactfully draped blanket. Even as I heard my friend gasp in horror, I was already calling Kelly out of the vehicle, grateful that she responded quickly by sailing out as gleefully as she had leaped in. Eyes wide, my friend wailed, "I thought you said dogs were respectful of the dead!"

Bewildered myself, I hastily explained that in Kelly's excitement she had probably not noticed anything and just thought she was going for a ride. Before my friend could see through the flimsiness of my answer, I continued in my very best dog trainer's voice, the one filled with confident assurance that students will follow my instructions: "Now is a good time to use all that training Kelly has. Why don't you put her on a down stay near the grave while we move Blaze?" Numbly, my friend walked off with Kelly, leaving me looking in amazement at the pawprints still visible on the blanket over Blaze. As I reached in, I whispered an apology to the dead dog. "Who knew Golden Retrievers didn't take funerals as seriously as German Shepherds do?"

At last, Blaze lay in the grave, her body arranged with care so that she looked comfortably asleep. As we gazed down at this fine old dog, we cried a little more and said a few prayers. "Let me finish this now," I gently suggested, but my friend reached out to stop me. "Wait," she said. "There is something missing. Blaze always loved her tennis balls, and I'd like to bury one with her." She began to cry again but struggled to speak through her sobs. "That way, I'll be sure that she's playing ball up in heaven." This started my tears again, and I just waved a hand toward the house, indicating that she should go find a tennis ball.

Through all this, Kelly had quietly lain near us. Tired of crying, I called Kelly to me, playing with her a little as we waited for my friend to return. I saw Kelly's eyes brighten when she saw the tennis ball in her owner's hand, but I quickly discouraged her interest with a quiet "Leave it." With a small sigh of regret, Kelly sat down at the grave's edge, watching as my friend lovingly placed the bright new ball near Blaze's muzzle. Brushing dirt from her hands and jeans, my friend took a deep, ragged breath as she looked down at her old friend's body. Turning to give her a hug, I caught a movement out of the corner of my eye. It was Kelly, leaping into the grave. In perfect unison, my friend and I exclaimed in shocked tones, "Kelly!" There was no guilt or shame in the dog as she stood on Blaze's body, tail madly wagging, triumphantly holding the ball in her mouth. Her message was crystal clear and contained a goofy wisdom we both understood: Life goes on, so why waste a perfectly good tennis ball?

Remembering the Way Home

After a lifetime with animals, I believe that animals are aware of and understand death. Though some may choose to interpret an animal's quiet acceptance of another's death as evidence there is no awareness, there is another interpretation that better fits what I have experienced. Animals accept death for what it is—a natural process that none of us may escape. I believe that animals have a deep connection to the eternal rhythms of spirit and the universe, a connection that we have as well, but ours is corrupted with complex overlays of knowledge, fear and civilization that draw us ever further from the natural tides of life and death.

There are those who point to the animal's lack of fear in the presence of dying and death as proof that animals have no awareness of death. It has long seemed to me an odd and telling supposition that an awareness of death must equal a fear of death. This is not to say that animals do not die fearfully—they sometimes do, as do we. This is not to say that they readily give up their hold on life. Just as we do, animals struggle, sometimes mightily, to hang on to life. I have held many animals as they fought, sometimes successfully, sometimes in vain, the battle that we all eventually must lose. But I have also seen animals welcome death without fear. Because I was there, riding the moments down the homestretch to the final heartbeat at the wire, I can say that I have seen the awareness in their eyes.

John's first dog, a Golden named MacIntosh, had spent his entire life unable to even look at any needle. Though a brave dog in so many ways, when the vet prepared a routine vaccine or approached to take a little blood for a test, Mac would always look away, his head turned and his eyes closed until the procedure was complete. He was fourteen years old when a tumor on his spleen ruptured. Though we were unaware of this particular tumor, we had been fighting another cancerous growth for several months and had known for quite a while that Mac's time with us was growing short. When he collapsed that last day, we were not sure why, but it was clear that Mac was tired of fighting. Unwilling to surrender hope, we rushed him to the veterinarian, but as Mac's eyes had already told us, the prognosis was not good. We stood agonizing over the choices that lay before us: Put Mac through difficult surgery with only a very slim chance he would survive the surgery, or let him go quietly without further pain or struggle. Looking back at this good dog's life, gazing into his eyes with a question no one wants to ask, we knew he had already given us all that he had to give. As the veterinarian prepared the needle, we held Mac in our arms, nodding mutely when the doctor asked if we were ready. Whatever doubts we had about our decision vanished with Mac's last message to us. As the needle approached his leg, Mac turned his head to look at it, his eyes calm and unworried, watching as it found his vein. He was ready. He laid his head in John's hand and fell asleep for the last time.

MacIntosh died as he had lived, without fear, taking each moment as it came, and welcoming death as the release of his spirit. Animals offer important lessons on being in the moment, even when it is the last. Our fearfulness about death and the process of dying, though understandable, may be unnecessary. Taoist philosopher Chuang-tzu asked, "How do I know that love of life is not a delusion after all? How do I know but that he who dreads death is not as a child who has lost his way and does not know his way home?"

NO REGRETS

I cannot say how McKinley died—I was not there and so do not know if he welcomed death or fought against it. When I found his body lying at the back door, there was no fear on his face, only a surprised look, as if death had caught him unaware. For a blessed, fleeting moment, I thought he was simply sprawled out on his side as he often was after a good romp in the yard. But that moment was only a heartbeat, and then I knew, even as I stepped toward him, long before I touched him. McKinley had found the way home. Grief mixed with relief. This was the moment I had dreaded, the moment I had anticipated with so many tears. The grieving had begun a long time ago, in a veterinarian's office, with a puppy in my arms. The waiting was over; now, at least for a while, I could push death's hovering presence away from me again.

There was also elation, difficult to explain. Stroking his head, calling his name, I realized that I had met this moment as I hoped I might. I had learned that no matter how much you love something, it is impossible to hold it so tightly that death cannot slip it from your grasp. But you can hold on so tightly that life cannot get through. I had held McKinley as lightly as I knew how, trying hard not to wait fearfully for the moment that he was gone but with gratitude for each moment that he was here. I had no regrets, no apologies to make, no actions or words that I would change or take back. Guided by McKinley himself, I had kept my promise and given him a full life. He was not quite eight months old. Had he lived longer, perhaps I would have failed him. Time is both a blessing and a curse to any relationship—time to get it right, time to get it wrong. But somehow, I had succeeded. He taught me, more than any other animal or person I had known thus far, that to live fully is to let go of fear.

Even in death, McKinley continued to teach me. A few days after he died, I was emotionally drained, trying to adjust to the immense emptiness his absence created in our lives. Work demands seemed relentless, and I was feeling increasingly angry. My dogs tiptoed away from me; my husband tried to appease my inarticulate wrath. Although I could see how stupidly I was behaving, I was unwilling to stop myself. Frustrated and trapped by my feelings, I decided to surrender the day and go to bed, hoping that sleep would ease me to a better place. Still wrapped in anger, I lay beside John, listening to his breathing as he relaxed into sleep. Seeking some outlet for the emotions working in me, I began to think about McKinley, and the tears—never far from the surface in those raw days—came quickly. Though nearly asleep, John sensed my misery and reached for me, meaning to hold and comfort me. I jerked away from him, only to find myself even more wretched when he did not repeat the attempt but fell captive to sleep's pull. This was fuel for my self-pity bonfire, and I fanned the flames with vivid images of McKinley's dead body.

Miserably reviewing McKinley's death, I felt his presence, and saw and heard him in my mind as clearly as ever. "Do you have any regrets?" he asked, referring to my relationship with him. My answer, mercifully, was that I did not. Then the image of his body transformed into a scene of John leaving abruptly in the night, which as a volunteer firefighter, he often did. In this movie, I could see myself asleep, only vaguely aware that John was gone.

McKinley spoke again. "What if John left right now and never came back? Would you have regrets?" It was a terrible thought that John should leave on a fire call but not return, never hear me apologize for my self-ishness, never hear me say again that I love him. "There does not need to be regret. If you would wish for a chance to do differently what you have done, if you would regret what you have left undone, make it right. Now. Now may be the only time you have."

I saw McKinley's face, his eyes steady and wise, and felt the peace I had known when I realized that at least with him, I had no regrets. Despite the hour, I woke my sleeping husband, told him that I loved him, that I had been a fool. As forgiving as a dog, he folded me into his arms, and with no regrets, we fell asleep.

THE FRAGILE CIRCLE

Mine is not an elevated existence lived in a state of constant, deep appre-ciation and awareness. Like anyone else, I find myself annoyed by dogs underfoot, by puddles on the floor, by papers cleared from tables by wagging tails. I sometimes forget to be thankful for the warm animal bodies that curl next to me in bed, and instead complain about a lack of blankets to call my own. I pull dog hair from our food and long ago surrendered to the impossibility of keeping home and self spotlessly clean against an endless onslaught of muddy paws and sloppy wet kiss-es. I daydream occasionally of an animal-free life where my time, ener-gy and resources are squandered on me and me alone. But the lesson of

McKinley has spilled over, far beyond the immediacy of his life and his death. Now, when my dogs offer a kiss or invite me to play, I am less quick to push them away if I am feeling pressured or busy. I know that when they are gone, I would happily trade every moment spent complaining for a chance to give them another hug or to stroke their heads once more. I try to accept their gifts of the moment, reminding myself that I am a poor person indeed if I can't spend time accepting the unconditional love offered so often every day by my dogs. On my left shoulder, death sits quietly, not a horrific figure but a source of wisdom on loving and living.

There is a cycle of love and death that shapes the lives of those who choose to travel in the company of animals. It is a cycle unlike any other. To those who have never lived through its turnings or walked its rocky path, our willingness to give our hearts with full knowledge that they will be broken seems incomprehensible. Only we know how small a price we pay for what we receive; our grief, no matter how powerful it may be, is an insufficient measure of the joy we have been given.

Writing in his essay, "The Once Again Prince," animal lover and gifted writer Irving Townsend summed it up:

> We who choose to surround ourselves with lives even more temporary than our own live within a fragile circle easily and often breached. Unable to accept its awful gaps, we still would live no other way. We cherish memory as the only certain immortality, never fully understanding the necessary plan.

It is a fragile circle. But it goes round and round without end.

20

COLD NOSES, NO WINGS

*Soul is most pregnant and ready to be born in relationships, since we can't be
human without them. We cannot save our soul, much less find it, alone.*

GARY ZUKAV, *SEAT OF THE SOUL*

TO INCLUDE SIX DOGS IN A WEDDING is to invite Loki, the Norse god of
mischief, to attend and bring a date. Even with Loki's giggles in our ears,
we designed a wedding ceremony that included our most beloved
human friends and also our animal ones—dogs, horses and even our
donkey. Friends took the dogs on leash as part of the entire procession
of guests as all made their way out into the pasture, where John and I
would follow on horseback later. Along with all our much-loved guests,
the excited dogs stood near the back of the group, waiting for the
moment in the ceremony when one by one we would call them to us.
Each dog exemplified and brought to us qualities and characteristics we
wanted to include in our marriage, and before calling out each dog's
name, we announced to all the gifts and lessons each dog brought us as
they eagerly galloped to join us. In calling Molson to us, we asked for
gentleness, maturity and determination. Bannockburn brought us power
tempered with kindness, and wisdom. Vali brought us gracefulness, intensity, faithfulness. Carson—only a few days away from delivering the litter that brought us McKinley—offered us nurturing, watchfulness and
fierceness. Chilkat carried with him beauty, nobility and courage. And
Otter gave us laughter, joy and playfulness.

In calling our dogs to us and naming their gifts and lessons, we
acknowledged what they helped create in our lives and honored their
role in our lives as teachers. We could have just as easily called out each

friend's name and told of the blessings and lessons they had brought to our lives. All relationships, no matter how brief, no matter whom they may be with, are opportunities for learning. The lessons we need to learn and the messages that we need to hear in order to heal and grow are all around us in the natural world, in the people that fill our lives, and in the animals in our lives. The very moment we open ourselves to hearing and seeing the possibilities at work in our lives, even our ugliest or unhappiest moments can teach us about ourselves and our interconnectedness with all others. In every friend's weakness, I may see a cautionary note for my own life, or recognize the blessing of being a bit stronger where my friend may falter. In every friend's strengths, I may see the power of gifts used with love and integrity, or realize that my own weaknesses need to be acknowledged and dealt with. Without the contrast between myself and others, I might all too easily forget that there are as many paths through life as there are feet to walk them, and that mine is not the only way to travel. Just as lessons about cooperation and industrious effort can be understood in simply lying on your belly and watching ants for an hour or so, our dogs offer us lessons if we are willing to open our hearts to hear them.

To ask "What can I learn from you?" acknowledges that all of us—including animals—serve at one time or another as teachers for each other. This humble question reminds us that we are, all of us, students of life; learning and growth are not phases we pass through on our way to adulthood, but constant companions in our daily life. When we are willing to ask this most fundamental of questions, something profound shifts inside us, creating an awareness that wherever we look, there are teachers bearing truths great and small for our lives.

Physicist John Archibald Wheeler noted, "The observer's choice of what he shall look for has an inescapable consequence for what he will find." Here we come full circle back to the responsibility of choice that is the very heart of every relationship. We can choose to move toward greater intimacy or away from it, to act out of love or out of fear, to bring our attention and energy to a moment or to live unconsciously. Far beyond our relationships with our dogs, even at the level of electrons and quarks, what we think and how we choose to observe our world, how we shape our expectations—all help to create our reality.

The mind is a powerful thing but, like all power, may not be used wisely. Years ago, while traveling in Germany, I had an amusing but unforgettable lesson in how our assumptions can lead us to block the information that is available to us. Watching television, I struggled for a while to make sense of the German dubbing over a familiar American show, but it made me quite queasy to watch lips move with no relation to the words my ears were hearing—if there's an auditory form of motion sickness, this is how it is triggered. Giving up my attempts to understand what was being said, I settled into simply watching the program as if it were a silent movie, using this opportunity to focus on the subtleties of facial expression and gesture, which told a surprisingly amount of the tale. An hour or so later, having halfheartedly watched several programs broadcast in German, I realized that some of what was being said was making sense to me, the foreign sounds of German resolving themselves in my mind so that with each passing moment, I could understand more and more of the words. This was astonishing. Elated with my newfound comprehension, I was about to announce this development to my hostess when a commercial came on. In German. And not one word made any sense to me. When the television show continued, I realized to my chagrin that it was not dubbed in German but broadcast in the original English.

How had I missed this? I was so sure that the television shows were in German that even when a new show began in English, my brain refused to accept what my ears were receiving—the familiar sounds of my native language. The filter of assumption is so powerful that though I was physically learning English, I could perceive nothing but what I assumed I was hearing: German. Assumptions about dogs may lead us to block what the dogs have to tell us, even when the message is clear and unmistakable. We may assume that animals have nothing of value to say, or even if we do accept that there are messages being sent, we believe that we are incapable of understanding them, reserving that for exceptionally gifted horse whisperers and Dr. Doolittle types.

What we choose to look for heavily influences what we will see. Someone seeking evidence of God's mercy or goodness will see it; someone seeking the faithlessness of men will find it. If all we look for is proof that animals are little more than lovable, pleasant jumbles of instinct and conditioned behaviors, then that is all we will be able to see. Believe in something more, and you risk being scoffed at as naïve, sentimental, foolish, irrational. Why do these scoffs frighten us so? The scoffers do not enlarge us or enrich our lives, and yet we fear them and give them the power to make us shy away from what our hearts pull us toward. Hungry for connections with others, reaching outward from ourselves from the moment of our birth, we somehow still manage to build walls between us and those around us, to draw the blinds and, huddled in the lonely darkness we have created for ourselves, sadly wish for more.

Whether my beliefs about animals are a delusion I've created for myself or an acknowledgment of what actually exists is fairly irrelevant. I am not as concerned with why I may believe what I believe so much as I am with the effects of what I believe. The effects of believing as I do are good ones, ones that enlarge me, make me kinder, more patient, more forgiving, more compassionate, more loving. In short, I am a better human being for having loved dogs and more specifically because of the ways that my personal beliefs shape the expression of that love. Ultimately, this belief in dogs as cold-nosed angels has pushed me hard to explore myself and to clear away more and more of the obstacles within me that prevent life and love from flowing unimpeded through me.

Raised with the life philosophy that everything happens for a reason, I don't pretend to understand the reason or purpose behind all that happens in my world, but I have faith that there is a grand design at work. Choosing as I do to look for evidence of such a grand design, I cannot help but find it. And what I also find, perhaps only because I choose to look for it, is confirmation of my belief that there's a lesson in every experience, some valuable nugget of wisdom or awareness or understanding or self-knowledge. Because of the power of this belief, even the hardest, saddest, most frightening times in my life have served me well as the rough ore from which I have mined some precious gems. All around me are potential teachers, every encounter a lesson if I am only willing to keep myself open to this.

Though it may be easy to dismiss my philosophy as the workings of a mind bent in rather mystical ways, quantum physics reveals that to an astonishing (even disturbing) extent, how we focus our attention has tremendous impact on the shape of our reality, right down to altering how subatomic particles behave. Commenting on a quantum physics experiment in which the behavior of electrons in an environment varied depending upon what the observer was trying to measure, Wheeler stated, "The observer is inescapably promoted to participator. In some strange sense, this is a participatory universe." The very moment that we ask "What can I learn?" we become participants and not merely spectators.

PARTICIPATING IN THE UNIVERSE

To ask "What can I learn from you?" is to open the door to an entire world of possibility in which our dogs can and do serve as our teachers. This is a participatory universe, and this simple question declares our willingness to participate in a very specific way. Much earlier in this book, I wrote that in order to hear what your dog might have to say, you have to take the first critical step of accepting that he has something of value to communicate to you. Block that most fundamental belief, and chances are good that even if your dog began speaking to you in plummy, cultured tones and the queen's own English, you'd not be able to hear him. Equally so, until we have opened ourselves to an acceptance of the spiritual being in canine form we may block up our souls' ears. If our assumptions about dogs and other animals do not include the possibility that these are voices that might carry important messages for our lives, then we may not be able to hear them. Not because they are speaking in mysterious ways beyond our comprehension, but because we have blocked ourselves to the possibility that there's something to be heard.

When we ask "What can I learn from you?" we can suddenly hear and see in new ways. What was once unintelligible or meaningless becomes fraught with potential, pregnant with possibilities. A whole new world of communicating with our dogs and other animals unfolds before us. And something amazing happens. You see more than you ever did before, and the animal now responds in ways you did not expect were possible, ways you did not anticipate or even ways you had hoped for but could never elicit before this. Inevitably, you come to wonder what exactly has brought about this change. Perhaps, you ask yourself, the animals have sensed this change in you and responded by offering more? Have the animals changed, or—uneasy possibility—have they always been this way? My experience is that both are true. The animals in and of themselves are exactly as they have been all along, just as waterfalls roar whether we stand at the cliff's edge or not. At the same time, we are not who we have been all along, which in turn means that in the context of their relationship with us, the animals are also in a new place. One simple question shifts the entire spirit of what happens between us and an animal. We find ourselves living the truth of the Arapaho saying, "When we show our respect for other living things, they respond with respect for us."

This wondrous and good change is the result of a profound shift within us. "We create ourselves by how we invest the energy of our attention," Mihaly Csikszentmihalyi wrote in *Finding Flow*. A shift in our focus, a new or renewed investment of our life energy—our attention—creates new realities. Our focus alters our perceptions, our perceptions inform and alter our behavior, our behavior in turn affects the experience and behavior of others, and we then have new perceptions, which lead to shifts in our behavior. And so it is that we create our reality. New questions arise, because new choices present themselves. Both we and our dogs have new options for how we will behave. We encounter new responses; we offer new opportunities.

When Badger came to live with us, he had a repertoire of behaviors that, though few in number, had been successful ones, at least in his experience thus far. Asked to do something he found unpleasant or senseless, he would simply stiffen and show his teeth, an impressive dental display against his dark brindle face. Until meeting me, this had proven to be a rather successful ploy; most folks he had known would simply back off instantly.

To Badger's great puzzlement, I did not respond to these toothy warnings as he expected I might. Though I acknowledged with some sympathy how difficult he was finding my requests, I did not back away. Initially, he seemed to think that I had inexplicable moments of intense density that left me unable to comprehend his very clear signals. Puzzled by my bouts of stupidity, it occurred to him that perhaps he needed to emphasize his point, and he did so by peeling his lips so far back from his teeth that I thought the lips might meet atop his muzzle. (His response would have been comical if not for the grim reality that this behavior, in most homes, might have resulted in his death as an aggressive dog.) That failing as well, he would usually sigh and cooperate, pleased though a bit puzzled by my enthusiastic praise and the tasty rewards. This was not how he thought the world worked, but as time passed, the very fact that I did not respond in the usual ways led to new possibilities of how Badger could respond. He still has his moments where he grits his teeth and resists, still flashes his teeth at us in annoyance from time to time. These are, after all, old habits with a long history of success behind them. Slowly but surely, replacing these habitual responses is a new thoughtfulness, a pause to consider what's being asked, a weighing of how persistently we'll ask, and finally, a cooperation that may be grudging but that is, most of the time, voluntary.

In opening to the possibility that more may exist, we have primed ourselves to a greater receptivity of what has always been before us. It is as if we were comic figures, stooges groping in the dark and claiming that we cannot see—only to realize that we had our eyes closed. When our eyes are open, new options spring into existence, and from that moment on, our relationships with our animals take on new dimensions and greater depth.

This is not a painless or certain process. *New* is not synonymous with *better*, and exploration is at times tiring and confusing. Though the opportunity to learn more about ourselves and others around us is a welcome one, it is not without price. We are held accountable for what we know. Nothing more, nothing less. But with each increase of understanding, awareness and knowledge comes a corresponding increase in responsibility. Weary at times of this new responsibility, we may long for the old, familiar way that did not require so much of us, and we may forget that it was some lack, some unease within us that prompted us to crack open the door of possibility and let in the light from this new world. Slowly, with stumbles and wrong turns, we begin to find our way and more easily shoulder the responsibility.

And as we learn to walk in this newfound awareness, we must be careful. Included within the possibilities that lay before us is also the possibility that we will mistake the grace within the message for the goodness of the messenger, confuse the value of the lesson with adoration of the teacher.

SAINTS NEVER NEED HOUSEBREAKING

Acknowledging and honoring our dogs as our teachers does not mean that we place them on pedestals where they can do no wrong. If we do this, then we have missed the Buddha nature of the dog—missed the entire point that, as a Zen saying notes, "After the ecstasy, the laundry." Life is an oddly complex blend of the lofty and the laundry, an ongoing tug-of-war between the magnificent heights our spirits may soar toward and the mundane realities of more earthbound realities like grumbling tummies and a need for a warm, dry place to sleep. And while it is quite interesting, and I believe important, to live with an awareness that the dogs at our feet are spiritual beings, just as we are, just as the birds outside our window are, we are also bound to acknowledge that these spirits are held in physical form. I may find great joy in contemplation of Grizzly's spirit, but I also must teach him not to vault from the open car door until asked. Pondering her dog nature does not relieve me of the responsibility for trimming Bird's nails or teaching her good manners. Left unsupervised or uneducated, these generous, kind spirits we call dogs may rummage through your garbage, chase and perhaps even kill other animals, clean the litter box for you, roll in dead things, and in short, live life by very canine guidelines.

While I remain grateful for what dogs make possible in my life, and while I welcome the lessons they have to bring, I will not put them on a pedestal as beings superior to me. The only thing that belongs on a pedestal is a completed work, something finished, done, as good as it can ever be. No living being deserves confinement in such a lifeless space; it is not something you do to anyone you love. Placing anyone on a pedestal implies sainthood, something possible only with finished lives, lives that weighed as a sum total were found to be far more heavily weighed toward the good and light than the lives of most. While many dogs I know can draw their last breath and have the people who knew them say without hesitation that the dog lived a blameless life, this kind of sainthood is possible only when a life is over, when the mistakes have been made and the lessons learned. If we assign them sainthood before their lives are completed, before we have lowered them into the grave or cast their ashes to the winds, then we have blocked ourselves from participating in the dynamic flow of their lives, and we may be denying our own responsibility as participants in their lives.

An animal to whom we have attributed sainthood or moral superiority would not need—nor would we dare to apply—reminders that living with humans requires certain manners, agreement to abide by (what must seem bizarre) rules, and an inhibition of many natural behaviors. A balanced relationship of respect, trust and compromise is not possible with a saint, nor is there any sense in such a relationship of the responsibilities that we have for providing leadership and supervision. And this is a very real danger of viewing animals as pure, wholly good and morally superior to us: We will fail them terribly precisely because we have not honored who they are as complete beings but have merely placed them on a pedestal so that we might admire what we would like them to be. No pedestal, however generously sized, permits freedom.

The real animal, a spirit housed in physical form, inhabits the real world just as we do. However wise the spirits may be that inhabit our dogs' bodies, we cannot forget that these are not saints, but souls here with us in dog form, not as wild wolves or even the sparrows that flit outside our windows without need of our assistance or guidance.

REACHING FOR THE GOD IN ALL

I have developed an odd form of dyslexia in which meaning to type *god* I instead type *dog*. For a while, I brushed it off as simply a bizarre habit born of a year where I wrote almost daily about dogs. That was followed by a phase where I actually grew mildly concerned that I was losing my grip on reality and perhaps taking the topic of dogs far more seriously than I ought. Looking for and finding reasonable balance in my life, I was able to dismiss this concern. I ended up pondering the notion flippantly posed by a friend: What if *dog* is simply an anagram for *God*? I do not think my friend meant for me to actually spend time contemplating this, but I have. What if God is dog, and dog is God? Upon some contemplation, I discovered that in my mind's eye I could easily replace the image of God as a fierce, bearded old man with the vision of a kindly eyed, tail-wagging, absolutely immense dog. Of all animals with which I am familiar, the dog best embodies the godlike qualities of unconditional acceptance, forgiveness and a deep love for humankind.

This notion of dog/God is not as big a leap or as profound a sign of madness as it might seem. To steal from the title of Machaelle Wright's book, I have long tried to behave as if the God in all things mattered, honoring the expression of God wherever I meet it, however it is expressed, whether in the beauty of an orb weaver's web or the dark depths of a dog's eyes. A long, long time ago, walking a coonhound into Sunday school, I believed as I do now that we are all creatures and creations of the same mighty force. As mystic Teilhard de Chardin wrote, "By means of all created things without exception, the divine assaults us, penetrates us and molds us." Call it soul, the God force, spirit or divine—name it what you will, it is precisely this unnameable thing that floods us with the joy and peace we feel in our most intimate connections. It is this that opens us to new—even ecstatic—experiences of our world and ourselves and others around us.

It is, I realize, one thing to acknowledge our dogs as thinking, feeling, sentient beings. Anyone who spends their days in the company of dogs cannot help but become aware that though they may feel and think differently than we do, dogs do think and they do feel. (There are, of course, those who refuse to grant this, and I can only assume that at this point, they've long ago given up this book as the work of a science-challenged mystic.) But even for those who would readily agree that dogs do think and feel, taking the next step into an acknowledgment of the dog as a spiritual being may be, for some readers, difficult to get their minds around.

"Let me get this straight," some might say with considerable skepticism and no small degree of alarm that perhaps I'm really treading water a little too far out from the shore. "Are you saying the goofball who is lying at my feet contentedly squeaking a rubber hamburger over and over is a spiritual being?" Or perhaps your four-legged spiritual being is out in the yard rolling on her back, or maybe she's barking at a squirrel or rummaging through the bathroom garbage or licking herself in a most indelicate way. This is a spiritual being who may have profound, important lessons to teach us?

My answer is an unequivocal yes.

We are made uneasy by this idea, mostly because we would prefer that our spiritual teachers and guides be different from us. There is an expectation (one not always articulated or even acknowledged) that any who might serve as our spiritual guides be purer, wiser, even superior in some way to us. We'd prefer important spiritual lessons and messages be delivered to us via such astonishing and amazing mediums as burning bushes or honest-to-goodness angels, not from Mary Lou at the grocery store or Tony down at the dry cleaners and certainly not from a being who chases cats, adores liver and drinks out of the toilet.

We are not, Jean Shinoda Bolen writes in her book *Close to the Bone*, human beings on a spiritual path but spiritual beings on a human path. This distinction offers the implication that spiritual beings might be on other, nonhuman paths, an implication supported by the most enduring human beliefs that we are not just in the world but woven into its very fabric as are all other beings. If we can accept that what connects us is far greater than anything that separates us, the differences in how we physically house this spirit become relatively unimportant. The Sioux believe "in all things and with all things, we are relatives."

I am not going to attempt to convince any reader that God resides within the dog at their feet and the cat next door and the bird singing outside their window and the tree across the street. I can only state that I believe it is so, and because I believe it is so, my experience of what happens when I am with the dog at my feet is, of necessity, different from the experience of someone who believes that a dog is nothing more than a lovable jumble of instinct and conditioned responses. I have no doubts that the dogs sprawled at my feet are spiritual beings, no more than I doubt that my husband who sits sipping his coffee and reading a magazine is a spiritual being. Gazing out the window at the ancient maple just outside the back door, I would say that this tree also contains a spirit. And the owl who perches on a fence post beneath the maple, waiting for the day to yield to a familiar, deepening darkness—he too is a being of spirit. We are, all of us, merely different-shaped containers, each holding for a brief while a small measure of the universe.

Our dogs, like all spiritual beings, have lessons to learn as well as to teach. Whatever the physical form that expresses our small cup of the spiritual ocean, each of us contains the light and the dark, the fullness and the emptiness, the good and the bad. Woven through our lives are flaws of understanding, failures of compassion, places where we have not yet learned to sweep away the fear and let the love pour in as it wants to do. Our lessons in this lifetime are simply our struggles to smooth the flow of life through and around our particular flaws.

What I find so deeply moving is the animal willingness to let love flow and not block it. Never once have I seen a fat dog draw back in shame from a loving hand that offered a belly rub, nor a dog who would turn away affectionate attention because of guilt over past misdeeds. But moved by fearful reasons, I have countless times shrank back from love extended to me, turned away the gifts freely and generously offered, set walls against the flow of love through me. In doing so, I limited myself as an instrument through which love and life could flow. It seems to me that dogs and other animals are such effective angels for the human spirit because, like very young children, so little blocks the flow of love and life through them. I watch dogs, and over and over again they teach me by example. They do not refuse the dynamic flow of life pouring through each moment. Whether we can articulate this or not, we recognize the power of such unimpeded flow and welcome its presence in our lives.

I have known dogs who were broken beings, victims of human neglect and anger and fear, and for these poor creatures, the flow of love was interrupted. And still, even when damage seemed too great, the flow of time and love offered without cessation did the work it does best and healed much of what had been put askew. Though not all that is broken can be put right, this too is a lesson about the power of love: In its presence, great things can be done; in its absence, the wounds created can be terrible.

For readers who find themselves drawing back at the notion that a dog is also a spiritual being, try this: Just crack open the door of Maybe. Emily Dickinson wrote about the need for the soul to remain ajar, open to the ecstatic experience. You need not enter nor even peek inside.

Simply leave the door of possibility open, and see what happens. Matters of spirit flow past and through and over the barriers we set in place, and given even a small crack in our fearful fortresses, spirit can move us deeply, and in surprisingly profound ways. See what happens when you examine an experience with this question in mind: "What can I learn from you?" It is surprising what unfolds when you approach another being with that question humbly posed and a sincere curiosity about what the answer may be.

MY LIFE AS A DOG

This book opened with me under a table, licking my aunt's knee. In my childish desire to be a dog, I could not possibly have understood just what I was asking of myself. My childhood version of being a dog consisted of little more than barks and wagging tails and gnawing on bones, a concept of dog no more sophisticated than a child's concept of what it is to be a mother. Now, as an adult, my desire to be doglike is more fervent than ever but tempered with a fuller understanding of just what that means. And it requires much of me that I did not expect, focused as I was on the dogs themselves.

There have been inklings, hints, quiet murmurs just at the edge of my awareness for many years. Each time I heard someone say "I'm more an animal person than a people person" or "I just understand animals better," something moved uneasily within me. Inevitably, these admissions were accompanied by an earnest listing of how it is that animals are easier, less frightening, less painful, more honest and more forgiving. All of us know firsthand that other human beings can be cruel, hurtful, deceitful, angry, violent and plainly callous. By comparison, animals seem nearly angelic, love made real with a wagging tail. We may cling with almost zealous fervor to the notion that animals alone are safe, that only in a dog's eyes or a cat's purr can we find unconditional acceptance of ourselves, that only animals are capable of truly appreciating us as we are.

Gary Zukav writes, "When you interact with another, an illusion is part of this dynamic. This illusion allows each soul to perceive what it needs to understand in order to heal." In no small part, it is precisely the illusory part of the dynamic that makes animals so attractive to us, especially if we have been wounded or hurt by other people. Throughout my life, animals have provided a safe haven for me when the people in my life could not; the oft-heard sentiment "the more I know of men, the more I love dogs" is one I certainly understand. In my teenage years, my woes were poured into interested ears that pricked toward me, my sadness absorbed in dark eyes that watched without judgment or rebuke, and ultimately, all of my words lay spent in the quiet space between me and the dog. And in that silence, in the quiet that offered no recommendations for action but merely a place where even the world's greatest woes could be poured without end, the healing occurred. The dog need not do anything except to be there, his silence a soothing balm and a stoppage against the harsh and angry words that filled my mind. Long before I encountered them on a page, I knew the truth of Max Picard's wise words: "Many things that human words have upset are set at rest again by the silence of animals."

Though I understand the safe haven that animals offer us against the slings and arrows of life, I am just now coming to understand that this is not an end point, a place to rest in safety, free from the complications and grief that may attend our human relationships. While valuable in and of itself, it is also a springing-off point, a place where we may begin the real work of love. Animals do not offer us a safe haven so that we may turn our back on our fellow humans. All that I have learned from the animals in my life up to now were preparatory lessons, prerequisites if you will, for the greatest challenge of them all: learning to love other people with the same grace and the same generous forgiveness that our dogs bestow upon us every day.

I realize this is not a notion that slides easily into our minds. Casting about for some alternative—one that won't require that we learn to love other people—it may be easier to think that our dogs love us as they do because they are not capable of understanding. This "sweet ignorant darlings" approach certainly takes the burden off us; a dog's naïve or ignorant adoration does not oblige in any way, as a fully aware and deliberate love might. In the same way, we often discount the love of children as uninformed. But what if our dogs and children are the ones who are not seeing an illusion? What if, unfettered by the fears and logic that tangle our adult minds, they are the ones who see past our surface imperfections, past our petty fears and straight to the heart of the matter to our unblemished, shining souls. What if what they love is simply this: the uncorrupted good within us, what we can be when we let love flow through us. It is perhaps a hackneyed phrase featured on refrigerator magnets, but this is not such a terrible thing to pray: "Help me become the kind of person my dog believes I am." This is not such a terrible shape to give a life.

As Forgiving as a Dog

In search of a way to find the dance between man and animal, I did not yet realize just where my journey was leading. Focused on the animals and by association on the people with them, I could feel something else at work within me, something that pushed me to consider the people around me with a newfound compassion. Having kept most people at a distance, I found myself more aware of them in new ways, and to my surprise, more able to see them more fully beyond the context of their relationship with their dogs. This was far from complete but occurred rather in odd flashes of insight. Though intrigued, I was also uncomfortable with the pricklings I felt when I considered what this might mean, and so I did not invest myself in an exploration of the phenomenon until three separate incidents shook me on a very deep level.

The first came on a winter morning as I sat silently watching the sun rise through the trees across the field. I was thinking about the many ways that we humans fail dogs, and how it sometimes cost dogs their lives. Specifically, I was thinking of Gillian, a beautiful young dog I had bred who, later that day, would be put to sleep for being a dangerous dog. Into my sad contemplation of the part I may have played in this tragic scene, the phone rang. Startled, I answered, and felt a wave of anger flood me when I recognized the voice of Gillian's original owner. Without question, I blamed her for the largest part of the whole situation (and blamed myself for even selling her the dog in the first place), and now, on a morning when I wanted only to be alone with my sad thoughts and apologies to this dog's spirit, her voice in my ear infuriated me.

Gritting my teeth, I answered her questions in tersely worded replies, unwilling to grant her anything but the most rudimentary courtesy. I listened in angry silence as she spun out her explanation of how and why it had all come down to this: a dog who would be dead in a few hours, Gillian the only one who would pay full price for promises made and broken. It began to dawn on me as she talked that she had called me because she was seeking forgiveness; I could hear it clearly in her tearful admission that she had failed this puppy. Hot righteous anger flared up in me, and as I swung up on my high horse, I felt a heavy weight on my knee. Glancing down, I saw my old dog Banni's head resting there, his dark eyes fixed on my face, his gaze steady, unblinking, telling me something. I shifted my focus to this old friend and silently asked what he needed to tell me. He answered with a quiet question: "What would she do?"

The question, so clearly posed in my head, confused me at first. What would who do? The woman I was speaking with? I struggled for an answer, the woman began to cry, and Banni's eyes locked on mine. The next image in my head was so startling that I nearly dropped the phone: I could see Gillian reaching up to lick away the woman's tears, eyes soft, tail wagging gently, the essence of forgiveness given physical form. Suddenly, I understood the question—"what would she do?"—and knew that it was what Gillian would do. She would forgive this woman, this flawed human being who had loved her but still failed her.

My challenge was this: Could I offer the same simple acceptance and forgiveness? I did not think I could, and I told myself that to forgive this would somehow equal condoning what she had done. Again, the steady gaze of Banni pushed me onward, and inexplicably, I was hurtling back years in time to Banni's youth and a gorgeous spring day when, as a young dog enjoying the day, he had ignored my repeated commands to come inside so I could leave for an appointment. In a rush, unreasonably angry, I had marched across the yard and grabbed him by the scruff of the neck, dragging him unceremoniously to the back door, where I scolded him far past any sane reprimand. He sat frozen, his eyes wary, until at last, realizing how stupid my own behavior was, I had sagged into a chair nearby. Holding my hands out to him, I apologized and asked for his forgiveness. And it had come faster than the speed of light. His forgiveness did not equal in any way an acceptance of what I had done; it simply acknowledged my apology and opened a way for me to go on, for us to go on and hopefully find another way next time.

So many years later, his graying muzzle laid on my knee, it occurred to me that if I were a good dog, I would be able to forgive this woman. It would not undo what had been done, and it would not change the sad reality that a dog she had loved would die that day. Forgiveness would not shift the responsibility for her failures onto anyone else, but it would be a way of saying that just like me, she was a flawed human being. I too had made terrible mistakes, broken promises, failed the ones I loved, and far past the biblical seven times seven, I had been forgiven by the animals and the people who had suffered at my hands. To deny her forgiveness was to act arrogantly, as if I had never needed to be forgiven, as if I would not need to be forgiven countless times in the future. Surely, I told myself, I could find a way to do what any good dog could do any day and sometimes a dozen times before breakfast: forgive a human being for being human. And so I did. It was not easy. But it was important.

The dog still died a few hours later. I never spoke to the woman again; what little we had between us had died that day. There is still great sadness in me for Gillian, a promising young dog who did not receive what she had been promised, what she deserved and needed. And there is deep gratitude in me for Gillian's lesson, for it was the first major crack in the wall between myself and other people.

TREAT ME LIKE A DOG

The next lesson came only a few months later, when a longtime friend unexpectedly began a verbal attack on me, laying at my feet a mountain of blame for her unhappiness with her life. Stunned, I listened in growing disbelief, the pain caused by her words a physical sensation as distinct as if I had been punched in the solar plexus. My initial response was one of anger, and yet, even as my snarled response rose up in my throat—"I'm not going to stand here and listen to this—screw you!"—something bizarre happened. Her words, shooting in painful trajectories from a face screwed tight, floated away so that their specific meaning was lost to me; all that was left was the pure sound of her feelings, and I was struck by the anger and fear that I heard in her voice. Without words, it seemed as if she were pouring out snarls and yelps and desperate, frantic barking.

If she were a dog, I asked myself, what would make her act like this, attack like this, without warning? Immediately, I corrected myself. There *had* been warning, hints in telephone conversations prior to this, and from the moment we had met on this day, I had felt the connection between us taut with tension though I could not determine why this was so. I was aware that I had to choose my words and actions carefully to avoid setting her off—in other words, I had warning. Transforming her into a dog who was snarling and snapping in fearful frenzy was a way of setting aside my own hurt response. Seeing her as hurting and terrified stilled my reflexive reaction, and though still hurting myself, I found I was able to listen compassionately and then walk away from that encounter knowing that I had done nothing to pour fuel on her fire.

The relief of finding a perspective that allowed me to stay calm and not react out of my own fear and anger was short-lived. Long after the incident had passed, I was deeply shaken by the realization that once I saw her—truly saw her—with the same clarity that I usually can bring to my interactions with dogs, I was obliged to respond to her with at least the same compassion I would show any dog brought to me. This was not a new concept for me. For years, I'd given it lip service and even some genuine effort, and at times, was even able to actually be kind and fair to many people. But never before had I been struck so deeply with how serious an obligation I had to live these words—or how difficult this really was.

Long ago, I had read Leo Buscaglia's wise words, "We must treat each other with dignity. Not only because we merit it but because we grow best in thoughtfulness." Living these words, I was discovering, was not an easy matter. An examination of my own behavior showed that while most people fared well in their interactions with me, not all did. With every animal that I came into contact with, I strove mightily to be compassionate, to demonstrate respect and kindness even in the face of their anger or fear. It seemed quite sad to me that if my friend had been a dog snapping fearfully at the end of the leash, I would instantly have responded in a way that I could manage only with effort on her behalf.

This was a terribly uneasy moment of awareness, one that nagged at me for many months. Watching myself, I could see that there was quite a difference at times between how I treated animals and how I treated some people. I could readily excuse my behavior with a recitation of my homemade litany of how "he done me wrong" and "she done me wrong" and "folks will do you wrong," but . . . the uncomfortable truth was that I wasn't bothering to make the distinction between past wrongs of others who had indeed hurt me, and the people in my life right now and their current behavior. To tar all people with my mistrust and fear was as silly as the prejudice I encountered daily when walking German Shepherds down the street. Despite my dogs' calm demeanor, good manners and tail-wagging greetings, they would often be viewed as aggressive, dangerous or even deadly, depending on how another German Shepherd at some other time had acted toward the person who now viewed all prick-eared, black-and-tan dogs with fear and loathing.

ACTING AS IF IT MATTERED

On the last day of her life, Vali did what she had done her entire life: She taught me. I knew we were making our way through the last few ticks of the clock, and each passing hour was treasured and savored. Leaving her in the cool shade where she could lie and watch the comings and goings on the farm, I picked up the hose to refill her water bowl, letting the water run for a while to be sure it was cold and pure. Hearing a noise behind me, I first thought it was Carson, Vali's sister, coming to play in the water as both of them had done since they were puppies. Instead, what I saw was Vali, her dimming eyes grown bright and alert as she fixed her attention on the hose. So weak she could barely stand, she made her way across the lawn while I stood dumbstruck. Reaching me, she stretched herself to bite gleefully at the stream of water as she always had, and then, as she steadied herself to try again, I saw in her eyes the terrible moment that she knew this was truly more than she could do.

She stood for a moment, her muzzle dripping, her frail body held unsteadily by pure effort, and then, with resignation, used the last of her strength to stagger back to the shade where her sister Carson lay.

"Why would you do that?" I asked Vali as I stretched out beside her and stroked her head. I knew she had loved any water game, always had, but from my perspective, it hardly seemed worth using what precious little energy remained in a life to snap one more time against that which could never be caught no matter how powerful the jaws brought to bear. Her answer came quietly: "If something matters to you, you give it all you have to give." I did not know that only hours later, when the stars hung bright but silent in the sky, her heart would finally beat its last beneath my hand and she would be gone. I never suspected that just hours after her death, her final lesson to me would need to be put to the test.

A short time after the sun rose as it does on both the grief and joy awaiting in each day, I went to tell a friend that Vali was dead. This was the same friend who had lashed out at me a few months earlier. Foolishly, hurting, needing to talk to someone who had known Vali all her life, I hoped for a little tea and sympathy. And for a few minutes, that's what I got before the sympathy evaporated and the conversation turned to my friend and her troubles. The tea in my cup had not yet cooled when what had begun as a sharing of loss became an intense exploration of my friend's problems and fears. With a huge wave of fatigue, I thought to myself that I did not have any energy for this, that right at this moment I was much too emotionally exhausted to be able to respond to or even care much about someone else's woes. More than anything, I wanted to curl up in sad silence and grieve for a good dog.

As I tried to shape the sentences that might let me escape this moment and my friend's needs, I suddenly saw Vali moving unsteadily in the sunshine to bite the water. It mattered to her, and she gave it all she had, even when all was very little indeed. My friend continued to cry and talk and accuse, and watching her from a calm, quiet distance, I asked myself, Does this friend matter to you? The answer was that of course she did. The next question was that if I knew this was her last day or mine, would I still be willing to walk away, holding my weariness and sadness as a shield against hearing her and offering what I had to offer? I did love this woman, and this relationship was critically important to me. Though my sorrow was real and my grief deserved time to be honored, this was a need of the living. And so, reaching deep inside me for that same determination that moved a dying dog to one last round of a favorite game, I opened myself to listening to the hurting, lonely woman who needed to be heard.

I do not know what would have happened if, having finished my tea, I had chosen the easier route and extricated myself from that situation. I do know that what I did that morning made a difference in that friend's life. Yet even if it had not, the difference this made in my life was important in and of itself. Vali's lesson for me was an extension of McKinley's: If we choose with awareness, there need not be regrets. Make no mistake. Vali's lesson has not mutated into an unrealistic martyrdom where no matter how I'm feeling, I can always find time for someone else's needs. That was not the lesson. It was about making aware investments of my life's energy.

The Most Difficult of All

There was once a time when I would have said that the greatest lesson our dogs could help us learn was how to be humane as well as human. Foolishly, as all beginners do, I thought that this was my destination, this beautiful white space between me and an animal, this place where an invitation to dance is sent and accepted. Here, I am now learning, is simply the place to which I had to come so that I could begin the real work of life: learning to love other human beings. In his *Letters on Love*, German poet Rainer Maria Rilke wrote, "For one human being to love another: that is perhaps the most difficult of all our tasks, the ultimate, the last test and proof, the work for which all other work is but preparation."

It is ironic that in all the times I've both said and heard "I prefer animals to people," never once had I stopped and wondered, What if animals said the same to us? What if our dogs looked at us and decided, as we ourselves may have long ago decided, that people really are rather cruel and terrible and, frankly, not worth being with. "Wait," we would wail, "it's other people who are like that, not us! Not us, the animal lovers, the ones who love furred and feathered ones more than we love our own kind. Look how kindly we treat you, how fervently we defend you, how much love and attention we shower on you! You can't turn away from us," we would cry. And if the animals continued on, their backs to us, unwilling to be with us, a quiet whimper might be heard, "If you leave us, who then will love us?"

And the dogs might look back at us and softly ask, "How is it that you've missed the most important lesson of them all?" By example, relentlessly, willingly, and so very well, dogs show us the importance of love offered without judgment or condition. They show us the value of being accepted as we are. And they show us, over and over again, that a life spent loving even misguided, confused, unsure human beings is a life well spent. All that our dogs might bring into our lives pales before this challenge to learn how to love each other as they love us. It is the work of a lifetime, to be sure, but we've chosen well when we choose to keep our cold-nosed angels at our side for the journey.

Just above a dog's paw, where rough pad curves in fullness outward and upward and then, giving way to fur, turns back in toward the body, there is a hollow. Framed by the living steel of sinew and bone, that hollow fits my thumb as if made by my own thumbprint long ago, perhaps in another lifetime when I was handmaiden to a minor goddess. If even a minor goddess is granted the powers to shape things in small ways, then I might have asked for just one thing for the future me: this hollow here just above a dog's paw. And I would have asked for this so that at some moment in the future the perfect fit of my thumb into that place would serve as a reminder that since time out of mind, for lifetimes without measure, my soul and this dog's had been together, intertwined in the great ocean of life. In wondering if the hollow was shaped to fit my thumb or my thumb to fill that hollow, I would remember that we are all holder and held, teacher and taught, guide and guided. I would set this hollow here for my future self to remember that even when a heartbeat no longer pulsed faintly under my hands, when my thumb reluctantly stilled its gentle rhythms of stroking the soft fur, our connection would go on. In this simple, sweet hollow, I would mark the dog as my fellow traveler, and my teacher.

How do we possibly measure the grace granted us by our dogs?

Capable of dramatic teachings, our dogs also move subtly but as relentlessly as water, the flow of their spirit working within us in ways we may not even know. How do we know what it is they have helped us to learn? Sometimes, this is how we discover the changes: Every step we take is different, easier, informed by knowledge that has quietly, surely soaked deep into our bones. This understanding seems so right, answers the thirst within us so well we may forget how freshly we have come to this, forget who we were before we embraced this wisdom. Our heads tell us that once, somehow, in a way we can no longer remember, we did move through the world without the understanding that we now possess. We are grateful but mystified, and we wonder how we ever found our way with such a faulty map. Somehow, we did find our way, and we will keep moving forward. And always, traveling beside us, the angels who both guide and guard us.

Coursing through our veins as surely as our own blood are the lessons we have mastered through effort, and through no small measure of grace gifted us by the animals who serve as our teachers. We could no more separate ourselves now from what we know, what we have learned, than we could strip the marrow from our own bones. Folding into ourselves what we have learned as well as what we have blindly accepted in faith, often without fully understanding it, trusting simply that it was a great and good gift, we grow. And as we stretch, the bonds of fear that seemed so mighty once, when we were smaller than we are today, begin to fray, become weak attempts to bind us to a lesser version of ourselves. When we drink from the well of wisdom, our souls begin to stir and stretch, awakening from a slumber we did not know was so deep. With growing hope, we understand that we can learn to fly. Fledglings, we perch on the edge of our lives and begin to flap our wings in the sure knowledge that we are growing toward the day when we throw ourselves onto the wind and trust to its flow.

ACKNOWLEDGMENTS

IN EARLY FEBRUARY 1997, I wrote a letter that began "It's only fair to warn you. There's something in my brain, and it's trying to get out." And friends and supporters answered with the help I needed. I was right—there *was* something in my brain, and it's now made its escape. But on that cold February night, I could not have foreseen that it would be almost exactly four years later before I was able to say "Here. This is what your love and support have made possible." For their patience, generosity and belief that I had something of value to say, I offer this book to the people who answered that letter. Though I would love to say something about each and every one of these fine folk, it is best perhaps to simply say that they and their dogs have made a profound difference—each in their own way—in my life. The dogs listed for each person may not be the dogs who accompany them today through life, but they are the dogs that appear in my mind's eye, forever and always at the side of the person they loved and who loved them:

Annabell Minty (*Misty, Shane, Meggie*); Steve Reiman (*Lily, Jordan*); Sarah Johnson (*Nokomis*); Mike Johnson; Kit Burke and Terry Modlesky (*Destiny*); Nancy Beach (*Rosie, Honor*); Bill Carroll (*Tasha, Kansas*); Barbara Warner (*Casey*); Marge Wappler (*Joker*); Linda Caplan (*Jagger, Dodger, Queenie, Brutus*); Deb Gillis (*Nugget, Strider, Sterling*); Claire Moxim (*Andy*); Betty Ferrare; Pat Barlow (*Schoen, Gina*); Harriet Grose; Wayne Rebarber (*Misha*); Anne and Ray Smith; Marian Nealey (*Sam*);

Mary Legge (*Utah, Chance, Tira, Cruiser, Trooper*); Bonnie Goldberg Rubin; Beth Taylor (*Woody, Tessa*); Chris Civil (*Indy, Alex*); Joy Nutall (*Devon, Halo*); Cliff Peabody (*Little John, Gunner*); Rose Ellen Dunn (*Blaze, Kelly, Finn*); Dale and Peter Demy (*Lucky, Rowdy*); Sherry Holm (*Jim, Dax*); Paul Koehler (*Ilka, Cree, Redbone*); Amelie Seelig (*Sailor, Tammy*); Gail James (*Buddy, Chance*); Deb Hutchinson (*Joppa, Gage, Josh*); Jane Guy (*Jenny, Kosmo*); Cecilia Hoffman (*Mouse, Charlie*); Janet Devich (*Aneaka, Cyrus, Morgan*); Marietta Huber (*Licorice*); Billie Rosen (*Cara*); Rosemary Rybak (*Jamie, Teddy, Zena, Sesame, Hannah*); Lynne Fickett (*Jazz, Sizzle, Chase*); Diana Hoyem (*Lana*); and Tom O'Dowd (*Buddy*). Special thanks to my friends Cheryl Smagala (*Prince, Token, Nikki, Axel*); Karen Lessig (*Tonya, Castor, Reveille, Ana, Caber*); and Kathy and Karl Huppert (*George, Ruffy, Mr. P, Samara*). They have seen me through more than a few ups and downs and a few head-on collisions with life.

For her unflagging encouragement to make this book a reality, my thanks to Dr. Helen Greven (*Angus*). For her diligent work as critical reader, my thanks to Beth Levine (*Owen, Wren*); someday she'll learn not to talk to strange manuscripts. For helpful suggestions and comments, I would also like to thank Dr. Thomas Blass and Dr. Marc Bekoff (*Jethro*).

To my agent, Lisa Ross, I offer my immense gratitude for her wise, patient guidance through strange waters. Without her, I would surely have lost sight of the shore. Many thanks to my editors, Jackie Joiner and Jessica Papin, for their support. To all at Warner Books, my thanks for working so diligently to polish up *Bones* and dress it in its Sunday best. With so many talented people dedicated to this task, *Bones* cleaned up right nice.

For extraordinary service as cheerleaders, counselors, critics and sounding boards, for having poured hours of their own lives into mine, for the love and support and tireless reading of yet another version, and for unwavering belief in me, I thank Wendy Herkert (*Chance, Panda, Quill*), Katrene Johnson (*Danny, Morgan*), Ginny Debbink (*Doc, Annie, Beckett, Crow, Hudson*), Terry Wright (*Kaji*), Janie Dillon (*Tristan*), Kathy Marr (*Pork, Krista*), Nancy Sickels (*Brook, Lark*), Judy Gardner (*Garen, Tasy, Bo* and so many others) and Carter Volz (*Trina, Bisser*). For reading on the deepest level of all, I thank Marlene Sandler (*Charlie, Gaia*). These are friends beyond compare, friends who would make very fine dogs indeed.

For a lifetime of putting up with a barking daughter, wild tales and sometimes strange projects, for her proud support of all that I have been and might still be, much love and unbounded thanks to my mother, Betty Livingston. For struggling with a mother not yet made even slightly wise by dogs and other creatures, I thank my beloved son, Christian Clothier.

It is important to gratefully acknowledge the teachers who have shaped who I am. I hope that their influence on me is evident: Linda Tellington-Jones, Ian Dunbar, Jack and Wendy Volhard. I would also like to thank the teachers—or, more accurately, the heroes—I have never met but whose work and thoughts have informed my own to a great degree: Konrad Lorenz, Jane Goodall, David Mech, Franz de Waal, Temple Grandin, J. Allen Boone, John Bradshaw, Gary Zukav, Alan Watts and Dr. Bruce Fogle.

I believe that messages and lessons are all around us; we need only tune our hearts to hear them. For the music that poured into me on a summer night in Saratoga, pulsing through me at a moment when I needed it most, for the urging to surrender the fear and fly and for providing a remarkably inspiring example of what is possible when you do, I thank Michael Stipe and REM. Though writing this book was an adventure in pushing an elephant up the stairs and trying to keep those flowers in full bloom, my feet were made lighter on this journey by the music of REM beating in time with my heart.

Writing is a solitary act, and in moving toward that solitude, I had to move away from my best friend, my partner, my husband, John Rice. Of all the gifts that dogs have brought me through the years, none can compare with this wonderful man. Without complaining, with unfailing patience, good humor and generosity, he shouldered an ever-increasing burden of responsibility for our farm and animals. Only he knows the true cost of writing this book. What he does not fully understand is that it would have been nearly impossible without him. And yet he still smiles at the idea of the books yet to come. Proving, of course, that he's much too easily amused.

And this would not be complete without acknowledging each and every animal who has touched my life and allowed me to touch theirs. My life has been richly blessed by these gracious teachers. I cannot possibly repay them, only share what they have helped me learn. If this book helps just one person find their way to the dance, then I will have begun in some small measure to give appropriate thanks for the gifts I have received.

Suzanne Clothier
Hawks Hunt Farm
February 2001

RECOMMENDED READING

SINCE I AM FREQUENTLY ASKED what books or people have influenced my own thinking, I offer this list of recommended titles. Mind you, not all of these titles are here because I agree wholeheartedly with what is found between their covers. Each of these are books that were valuable in one way or another for me, and I believe they may also be valuable for some readers who thirst for deeper understanding. Some of these titles were written by people I would consider kindred spirits who see the world very much as I do. Some books are listed here because they provoked me to carefully consider perspectives that I might have missed but for the author's encouragement to think or feel or view the world in a certain way. Some of these books annoyed or even angered me, and so provoked thought and discussion and a search to make more concrete in my own mind what was more in alignment with my soul and my philosophy.

It is never enough to flatly state "That makes no sense to me!" or "Bah, I don't believe that!" You must also be willing to do the work of discovering and knowing (truly, deeply knowing) what *does* make sense to you and what it is you actually do believe, and which direction you wish to go and why. To the extent that you are willing to do that work, any book or viewpoint or teaching or teacher—even if they stand in direct opposition to what you believe—can work to your benefit and on your behalf, strengthening your understanding of yourself and your preferred paths through life.

In addition to these titles that shaped my philosophy, there were so many events, people and animals that cannot be referenced. Would that I could recommend to each reader the great experience of time spent in the company of any of those who have taught me so much: the incredible McKinley or Valinor or my beloved Bear, to name but a few. But I trust that when you curl up with one of the books listed below, your own special teachers and guides are there beside you. Listen carefully to what they have to tell you.

I've deliberately avoided any brief description, synopsis or even short review of these books. I leave it to the reader to follow their own curiosity and their own hearts and minds. Explore. Enjoy. Stretch yourself. Listen with an open heart . . .

Arluke, Arnold, and Clinton R. Sanders. *Regarding Animals*. Philadelphia: Temple University Press, 1996.

Beck, Alan, and Aaron Katcher. *Between Pets and People: The Importance of Animal Companionship*. West Lafayette, IN: Purdue University Press, 1996.

Bolen, Jean Shinoda. *Close to the Bone*. New York: Simon and Schuster, 1996.

Boone, J. Allen. *Kinship with All Life*. San Francisco: Harper, 1954.

Bradshaw, John. *Creating Love*. New York: Bantam Doubleday Dell Publishing, 1993.

Csikszentmihalyi, Mihaly. *Finding Flow*. New York: Basic Books, 1998.

———. *Flow*. San Francisco: HarperCollins, 1991.

Dawkins, Marian Stamp. *Through Our Eyes Only? The Secret for Animal Consciousness*. Oxford University Press, 1998.

de St. Exupéry, Antoine. *The Little Prince*. New York: MacMillan Reference Library, 1995.

———. *Wind, Sand and Stars*. New York: Harcourt Brace and Company, 1939.

de Waal, Franz. *Chimpanzee Politics: Power and Sex among Apes*. London: The Johns Hopkins Press Ltd., 1989.

———. *Good Natured*. Cambridge, MA: Harvard University Press, 1996.

Derr, Mark. *Dog's Best Friend.* New York: Henry Holt & Co., 1997.

Dossey, Larry, M.D. *Healing Words: The Power of Prayer and the Practice of Medicine.* San Francisco: Harper, 1997.

Dunbar, Ian. *Dog Aggression: Biting.* Oakland: Kenneth & James, 1998.

———. *Dog Aggression: Fighting.* Oakland: Kenneth & James, 1998.

———. *Dog Behavior.* Neptune, NJ: T.H.F. Publications, Inc., 1979.

———. *How to Teach a New Dog Old Tricks.* Oakland: Kenneth & James, 1991.

———. *Sirius Puppy Training.* Oakland: Kenneth & James, 1998.

Fogle, Bruce. *The Dog's Mind.* London: Stephen Greene Press, 1990.

Goldstein, Martin, DVM. *The Nature of Animal Healing.* New York: Alfred A. Knopf, 1999.

Greven, Philip. *Spare the Child.* New York: Alfred A. Knopf, 1991.

Griffin, Donald. *Animal Minds.* University of Chicago Press, 1992.

Hearne, Vicki. *Adam's Task: Calling the Animals by Name.* New York: Alfred A. Knopf, 1986.

———. *Bandit: Dossier of a Dangerous Dog.* New York: HarperCollins, 1991.

Katra, Jane Targ, and Russell Targ. *The Heart of the Mind.* New York: New World Library, 1999.

Kowalski, Gary. *The Souls of Animals.* Walpole, NH: Stillpoint Publishing, 1999.

Lorenz, Konrad. *King Solomon's Ring.* New York: Harper & Row, 1952.

———. *Man Meets Dog.* Boston: Houghton Mifflin Co., 1955.

Mech, David. *The Wolf.* Minneapolis: University of Minnesota Press, 1970.

Newby, Jonica. *The Animal Attraction.* Sydney: ABC Books, 1999.

Nørretranders, Tor. *The User Illusion.* New York: Penguin, 1998.

Page, George. *Inside the Animal Mind.* New York: Doubleday, 1999.

Peck, M. Scott. *The Road Less Traveled.* New York: Simon and Schuster, 1978.

Pert, Candace B. *Molecules of Emotion.* New York: Simon and Schuster, 1997.

Pirsig, Robert. *Lila: An Inquiry into Morals.* New York: Bantam Press, 1991.

———. *Zen and the Art of Motorcycle Maintenance: An Inquiry into Values*. New York: William Morrow Publishing Co., 1979.

Rogers, Lesley. *Minds of Their Own: Thinking and Awareness in Animals*. Boulder, CO: Westview Press, 1997.

Roocroft, Alan, and Donald Atwell Zoll. *Managing Elephants*. Ramona, CA: Fever Tree Press, 1994.

Rugaas, Turid. *On Talking Terms with Dogs: Calming Signals*. Sequim, WA: Legacy Publications, 1997.

Sanders, Clinton R. *Understanding Dogs: Living and Working with Canine Companions*. Philadelphia: Temple University Press, 1999.

Schoen, Allen M., D.V.M., M.S. *Kindred Spirits*. New York: Broadway Books, 2001.

———. *Love, Miracles and Animal Healing*. New York: Simon and Schuster, 1996.

Serpell, James. *In the Company of Animals: A Study of Human-Animal Relationships*. Cambridge University Press, 1996.

Smith, Penelope. *Animal Talk*. Pt. Reyes Station, CA: Pegasus Publications, 1982.

Tellington-Jones, Linda. *The Tellington-Touch*. New York: Viking Press, 1992.

Townsend, Irving. *Separate Lifetimes*. Exeter, NH: J. N. Townsend, 1992.

Wright, Machaelle Small. *Behaving as if the God in All Life Mattered: A New Age Ecology*. Warrenton, VA: Perelandra Limited, 1987.

Zukav, Gary. *Seat of the Soul*. New York: Simon and Schuster, 1989.